JOHNS HOPKINS UNIVERSITY STUDIES

IN

HISTORICAL AND POLITICAL SCIENCE

EXTRA VOLUMES   NEW SERIES, NO. 28

MAJORITY RULE IN INTERNATIONAL ORGANIZATION

A STUDY OF THE TREND FROM UNANIMITY
TO MAJORITY DECISION

MAJORITY RULE IN INTERNATIONAL ORGANIZATION

A Study of the Trend from Unanimity to Majority Decision

BY

CROMWELL A. RICHES

Associate Professor of Political Science
Goucher College

BALTIMORE
THE JOHNS HOPKINS PRESS
1940

PRINTED IN THE UNITED STATES OF AMERICA
BY J. H. FURST COMPANY, BALTIMORE, MARYLAND

TO
S. M. R.

PREFACE

Several years ago the writer made a study of the unanimity rule in the practice of the League of Nations (*The Unanimity Rule and the League of Nations,* Johns Hopkins Press, 1933). The study was undertaken for the purpose of discovering the extent to which the rule of unanimous consent, laid down in Article 5 of the Covenant, had hampered the functioning of the Council and the Assembly. The findings revealed a rather astonishing number of ingenious devices by which the League organs, especially the Assembly, had escaped the rigors of the restrictive unanimity rule, in many cases approximating majority decision. This led the writer to investigate the extent to which other permanent international organs have accepted in their practice some form of majority decision. The results of the investigation are set forth in this volume.

The generosity of the Carnegie Endowment for International Peace in granting to the writer one of its fellowships in international law made possible the undertaking of this study. The encouragement and friendly interest of Professor H. Lauterpacht of Cambridge University, as well as his many helpful suggestions, are gratefully acknowledged. The writer is also indebted to Mr. S. H. Bailey, Reader in International Relations in the London School of Economics, who gave material assistance in locating some of the documents used, and to Dr. Johannes Mattern, Associate Professor of Political Science in The Johns Hopkins University, who read the entire manuscript. Dr. Mattern made many suggestions for improvement which the author was very glad to accept.

The manuscript of the study was completed before the present world war had entered its active phase. Undoubtedly, changes will occur in the nature of the state system and, consequently, in the nature of international organization. Nevertheless, many of the international bodies dealt with will continue to function after the war, and knowledge of their practices, as well as those of the international organs which may disappear, will be important in any attempt to establish a new world order.

C. A. R.

CONTENTS

CHAPTER I

INTRODUCTION

Municipal legislatures and other deliberative bodies within states are empowered, in general, to reach decisions binding upon the political community over which their jurisdiction extends through some form of majority rule. Effective collective action is not confined, as a rule, to those instances in which all are in agreement. It is generally accepted that, where a majority, or in some instances a qualified majority, has found a basis of agreement, that basis will stand as the common agreement of the whole group. The function of the deliberative body is to examine the divergent views expressed, selecting that acceptable to the majority as the view of the community, binding upon all, including the dissenting minority groups.

Although majority decision is widely accepted, there appears to be no universal principle of law which decrees that majorities may command obedience. A resolution adopted by majority vote at a public meeting of citizens is not necessarily binding upon those who do not concur in it. In England and the United States, as well as in other countries using English common law, a petty jury can not render a verdict in a felony case by majority vote. In Poland, unanimity was long required for enactment of laws by the legislative body. Majority decisions are binding upon the entire group or community only in those instances in which there has been express or tacit acceptance of a rule of law recognizing the validity of decisions reached in such fashion.

In municipal law, wide acceptance of such a rule has come by extremely slow process. Until there developed a corporative spirit, an appreciation that the group was something beyond the mere sum of its members, as well

1

as a recognition of the need for an effective method for expressing the collective will, acceptance of such a rule was not possible. Apparently the Greek city states, particularly Athens, were the first to employ successfully majority decision in their deliberative bodies.[1] Although the majority device had no complete acceptance in Roman law, certain of the Roman Assemblies applied what amounted to a system of concurrent majorities. The assemblies were composed of corporate divisions, each division reaching its decisions by majority vote. The decision of the entire assembly depended upon the action of a majority of the divisions.[2]

But with other peoples the principle had no such recognition. In the early stages of Germanic law, the majority device was unknown. The " will " of the group was made up of the " wills " of the individuals who assembled. If unanimity was not achieved, the " will " of the preponderant majority prevailed, but the minority was not obliged to accept it. By refusing acquiescence, they separated themselves from the group and subjected themselves to coercion by the majority. From this point it was no great step to hold that, from the nature of social relations, there arises a duty on the part of the minority to conform to the will of the majority for the sake of social unity. Final unanimity was still required, decisions becoming valid only if the minority actually accepted the majority position, but the way was prepared for the complete acceptance of majority rule. However, in the election of German kings, the original conception of the unanimity rule prevailed until the issuance of the Golden Bull by Emperor Charles IV at the Diet of Nuremberg in 1356.[3]

In canon law, unanimity was used for centuries as the one method of expressing the collective will. Majority

---

[1] J. G. Heinberg, "Theories of Majority Rule," *American Political Science Review* (1932), XXVI, 453.
[2] *Ibid.*, p. 455.   [3] *Ibid.*, p. 454.

decision was introduced only through use of the legal fiction whereby it was held that the majority will might appropriately be considered the will of all for the reason that the will of the many was more likely to approach truth than that of the few.[4]

In English parliamentary practice, which has had such great influence upon the development of political institutions elsewhere, majority decision does not appear to have been well established until the second half of the sixteenth century.[5] Not until 1554, in the reign of Queen Mary, do the records of the House of Commons reveal an instance of the passing of a bill by majority vote.[6] The House of Lords had taken a similar action as early as 1541 and several other cases are recorded in the years immediately following.[7] At this time divisions in both houses occurred infrequently and dealt, for the most part, with inconsequential subjects. As the English Parliament through the centuries had represented not the English people as a whole but numerous corporate bodies and powerful lords, unanimity was the rule, and divisions naturally occurred but rarely. Thomas Baty expresses the view, which does not seem unreasonable, that in all probability majority decision was first accepted as a simple and efficient means of disposing of indifferent matters and that insensibly members of Parliament came to believe they were obliged to accept majority decision in all matters. Thus he concludes that " mental indolence " was responsible for the acceptance of majority rule. " Never deliberately or of set purpose adopted as a political principle, it [majority decision] has drifted into casual acceptance through loose political thinking." [8] However, it should

---

[4] *Ibid.,* p. 456.
[5] T. Baty, " The History of Majority Rule," *Quarterly Review* (1912), CCXVI, 19; J. G. Heinberg, " History of the Majority Principle," *American Political Science Review* (1926), XX, 67.
[6] Baty, *Quarterly Review,* p. 11.   [7] *Ibid.,* p. 18.   [8] *Ibid.,* p. 27.

not be overlooked that acceptance of the majority principle appears to have been coincident with certain other events, namely, with the development of a considerable group consciousness in Parliament and with a sufficient extension of parliamentary powers to warrant adoption of a rule making rapid, effective decision possible.

Although, as seems probable, the majority device attained acceptance in municipal parliamentary practice and elsewhere largely because it afforded a convenient, rapid method for taking decisions rather than because of any ethical validity possessed by it, many publicists have in the past taken pains to justify it. The justifications were, for the most part, proposed only after the rule had been acknowledged and applied. As previously noted, the canonists had used the justification of truth. The majority was more likely to approximate the true and the good than was the minority. For a time the canonists even attempted a system of both counting and weighing votes, but ultimately discarded it for the more simple rule of counting.[9] In Germanic law, the justification of force had been used. The majority possessed greater force than the minority, hence the latter could be compelled by force of arms to join with the majority. To preserve social unity and avoid actual use of force it came to be considered the duty of the minority to acquiesce in the majority decision.[10]

But it was the natural law and social contract writers who finally brought the doctrine into wide acceptance by theorists. To Grotius, citing numerous classical writers in support, it appeared natural that the majority has the right to decide.

All associations have this in common, however, that in those matters on account of which the association was formed the entire

---

[9] Heinberg, "Theories of Majority Rule," *American Political Science Review*, p. 456.

[10] *Ibid.*, p. 454.

membership, or the majority in the name of the entire membership, may bind the individual members. In general it must be
believed that it was the wish of those who united in an association
that there should be some method of conducting business. But
it is manifestly unfair that the majority should be ruled by the
minority. Therefore, naturally, the majority has the same right as
the entire body, if due exception is made of agreements and laws
which prescribe the form of conducting business.[11]

Locke based the validity of majority vote upon necessity,
force, and the nature of society as well as upon " the law
of nature."

For, when any number of men have, by the consent of every
individual, made a community, they have thereby made that community one body, with a power to act as one body, which is only
by the will and determination of the majority. For that which
acts any community, being only the consent of the individuals of
it, and it being necessary to that which is one body to move
one way; it is necessary the body should move that way whither
the greater force carries it, which is the consent of the majority;
or else it is impossible it should act or continue one body, one
community, which the consent of every individual that united
into it, agreed that it should; and so everyone is bound by that
consent to be concluded by the majority. And therefore we see
that in assemblies, impowered to act by positive laws where no
number is set up by that positive law which impowers them, the
act of the majority passes for the act of the whole, and of course
determines; as having, by the law of nature and reason, the power
of the whole.[12]

Rousseau found majority rule justified by terms of the
original contract and considered it the appropriate device
for ascertaining the general will.

There is but one law which by its nature requires unanimous

[11] Grotius, *De Jure Belli ac Pacis* (" The Classics of International Law,"
ed. J. B. Scott), Book II, Ch. 5, sec. 17.
[12] J. Locke, *Two Treatises on Civil Government* (" The Works of John
Locke," London, 1824, IV), Book II, Ch. 8, sec. 96.

consent, that is the social compact. . . . Excepting this original contract, the vote of the majority always binds all the rest, this being the result of the contract itself. . . . When a law is proposed in the assembly of the people, what is asked of them is not exactly whether they approve the proposition or reject it, but whether it is comformable or not to the general will, which is their own; . . . and from the counting of the votes is obtained the declaration of the general will. When, therefore, the opinion opposed to my own prevails, that simply shows that I was mistaken, and that what I considered to be the general will was not so.[18]

The majority dogma has not been permitted to go entirely unchallenged. Numerous writers have questioned its validity.[14] However, these attacks have not been directed toward restoration of the old concept in accordance with which the will of the collectivity could only be expressed through explicit consent of all. Rather, they have been directed, for the most part, toward the imposition of some constitutional limitation upon the power of small or temporary majorities to commit the group to what are considered important changes from the accepted state of things. Thus, the discourses referred to advocate or are in defense of the imposition of qualified or, in some cases, concurrent majorities for the adoption of constitutional change or for taking other actions deemed to be of special importance. Modern constitutions afford many examples of checks upon rule by simple majority in legislative and other deliberative bodies. The provisions found in the Constitution of the United States by which extraordinary majorities are required in Congress both for

---

[18] J. J. Rousseau, *The Social Contract* (Translation by H. J. Tozer), Book IV, Ch. 2.

[14] A few may be cited: E. Burke, *Appeal from the New to the Old Whigs;* J. S. Mill, *Representative Government,* Ch. 7; J. C. Calhoun, *A Disquisition on Government;* Hamilton, Madison and Jay, *The Federalist;* A. B. Hall, *Popular Government,* pp. 146-171; M. P. Follett, *The New State,* pp. 142-155.

the proposal of constitutional amendments and the over-riding of presidential vetoes, and in the Senate for con-senting to the ratification of treaties, are illustrations of the revolt against simple majority rule.[15] Although such requirements tend to delay decision, in many instances preventing new situations being met with desirable dis-patch, it is important that there remain in deliberative bodies operating within states professing popular govern-ment *some* device short of unanimity by which the col-lective will may be expressed. The unanimity rule is recognized as incompatible with effective government within the domestic sphere. Should the requirement for decision be made too exacting to be achieved readily or should its achievement impose too great delay in critical situations, the result might well be to invite resort to extra-legal devices for securing the ends sought, or even to provoke the complete breakdown of constitutional government.

In the international sphere, much less progress has been made toward the acceptance of the majority device in reaching decisions. When the representatives of a group of states meet in conferences either of a formal or of an informal character, final decisions are generally, but not invariably, taken only by unanimous consent.[16] The col-

[15] It is appreciated, of course, that many provisions requiring exceptional majorities have been written into constitutions for the express purpose of preventing a particular action from being taken rather than because of any generally held view that ideally such action should depend for its validity upon the consent of more than a majority. The provision requiring two-thirds vote of the United States Senate for consent to the ratification of a treaty is a case in point, for it was written into the Constitution for the purpose of preventing a majority bartering away navigation rights on the Mississippi River. However, the two-thirds remains widely applauded as a safeguard against precipitate action in foreign affairs by the President and a majority of the Senate.

[16] Not infrequently the rule of unanimous consent is held to apply to all procedural questions as well as to decisions pertaining directly to the substance of the matter under discussion. Thus, in July, 1937, the London Non-Intervention Committee was deadlocked because the Italian and Ger-

lective will is expressed only with the consent of all states participating. The practice is much as it was in municipal deliberative bodies prior to the development of the spirit of group solidarity which characterizes states today, and prior to the time when the powers of those bodies were sufficiently advanced to cause them to feel the need for a device for rapid determination of the group will. Although many publicists have urged that, in the interests of effective international government, the rule of unanimity be abandoned in international practice,[17] those responsible for the determination of state policy have been singularly unwilling to commit the state to acceptance of a rule of law whereby the state is bound to accept the will of the majority, or even that of the quasi-totality of states, as its own.

Several defenses have been advanced for maintenance of the rule of unanimity in international practice. In the first place, it is asserted that the nature of the international community, resting as it does upon the independence or sovereignty of its component parts, makes acceptance of any other rule impossible.[18] The states are sovereign; no

---

man representatives refused to discuss the removal of volunteers before belligerent rights even though the twenty-four other governments represented agreed the propositions should be discussed in the order in which they appeared on the draft plan submitted by the British government. Cf. *The Times* (London), July 26, 1937.

[17] See F. B. Sayre, *Experiments in International Administration*, pp. 150 ff.; F. N. Keen, *A Better League of Nations*, pp. 65 ff.; Lord Davies, *Nearing the Abyss*, p. 146; L. S. Woolf, *International Government* (2d ed.), pp. 108 ff.; O. Newfang, *The Road to World Peace*, p. 47; H. Lauterpacht in *Peaceful Change*, ed. C. A. W. Manning, p. 160; C. K. Streit, *Union Now*, p. 139.

[18] See the statement of Secretary Hughes at the Conference on Central American Affairs in 1922-23 to the effect that "unanimity is a part of the consequence of the status of states in international law." (*Conference on Central American Affairs*, 1922-23, p. 80.) Also M. Nelidow's statement at the Second Hague Peace Conference that, since each delegate represents a different state of equal sovereignty, "no delegation has the right to accept a decision of the majority which would be contrary to the will of its government." (Quoted by L. S. Woolf, p. 109.) See also the

line of conduct, no legal principle can be imposed upon them against their will. Translated into juristic technic, this principle of sovereignty is held to mean, first, that no congress or conference of states, even if it includes a large majority of the states of the world, including all the great powers, is competent to take decisions having legal validity in respect to non-participating states; and second, that for decisions to be generally binding upon participating states unanimity in the meeting is required. Clearly, the sovereignty principle implies that, in the absence of express agreement, no state is bound as a matter of law to accept decisions reached by any number of other states. Nor could the mere fact of entering into conference with other states imply agreement to be bound by majority decision. However, there appears to be nothing in the doctrine of state sovereignty which would prevent states from agreeing to accept as binding decisions reached by majority vote of an international body. An undertaking on the part of a state to join with others in accepting as binding decisions reached by majority vote in an international conference or in some other international organ involves no encroachment upon state independence. It is essentially no different from the acceptance of any other treaty obligation. The state exercises its independence in deciding to attend or not to attend such a conference or in deciding to participate or not to participate in an international institution empowered to take decisions by majority vote. Indeed, as Dunn has pointed out, to hold " that sovereign states cannot submit themselves to majority rule without compromising their independence seems to carry within itself a logical contradiction of the premise of com-

---

report adopted by the First Committee of the Second Assembly of the League wherein they held " the essential characteristic of the unanimity rule . . . is that it serves to safeguard the sovereignty of states." (League of Nations, *Records of the Second Assembly*, First Committee, p. 177.) The Committee recommended that the rule be applied only in those cases in which the sovereignty of states was in jeopardy. (*Ibid.*, p. 178.)

plete freedom of action from which it is deduced." [19]
Furthermore, it should be noted that the independence
argument is entirely without validity when used in defense
of the unanimity rule in international conferences legislating as they usually do, *ad referendum*. Such conferences,
even though using the majority device for reaching decisions, impose no substantial obligation either on the
majority or on the minority in the absence of their express
consent given through ratification. The freedom of conduct of those states finding themselves in the minority is
only interfered with when the decisions take effect without subsequent signature and ratification being required,
and, even here, as has been pointed out, such interference
with freedom of conduct involves no violation of the
doctrine of state sovereignty provided that the states have
agreed to accept such a practice.

In the second place, it has been asserted by both statesmen and publicists that the rule of unanimity has received
such recognition in the practice of states as to stand as a
rule of customary international law. Thus, at the Geneva
Conference of 1864 for the amelioration of the condition
of soldiers wounded in armies in the field, General
Dufour, the chief Swiss delegate and president of the
conference, declared no vote could be taken as the majority
could not bind even an insignificant minority. Sir Ernest
Satow declares that without doubt this is the correct international doctrine.[20] At the Second Hague Peace Conference the president, M. Nelidow, stated that " the first
principle of every Conference is that of unanimity; it is
not an empty form but the basis of every political understanding." [21] J. B. Scott finds this ruling in accord with
established international practice. " The parliament, by

---

[19] F. S. Dunn, *The Practice and Procedure of International Conferences,*
p. 126.
[20] E. Satow, *A Guide to Diplomatic Practice* (2d ed.), II, 133 n.
[21] Quoted by Woolf, p. 109.

means of majorities, decrees or issues a law; the conference, by means of unanimous agreement, presents to the nations represented a draft which, when ratified by the nations, becomes with the approval of the internal and constitutional organs, the law of the ratifying nation. When ratified by the nations as a whole, it becomes *jus inter gentes*, that is, international law in the strict sense of the word." [22] In the course of the deliberations of the Commission charged by the Preparatory Peace Conference with drafting the Covenant of the League of Nations, Lord Robert Cecil declared that " all international decisions must by the nature of things be unanimous." [23]

Although it is undoubtedly true that the rule of unanimity has enjoyed wide acceptance in international practice since the formation of the modern state system, it seems questionable whether the rule can be appropriately described as having the status of customary law. In the first place, although the rule has generally been adhered to in international practice, its acceptance, as will be pointed out presently, has not been universal. Second, the fullest acceptance of the rule has come in conferences of a particular character, namely, those in which relatively small groups of states have come together for bargaining over interests of a political character, that is, over interests

[22] J. B. Scott, *The Hague Peace Conferences of 1899 and 1907*, I, 36.

[23] D. H. Miller, *The Drafting of the Covenant*, I, 161. For other evidence that the unanimity rule is considered to be firmly fixed in international practice by reason of long usage see the statement of M. Ostertag in an address delivered before the European Conference of American Professors of International Relations at Geneva, August 30, 1926 (*Michigan Law Review*, XXV, 108) ; also the authorities cited by Walter Schücking, *Der Staatenverband der Haager Konferenzen*, p. 210. See also K. Strupp, *Eléments du droit international public universel, européen et américain*, p. 66; P. Fauchille, *Traité de droit international public*, I, 245; E. Nys, *Le droit international*, II, 491; P. Pradier-Fodéré, *Cours de droit diplomatique à l'usage des agents politiques de ministre des affaires étrangeres des etats européens et américains*, II, 410; R. Genet, *Traité de diplomatie et de droit diplomatique*, III, 193.

which affect the states as political units.[24] It by no means
follows that the representatives of states serving upon
international administrative bodies or participating in
international conferences undertaking the formulation of
rules for the guidance of the entire international community upon questions primarily of concern to individuals,
should be governed by such a rule. If the interest of the
international community may be advanced, in certain circumstances, by express or tacit acceptance of some form
of majority decision in international deliberative bodies,
there would appear to be no reason in law why this should
be prevented through insistence upon application of a rule
devised to meet different circumstances and, at best, im-
perfectly observed in the conduct of states.

Third, while unanimity can not be said to be a consequence of state equality, it is frequently defended as a
device useful for its protection. So long as unanimity is
maintained the small powers are equipped to defend themselves against subjection to the will of the larger powers
even though the latter may exclude them from participation in preliminary discussions or from equal representation on conference committees or in plenary sessions.
Conversely, so long as the small powers insist the doctrine
of state equality justifies the maintenance of political
equality in all international bodies, the great powers, being
heavily outnumbered, will look upon the rule of unanimity
as essential for the protection of their dominant position
in the international society.[25]

Fourth, certain considerations of a practical character
are advanced in defense of the unanimity rule. In the first
place, it is asserted that the rule promotes international
consultation and cooperation. When it is known in advance that decisions in a particular meeting will be taken

---

[24] Cf. Dunn, p. 35.
[25] For consideration of the relation of the doctrine of state equality to
unanimity see below, Chapter X.

only by unanimous consent, it becomes very difficult for any state to refuse participation even though matters of high policy of the most controversial character are to be discussed. Thus the rule makes conference possible. There is not always a choice between a conference using unanimity and one using majority decision. Sometimes the choice is between a conference operating by unanimous consent and no conference at all. This would appear to be the case in respect to the deliberations of the London " Non-Intervention " Committee. In the second place, for conferences or other international bodies working *ad referendum* it is asserted the unanimity rule serves to prevent waste of time. With such a rule in use, propositions which have no chance of subsequent approval by all participating governments can not be pushed to adoption. When applied to the small bargaining type of conference dealing, let us say, with such a matter as limitation of naval armament, this reasoning is sound. In the absence of an agreement acceptable to all, there is no bargain and nobody is bound. However, when the argument is applied to what may be described as the legislative conference acting *ad referendum* the case is materially altered. The validity of the argument would then appear to rest upon the nature of the draft agreements or conventions under consideration. When it appears highly probable that states dissatisfied with the content of such agreements will refuse ratification, and if the agreements are of such a nature as to depend for their efficacy upon acceptance by all the participating states, then unanimity in the conference can not properly be dispensed with. However, when the conventions or agreements in question are of such a nature as to be suitable for application by part of the international community, in spite of rejection by some members, or when of such a nature that virtually all states find it to their interest to ratify in order to reap the benefits of the conventions or agreements even though not completely satisfied with their content, it would seem that unanimity might profitably be discarded in favor of some more effective means for reaching decisions.

Finally, maintenance of the unanimity rule is defended on the ground that it obliges the international conference or other organ to seek a formula acceptable to all. " The purpose of a conference is to reconcile divergent views, and, by conciliation and renunciation if necessary, to produce substantial agreement. This often means that progressive measures are discarded for more moderate formulas, just as the advance guard of an army halts that the laggard may catch up; for the purpose is not to secure the assent of the few but to bind the many." [26] However, too frequently unanimity in large gatherings is obtained only at the expense of accomplishment. To obtain the consent of all, the conference resorts to the adoption of mere platitudes on which all are, of course, in agreement, or to formulas so evasive in their wording as to be susceptible to a variety of interpretations.

In the actual practice of states, certain inroads have been made in the practice of deciding only by unanimity. This is, perhaps, most conspicuous in the field of international arbitration and adjudication. Here the principle has long been recognized that an award or judgment adopted by majority vote of a tribunal is obligatory for the parties, even though the members of the tribunal designated by them have voted against the award or judgment. Thus Article 78 of the Convention of October 18, 1907, providing for establishment of the Permanent Court of Arbitration at the Hague states that " all questions are decided by a majority of the members of the tribunal." Similarly, Article 55 of the Statute of the Permanent Court of International Justice provides that " all questions shall be decided by a majority of the judges present at the hear-

---

[26] Scott, *The Hague Peace Conferences,* I, 37.

ing." The majority principle has also been adopted for control of the internal affairs of the court, provision being made for selection of technical advisers, the president and vice-president of the court, and the registrar by majority vote.[27] Qualified unanimity is required for the dismissal of a judge,[28] this being designed, of course, to assure the independence of the individual members of the Court.

At first glance, it may appear surprising that majority decision should stand so completely accepted in the realm of international arbitration and adjudication and yet fail to attain a larger place for itself in the regulation of other relations among states. This appears even more striking when it is recalled that awards or judgments rendered by international arbitral tribunals or courts are obligatory and that such awards have, with remarkably few exceptions, been scrupulously observed by the parties. Where a state has refused to abide by such a decision it has generally been alleged, and with reason, that the arbitral body had exceeded its jurisdiction as defined by the *compromis*.[29]

The success of the majority rule in judicial determination has sometimes been made the occasion for assertion that, since majority decision is so widely and successfully employed in arbitration, it should be recognized as the appropriate method for taking decisions in other international deliberative bodies. However, acceptance of majority decision in arbitration and in adjudication represents much less concession to the community will than acceptance of majority decision elsewhere. In the first place, it must be remembered that international tribunals

[27] Rules 7, 9, 17 of the Rules of the Court, *Publications of the Permanent Court of International Justice* (cited hereafter as *Publications of the P. C. I. J.*), Series D, No. 1 (2d ed.), p. 23.

[28] Statute of the Court, Art. 18.

[29] For example, the award made in 1831 in the Northeastern Boundary Dispute between Great Britain and the United States was set aside by both parties for such reason. J. B. Moore, *Digest of International Law*, VII, par. 1082.

are not composed of representatives of states as such but of individuals. Hence, when a judgment is imposed by majority vote the state against which it is rendered has not been out-voted by a group of other states. Second, and much more important, in arbitration and adjudication states do not deem retention of the unanimity rule essential for preservation of their interests because they possess, in such cases, what amounts to a prior veto. The submission of differences between states to judicial determination depends upon the consent of the parties. This consent is generally given through treaties in which the parties have agreed in advance to submit to some form of judicial settlement disputes of a certain character. But before arbitration actually takes place under such a treaty there must be negotiated a *compromis* in which the parties define by mutual agreement the question or questions at issue, set the limits to the jurisdiction of the tribunal, and even, in some cases, determine the law which is to apply in the case. Hence, each arbitral award rests upon the consent of the parties given after the difference has arisen and to have validity the award must be strictly within the terms of that consent. The jurisdiction of the Permanent Court of International Justice likewise rests upon consent. True, those states accepting the optional clause have agreed to " compulsory jurisdiction " in disputes of a certain character, thus surrendering their power of control exercised in other cases through the *compromis*. However, although the optional clause has been widely ratified, the reservations have been so numerous and so far-reaching in character as to render the field in which states consent to " compulsory jurisdiction " small indeed. Finally, the use of majority rule in adjudication has resulted much more from the nature of the personnel of arbitral bodies than from any recognition that the minority should submit to the will of the majority. In general, the practice has been for each party to name one or more individuals to serve, these joining in the selection of a "neutral" or "neutrals" to complete the tribunal. Those designated directly by the parties are inclined to favor their own states, the vote of the "neutral" member or members being decisive. Thus arbitration developed much more as a submission to "neutral" determination than as a submission to the majority view. Even in the Permanent Court of International Justice the principle of representation of the interested parties survives in the practice of appointing *ad hoc* judges, the difference being that the neutral element represents a much larger proportion of the court than on an arbitral tribunal. Thus, while the adoption of majority decision in the practice of international adjudication must be regarded as an important deviation from the rule of unanimous consent generally adhered to elsewhere, it should be recognized that its use does not result in states being out-voted by other states as such, that it operates in a closely controlled field, and that its development can scarcely signify any recognition of the validity of majority decision as such.

In international conferences not associated with permanent organizations and devoted to work of a "political" character, that is, to work directly affecting the interests of states as political units, those responsible for the conduct of state policy have shown much greater reluctance to abandon the rule of unanimous consent. Although unanimity in such conferences has undoubtedly been the general rule,[30] even here certain deviations, some of considerable importance, have been permitted in order that achievement be facilitated. Frequently, procedural questions and matters considered as being of secondary importance only have been disposed of by majority vote. Thus, at the Geneva Conference of 1868 for the revision

[30] Cf. Satow, II, 133 n.; E. D. Dickinson, *The Equality of States in International Law,* p. 282; N. L. Hill, *The Public International Conference,* pp. 188 ff.; Pradier-Fodéré, II, 410 ff.; R. Genet, III, 192.

of the Convention of 1864 respecting the treatment of soldiers wounded on the field of battle, it was held that a majority vote should suffice for decision to discuss a particular subject, but that unanimity would be required for its final adoption.[31] In the Congress of Berlin of 1878, at the suggestion of Bismarck, it was unanimously decided that, in the interests of accomplishment, resolutions concerning procedure and not touching questions of substance should be held to be decisions of the congress when approved by majority vote unless the minority should register formal protest.[32] The committees of the Hague Peace Conferences of 1899 and 1907 made recommendations upon the basis of majority vote, and in the Second Conference majority vote was sometimes regarded as sufficient to entitle a proposal to be recorded as part of the proceedings, while in other cases unanimity was held necessary.[33] Occasionally, such conferences have taken decisions of a major character by something less than unanimous vote. The Congress of Berlin adopted a settlement in respect to Bosnia and Herzegovina without the consent of Turkey. Similarly, the resolution relative to the Chinese Eastern Railway, adopted at the Washington Conference of 1921, did not have the approval of the Chinese delegation.[34] The Inter-American Conferences for the Maintenance of Peace now take decisions by vote of an absolute majority of the delegations present at the meeting, extraordinary majorities being required in some cases.[35] More striking, however, are the departures made from the rule of unanimous consent in some of the political conferences organized under the auspices of the League of Nations. The

---

[31] Satow, II, 139.

[32] *British and Foreign State Papers* (cited hereafter as *B. & F. State Papers*), LXIX, 892.

[33] Satow, II, 172.

[34] Hill, p. 190.

[35] Pan American Union, *Regulations of the Inter-American Conference for the Maintenance of Peace*, Art. 22.

règlement adopted by the Conference for the Codification of International Law, 1930, appears particularly interesting. By virtue of these rules, decisions in each of the three standing committees were reached by majority vote. In order that a proposition be placed before the plenary session of the conference in the form of a draft convention or protocol, support by vote of two-thirds of those present in the committee was required.[36] However, on the request of five members, the commissions were authorized to decide by simple majority vote to include in special protocols open to signature or accession any proposition which had obtained a simple majority vote but which had failed to attract the support of two-thirds of the members present.[37] Finally, the conference in plenary session was authorized to adopt by vote of a simple majority of the delegates present any or all of the draft conventions, protocols, recommendations and *voeux* placed before it by its committees.[38] Although M. Guerrero (Salvador) and some other delegates to the conference questioned the propriety of departing from the rule of unanimous consent in a conference engaged in the codification of international law,[39] M. Rolin (Belgium) justified majority vote by asserting that in reality the conference was engaged in the preparation of conventions on international law rather than on a work of pure codification which would appear to require the assent of the entire international community.[40]

In the most ambitious attempt to provide permanent organization for the international community, namely, in the establishment of the League of Nations, the framers saw fit to provide, in general, for adherence by the Council

---

[36] Art. 18, Rules of Procedure. League of Nations, *Acts of the Conference for the Codification of International Law,* 1930, I (League Doc. C. 351. M. 145. 1930. V), 62.

[37] Art. 20, *ibid.*

[38] Art. 23, *ibid.*

[39] *Acts of the Conference,* 1930, I, 33.

[40] *Ibid.,* p. 34.

and the Assembly to the rule of unanimous consent. Article 5 of the Covenant provides:

> Except where otherwise expressly provided in this Covenant, or by the terms of the present treaty, decisions at any meeting of the Assembly or of the Council shall require the agreement of all the Members of the League represented at the meeting.
>
> All matters of procedure at meetings of the Assembly or of the Council, including the appointment of Committees to investigate particular matters, shall be regulated by the Assembly or by the Council and may be decided by a majority of the Members of the League represented at the meeting.

Yet even here, in the face of an apparently explicit legal formula, numerous exceptions, many of them important, have developed to the rule of unanimity.[41] In the first place, the Covenant itself provides for a number of exceptions from the general rule. New members are admitted to the League by two-thirds vote of the Assembly (Art. 1, par. 2) ; a majority vote of the Assembly is sufficient for approval of a Council resolution increasing the permanent or non-permanent membership of the Council (Art. 4, par. 2) ; procedural questions in either Council or Assembly are decided by majority vote (Art. 5, par. 2) ; a majority vote in the Assembly is sufficient to approve the appointment of the Secretary-General by the Council (Art. 6, par. 2) ; if a dispute between member states likely to lead to a rupture is not settled through arbitration, ad-

---

[41] For detailed examination of the deviation from unanimity made by the Council and the Assembly of the League see, C. A. Riches, *The Unanimity Rule and the League of Nations*. G. T. Éles, *Le principe de l'unanimité dans la Société des Nations*. Briefer accounts may be found in J. F. Williams, " The League of Nations and Unanimity," *American Journal of International Law* (cited hereafter as *A. J. I. L.*) (1925), XIX, 475 ; J. Stone, " The Rule of Unanimity: The Practice of the Council and Assembly of the League of Nations," *British Yearbook of International Law* (cited hereafter as *B. Y. I. L.*) (1933), XIV, 18 ; W. Schücking and H. Wehberg, *Die Satzung des Völkerbundes* (2d ed.), pp. 507-522 ; J. Ray, *Commentaire du pacte de la Société des Nations*, pp. 221-236.

judication or by Council mediation, the Council shall, either unanimously or by a majority vote, make and publish a report containing a statement of the facts of the dispute and the recommendations which are deemed just and proper in regard thereto (Art. 15, par. 4) ; under the same Article members of the League agree not to go to war with any party which complies with the recommendations of a report made by unanimous vote of the Council exclusive of the parties to the dispute (Art. 15, par. 6) or which complies with a report by the Assembly concurred in by the representatives of those members of the League represented on the Council and a majority of the other members of the League, exclusive in each case of the parties to the dispute (Art. 15, par. 10) ; any member violating the Covenant may be excluded from the League by vote of the Council concurred in by all the other members of the League represented thereon (Art. 16, par. 4) ; finally, amendments to the Covenant take effect when ratified by the members of the League whose representatives compose the Council and by a majority of the members of the League whose representatives compose the Assembly (Art. 26, par. 1), but a dissenting state, instead of being bound by the amendment, may cease to be a member of the League (Art. 26, par. 2). By amendment in force July 29, 1926, the Assembly " shall fix by a two-thirds majority the rules dealing with the election of the non-permanent members of the Council, and particularly such regulations as relate to their term of office and the conditions of re-eligibility " (Art. 4, par. 2 *bis*). In pursuance of this authority, the Assembly, on September 15 of the same year, adopted regulations which permit that body at any time to decide by two-thirds vote to proceed to a new election of all the non-permanent members of the Council.[42] This is tantamount to a power of recall.

[42] *Records of the Seventh Assembly,* Plenary, p. 79.

Further, the treaties of peace impose a number of functions upon the Council, to be exercised by majority vote. Thus questions relative to the Saar [43] and to investigation of the compliance of the defeated powers with the disarmament provisions of the treaties [44] could be decided by majority vote of the Council. Provisions of the minorities treaties may be modified by a similar vote.[45] Post-war treaties have added many instances in which the Council or Assembly may act by majority vote.[46] To cite only a few: the judges of the Permanent Court of International Justice are elected by majority vote of the Assembly and of the Council; [47] disputes relative to the Oriental Railways are decided by majority vote of the Council, the Greek and Turkish governments undertaking to carry out all such decisions; [48] changes in the composition and rights of the Memel harbor administration and in the regulations pertaining to transit through the Memel district were made by proposal of Lithuania approved by majority vote of the

[43] Treaty of Versailles, par. 40 of Annex to Part III, Sec. IV.

[44] Treaty of Versailles, Art. 213; St. Germain, Art. 159; Trianon, Art. 143; Neuilly, Art. 104.

[45] Treaty of St. Germain, Art. 69; Trianon, Art. 60; Neuilly, Art. 57. Similar provisions for majority action by the Council are to be found in the other minority treaties. See, for example, Art. 12, par. 1, of the Polish treaty of June 28, 1919.

[46] Conceivably, it might have been argued that Art. 5 of the Covenant prevented the Council or Assembly from acting under such a power. However, in the Rules of Procedure adopted by the Assembly in 1920, Rule 19 substitutes for the words of Art. 5 "by the terms of *the present* treaty" the words "by the terms of *a* treaty." A similar change was made in Art. 8 of the Council Rules of Procedure adopted May 17, 1920. These changes have not been altered by subsequent amendment of the rules of either body. All doubt on the matter appears to have been cleared away by the statement of the P. C. I. J. in the Mosul case: "No one denies that the Council can undertake to give a decision by a majority in specific cases, if express provision is made for this power by treaty stipulations." *Publications of the P. C. I. J.,* Series B, No. 12, p. 30.

[47] Statute of the P. C. I. J., Art. 10.

[48] Treaty of Lausanne, Art. 107. League of Nations, *Treaty Series* (cited hereafter as *L. N. T. S.*), XXVIII, 12.

Council including the representatives of all the Principal Allied Powers; [49] decisions of the Council relative to the Greek Refugees Settlement Scheme were taken by majority vote; [50] decisions of the Council concerning disputes arising out of the Bulgarian-Greek financial agreement of December 9, 1927, are taken by an absolute majority of the Council; [51] a two-thirds vote of the Council sufficed for decision on measures to be taken in event of violation of the de-militarization or neutralization clauses of the Aaland Islands Convention of October 20, 1921.[52]

Probably of much greater significance are the exceptions to the general rule of unanimity which have appeared in the practice of the Council and of the Assembly through liberal interpretation of the Covenant by those two bodies. Both Council and Assembly hold that abstention on the part of one or more of the delegates present does not prevent unanimity from obtaining.[53] The " matters of procedure," which Article 5 exempts from the general rule of unanimity, has been held by both organs to include much more than adoption or modification of the rules of procedure, election of officers, decisions in respect to

[49] Convention Concerning the Territory of Memel, Annex II, Art. 14, and Annex III, Art. 4, *L. N. T. S.*, XXIX, 86.

[50] Arts. 17, 18, 19 of Annex to the Protocol Relating to the Settlement of Refugees in Greece, *L. N. T. S.*, XX, 30.

[51] Art. 8, *L. N. T. S.*, LXXXVII, 199.

[52] Art. 7, *L. N. T. S.*, IX, 212.

[53] Express provision to this effect is made in Rule 19, par. 5, of the Rules of Procedure adopted by the Assembly in 1920. Although no such provision is to be found in the Rules of the Council, it is, nevertheless, accepted in practice. Cf. *Committee on the Composition of the Council* (League Doc. C. 299. M. 139. 1926. V) First Session, pp. 24, 26, 93. When Soviet Russia was excluded from the League, Dec. 14, 1939, by the Council acting under Art. 16, par. 4, only the representatives of France, Great Britain, Bolivia, Belgium, the Dominican Republic, South Africa, and Egypt assented to the resolution. Greece, Jugoslavia, Finland, and China abstained from voting and the representatives of Peru, Iran, and Russia were absent (*The New York Times,* Dec. 15, 1939). Thus " unanimity " was achieved by a vote of seven of the fourteen Council members.

agenda, and similar matters which are not likely to provoke controversy. The exemption has been held to extend
as well to the election of the non-permanent members of
the Council by the Assembly,[54] to the establishment of
committees of inquiry as well as to the selection of their
personnel,[55] and to the extension to a non-member state
of an invitation to sit with the Council.[56]

In the Assembly, the inconvenience of operating under
a general rule of unanimous consent has been greatly
reduced through the drawing of a distinction between
" decisions " within the meaning of Article 5, paragraph 1,
and resolutions which may be described as " *voeux* " or
" recommendations." The former includes only resolutions intended to impose definite legal obligations upon
member states. Recommendations to the member states,
to the Council, or to other international bodies clearly do
not fall within this category, thus eliminating from the
requirement of unanimity a large and important part of
the work of the Assembly. Although this practice of
adopting *voeux* or recommendations by majority vote has
been followed consistently in the Assembly since its first
year of existence,[57] it has never been accepted in the

---

[54] *Records of the First Assembly,* First Committee, p. 110; *ibid.,* Plenary,
pp. 423, 559.

[55] League of Nations, *Official Journal* (cited hereafter as *O. J.*), 1922,
p. 551; *ibid.,* 1931, p. 2378.

[56] There is some doubt as to the value of this precedent which arose, of
course, during the Sino-Japanese controversy in 1931. It may be alleged
that the substantive issue of American participation had already been
decided by earlier adoption of a unanimous resolution to keep the United
States fully informed of the progress made in settlement of the dispute.
In this view, the resolution merely introduced a change in the method of
keeping the United States informed. However, since Japan's protests were
unavailing, the incident does appear to establish that determination of
what constitutes a procedural question is itself a procedural question. A
contrary view was taken earlier by the Assembly. Cf. *Records of the First
Assembly,* Plenary, p. 426.

[57] Cf. *Records of First Assembly,* Plenary, p. 435; *ibid.,* p. 529; *Records
of Second Assembly,* Plenary, p. 888; *Records of Third Assembly,* Plenary,

practice of the Council. In that body, in the absence of explicit treaty provisions authorizing majority decision, all resolutions other than those dealing with procedural questions are adopted by unanimous vote regardless of whether they impose definite legal obligations upon the member states or merely recommend action. It would seem, however, that by the same line of reasoning employed by the Assembly the Council could, if it so desired, avoid use of unanimity for recommendations.[58] It appears illogical to interpret the language of Article 5 differently in relation to the Council and Assembly, respectively. However, both the Committee on Amendments to the Covenant and the First Committee of the Second Assembly have endorsed this distinction, justifying it largely upon the ground that the Council by reason of its smaller membership can more easily achieve unanimity.[59]

Further, the Assembly has held unanimity not essential in the proposal of amendments to the Covenant. Although Article 26 is silent on the vote necessary for proposing amendments, the article providing only that they shall take effect when ratified by the members of the League whose representatives compose the Council and by a majority of the members of the League whose representatives compose the Assembly, the Assembly has, by the same process of reasoning used in freeing recommendations and *voeux*, removed propositions of amendment from the category of resolutions falling within the term " decisions " within the meaning of Article 5, paragraph 1. Covenant stipulations are satisfied, the Assembly holds, when proposals of amendment are supported by majority vote of the

p. 350; *Records of Fourth Assembly*, Plenary, p. 114; *Records of Tenth Assembly*, Plenary, p. 121.

[58] In support of this view see J. F. Williams, " Sanctions Under the Covenant," *B. Y. I. L.* (1936), XVII, 130.

[59] *Committee on Amendments to the Covenant*; *First Report to the Council* (League Doc. A. 24. 1921. V), p. 12; *Records of the Second Assembly*, First Committee, p. 177.

Assembly including the representatives of the states having Council seats.[60] At least two amendments have been proposed over the negative vote of one or more members of the League, and one of these has actually entered into force.[61]

Finally, the rule of unanimity is mitigated considerably in the Assembly through the practice, quite consistently followed, of taking decisions in the committees by majority vote.[62] This appears to apply equally to the Assembly sitting in general commission.[63]

In certain other matters the League organs have been much less daring in interpretation. Uncertainty still exists concerning the nature of the vote required in the Assembly or in the Council for requesting an advisory opinion from the Permanent Court of International Justice. In the view of many, the request for an advisory opinion should be looked upon as a procedural question essentially no different in character from a decision to set up a committee of jurists to advise on questions of a legal character, a decision which either Council or Assembly admittedly can take by majority vote. Others hold that the matter can not properly be considered procedural for, even though the requesting body has, in theory, no legal obligation to

[60] Records of the Second Assembly, Plenary, pp. 733-735. See also Records of the Second Assembly, First Committee, p. 65. At the same time this interpretation was adopted the Assembly proposed an amendment to Article 26 providing that amendments should require a three-fourths vote in the Assembly including all members having Council seats. It also recommended that, until this amendment entered into force, amendments be proposed only by such a vote. Records of the Second Assembly, Plenary, pp. 733-735.

[61] An amendment to Article 6, in force August 13, 1924. It was proposed in the Assembly by vote of 40 for, 1 against (Greece), with 10 abstaining. Records of the Second Assembly, Plenary, p. 885.

[62] See the Report of the First Committee of the Fifth Assembly on the practice in the Committees (Records of the Fifth Assembly, Plenary, p. 411). The report was approved by the Assembly, thus giving official sanction to the practice (ibid., p. 113). See also the statement of Motta (Switzerland) in Records of the Fourth Assembly, Plenary, p. 114.

[63] See Records of Special Session of the Assembly, 1932, I, 43, 87.

accept the advice tendered, such a step amounts in fact to submission of the question at issue to adjudication. In the words of Politis, an advisory opinion is no longer looked upon as advisory but is " equivalent in the eyes of the Council, of public opinion and of the interested parties to a judgment." [64] Although the rule of unanimity has in all cases been observed in the requesting of advisory opinions, the League organs have carefully avoided any commitment to the effect that such a vote is necessary. Their position has been to hold the matter open for future determination.[65] However, on September 24, 1928, the Assembly adopted a resolution urging the " necessity for putting an end to the prevailing uncertainty " and calling upon the Council to submit the matter to study,[66] but the Council took no effective action in pursuance of this resolution. In September, 1935, the Belgian, Netherland, Swedish, Norwegian and Swiss delegations, disturbed by the declining use of advisory opinions and believing it a consequence of the unanimity rule observed in practice by the Council, suggested that the question be submitted to the Court for an opinion.[67] The Assembly, however, faced with the assertion that the Court could not decide on a question thus submitted to it in the abstract, merely reiterated in a resolution of September 28, 1935, its earlier request that the Council submit the matter to examination.[68]

In yet another matter, namely, the right of parties to a dispute to vote, the Council has wavered between a liberal

[64] *Records of the Ninth Assembly,* First Committee, p. 47.

[65] See particularly League of Nations, *Minutes of the Conference of States Signatories of the Protocol of the Statute of the Permanent Court of International Justice, 1926.* See also Sir Cecil Hurst's remark made in the First Committee of the Ninth Assembly that " it would be better to leave it to experience to show what would ultimately constitute the best and most useful rule for the League to follow," *Records of the Ninth Assembly,* First Committee, p. 45.

[66] *Records of the Ninth Assembly,* Plenary, p. 139.

[67] *Records of the Sixteenth Assembly,* Plenary, p. 76.

[68] *Ibid.,* pp. 95, 127.

interpretation of the Covenant which would permit it to be a workable document and a narrowly legalistic view which deprives certain articles of all meaning. As is well known, Article 15, paragraphs 6, 7, 10, and Article 16, paragraph 4, specify that the votes of the parties concerned are not counted in determining whether the vote required by the Covenant article in question has been achieved. No such exceptions are found in Articles 10, 11, 13, paragraph 4, Article 16, paragraph 2, or Article 19. Cecil and Scialoja, both members of the commission which drafted the Covenant, have testified that sheer oversight explains this discrepancy.[69] In a number of cases coming before the Council under Article 11, the Council appeared to hold qualified unanimity applicable in proceedings under that article, applying the rule of law, the applicability of which was suggested by the Permanent Court in its advisory opinion in the Mosul Case,[70] that no one can be judge in his own suit.[71] Yet in the Sino-Japanese controversy of 1931 the negative vote of Japan was permitted to defeat a Council resolution presented under that article.[72] The League committee of jurists, which met in June 1935, to consider possible action under Article 11 to deter treaty violation, were unable to agree whether the article required absolute unanimity or not.[73] The suggestion that Article 11 be amended to permit decision being taken without the consent of the parties to the dispute, made in a number of the replies to the Assembly request of July 4,

---

[69] *Minutes of the Committee for the Amendment of the Covenant of the League of Nations in order to Bring It into Harmony with the Pact of Paris* (League Doc. C. 160. M. 69. 1930. V), pp. 47-48.

[70] *Publications of P. C. I. J.*, Series B, No. 12, p. 31.

[71] *O. J.*, 1922, p. 1333; *ibid.*, 1923, p. 599; *ibid.*, 1925, p. 1700; *ibid.*, 1927, p. 1414. See also the statement of Paul-Boncour in *Documents of the Preparatory Commission for the Disarmament Conference*, Series 3 (League Doc. C. 740. M. 279. 1926. IX), p. 71 and the report of the Committee of the Council on Art. 11, *O. J.*, 1927, p. 833.

[72] *O. J.*, 1931, p. 2358.

[73] League of Nations, *Monthly Summary* (June, 1935), XV, 147.

1936, for proposals for strengthening the League, strongly suggests that, in the view of many Geneva statesmen, absolute unanimity is now required under the article.[74]

Finally, it might be added, the Assembly has never given any indication that Article 19 might be employed by any vote other than absolute unanimity, although it might reasonably have done so. From the wording of the article, both in the French and English texts, it would appear reasonable for the Assembly to classify resolutions adopted under it as recommendations or *voeux* to be adopted by majority vote rather than as " decisions " within the meaning of Article 5.[75] The tendering of " advice " to give up rights could impose no legal obligation upon member states to accept that advice—which is the test adopted by the Assembly for determining what constitutes a " decision." Clearly, the persuasive influence of such a resolution adopted by quasi-unanimity might be substantially as great as if absolute unanimity were obtained. To hold absolute unanimity essential for the adoption of a resolution under Article 19 is to deprive the article of all meaning.[76]

[74] See League Doc. A. 31. 1936. VII; League Doc. C. 376. M. 247. 1936. VII.

[75] For a contrary view see Q. Wright in *Proceedings of the American Society of International Law*, 1936, p. 71. However, Wright appears to arrive at his conclusion through a confusion in the nature of the practices of the Assembly in respect to recommendations. " It seems to be accepted," he states, " that so important a matter as advice under Article 19 cannot be regarded as merely procedural; consequently the practice of making recommendations by majority vote cannot be applied. It, therefore, seems that absolute unanimity, required for ' decisions ' by Article 5 of the Covenant, is necessary. . . ." But the Assembly has never held that recommendations must relate to procedural questions. On the contrary, examination of Assembly documents will reveal that they very frequently relate to substantive issues, often being resorted to when the unanimity requisite for a " decision " cannot be obtained, the word " decides " being changed to " recommends."

[76] It would not appear possible to exclude the votes of the interested parties in the absence of a Covenant provision to that effect since it is doubtful whether procedure under Article 19 can properly be regarded as dealing with a dispute between states.

But no adequate conception of the present status of the rule of unanimity in the relations among states can be obtained without examination of the place of the rule in the numerous international public unions and other permanent international bodies now existing for the performance of functions of interest to groups of states. In the chapters which follow, the results of such an examination are set forth together with some consideration of the closely associated, and quite inseparable, problem of representation. Here one naturally encounters great variation in the practices followed. Some of these organizations date from the second half of the nineteenth century, and have undergone little change since their establishment, while many others are post-war creations. Some perform functions very closely associated with matters of high policy while others deal with subjects which by no stretch of reasoning can be so considered. In some, the larger questions of policy involved in the activity are regulated by convention stipulations completely beyond the reach of the organization itself, while in others the international body is in a position to make, or at least to propose to the governments, changes in these stipulations. In some cases, the union is competent to impose an immediate legal obligation upon the member states, while in others all action is solely of an advisory character. Several of the unions have elaborate governmental organizations consisting of congresses or conferences, commissions, and bureaus while in others the organization is extremely rudimentary. Representation in some is diplomatic and in others technical. Delegates in some cases represent the states, as such, and in other cases only government departments. These very differences, however, may assist in arriving at conclusions of at least a tentative nature concerning the circumstances under which states in their relations with one another are willing to agree to a rule of law whereby the majority may bind the minority.

CHAPTER II

UNANIMITY IN CONFERENCES OF PUBLIC UNIONS

Decision by some form of majority vote has been widely adopted in the organs of many public international unions. However, a survey of the practices of the general conferences of existing unions reveals several which continue to adhere to the rule of unanimity for the adoption of final acts. Outstanding among these are the conferences of the Union for the Protection of Industrial Property (1883), the Union for the Protection of Literary and Artistic Works (1886), and the International Institute of Agriculture (1905). Before turning to a consideration of the many departures made from the rule of unanimity in other international bodies, it seems appropriate to examine the circumstances which gave rise to adoption of the rule in those conferences using it, the legal basis on which it rests, and the experience of the organs with it.

The Union for the Protection of Industrial Property, established because of the inadequacy of the protection afforded foreigners in industrial property rights by the domestic legislation of the countries of the world and through bipartite treaties, was created by the Paris Conference of March 20, 1883.[1] The Convention was signed and ratified by eleven of the states represented,[2] thus bringing it into force July 7, 1884, in conformity with

---

[1] *B. & F. State Papers,* LXXIV, 44. For the convention as revised at Brussels, Dec. 14, 1900, at Washington, June 2, 1911, at the Hague, Nov. 6, 1925, and at London, June 2, 1934, see L'Union Internationale pour la Protection de la Propriété Industrielle, *Actes de la Conférence de Londres,* 1934, p. 535.

[2] Belgium, Brazil, France, Guatemala, Italy, Netherlands, Portugal, Salvador, Serbia, Spain, and Switzerland. *Actes de la Conférence de Paris,* 1883.

Article 18. Membership in the Union has since increased to forty.[3]

The terms of the Convention establish a much less elaborate governing organization than has been created for many public unions performing less important work. Article 13, which remains substantially in the form adopted in 1883, provides for an International Bureau of the distinctly informational type under the authority of the Swiss Confederation. The Bureau is charged with the collection of information of every kind relating to the protection of industrial property. The term " industrial property," according to Article 1 of the Convention, is to be understood in its broadest sense, applying not only to industry and commerce properly so called, but also to agricultural industries and to the extractive industries generally.[4] The Bureau has no powers comparable to those possessed by the Governing Body of the International Labor Organization for calling the attention of member states to their failure to bring their municipal law into conformity with the terms of the Convention, or even to urge ratification of the revised texts of the Convention. For purposes of financial maintenance, the member states are divided into six classes, each state being permitted to designate, at the time of its accession, the class to which it will belong.[5] The annual expenditure of the Bureau is limited by terms of the Convention but in case of necessity the sum fixed may be increased by

[3] Bulgaria, Canada, Dominican Republic, Greece, Luxemburg, New Zealand, Germany, Australia, Austria, Belgium, Brazil, Cuba, Denmark, Danzig, Spain, Esthonia, Syria and Lebanon, the United States, Finland, France, Great Britain and Northern Ireland, Hungary, the Irish Free State, Italy, Japan, Latvia, Liechtenstein, Morocco, Mexico, Norway, Netherlands, Poland, Portugal, Roumania, Sweden, Switzerland, Czechoslovakia, Tunis, Turkey, and Jugoslavia. *Actes de la Conférence de Londres,* 1934.

[4] The definition was widened at the conference of 1934. *Actes de la Conférence,* 1934, p. 540.

[5] Article 13 of the Convention.

unanimous decision of one of conferences of revision.[6] Since 1888, the Bureau has also served as the central organ for the Union for the Protection of Literary and Artistic Works.

The only other governing organ provided for is the Conference of Revision. Article 14 of the Convention is as follows:

The present Convention shall be submitted to periodical revisions with a view to the introduction of amendments calculated to improve the system of the Union.

For this purpose, Conferences shall be held, successively in one of the contracting countries, among the delegates of the said countries.

The Administration of the country in which the conference is to be held will make preparations for the work of that Conference, with the assistance of the International Bureau.

The Director of the International Bureau will be present at the meetings of the Conferences and will take part in the discussions, but without the right of voting.

In accordance with the terms of this article, successive conferences of revision have been held at Rome in 1886, at Madrid in 1890, at Brussels in 1900, at Washington in 1911, at the Hague in 1925, and at London in 1934.

The Convention, it will be noted, contains no explicit statement concerning the vote necessary for taking decisions in the conferences of revision other than the statement made in Article 13 in respect to increases in the annual budget of the Bureau. Nor does it specify the number of votes to be cast by the various contracting

---

[6] At first the annual expenditure of the Bureau was limited by terms of the Final Protocol to 2,000 Swiss francs per annum for each contracting country. In 1891, this was changed to a sum not exceeding 60,000 francs and in 1925, to a sum not exceeding 120,000 francs. It was in 1925 that the convention was amended to give the Conference of Revision express power to increase the amount by unanimous vote. Consequently, the changes can now be made without awaiting ratification by the member states.

states. These omissions suggest that it was the intention of those drafting the Convention to permit modification only with the consent of all. Hence, it was unnecessary to provide, as the terms of many other conventions do, for awarding greater voting power to those states electing to supply greater financial support to the Union.

In the absence of detailed regulations in the Convention for the conferences of revision, each conference has adopted its own rules of procedure. It has been the practice, in conformity with Article 14 of the Convention, for the administration of the country in which the conference is being held to formulate, with the assistance of the International Bureau, draft rules of procedure to submit to the delegates. These are adopted, article by article, by majority vote.[7] As one would expect, these rules are in fact carried over from conference to conference with little change. At the 1934 conference only one innovation was introduced, namely, the placing of the English language on a basis of equality with French for purposes of debates in the conference.[8] This proposition was adopted by 17 votes for to 4 votes against, with ten abstentions.[9]

The rules of procedure are quite clear on the voting power to be exercised by each contracting state. Rule 2 provides that each country shall have a single vote. However, in case of necessity, member states may be represented by the delegation of another member state. Consequently, it is by no means unusual for some states, particularly those with colonial possessions which have been admitted to membership, to be casting more than a single vote in a given conference. Delegates from non-member states and representatives of the Economic Section of the League of Nations and the Organization for Intel-

[7] Cf. *Actes de la Conférence de Londres,* 1934, p. 321.
[8] Rule 9, *Actes de la Conférence,* 1934, p. 329.
[9] *Actes de la Conférence,* 1934, p. 328.

lectual Cooperation are permitted to take part in the debates, but have no right to participate in the voting. Equality of representation is provided for not only in the plenary sessions but in the commission and sub-commissions as well by the terms of Rule 6 which declares it to be the privilege of all delegates to attend all sessions and to take part in all debates.

The rules of procedure, however, contain no statements concerning the vote necessary for taking decisions in the plenary sessions, in the commission, or in the six sub-commissions into which the commission usually divides itself for consideration of the agenda. The rules on this matter are, nevertheless, well established by the practice of the conferences. Procedural questions in the plenary sessions and all questions in the commission and sub-commissions are settled by majority vote. In the plenary sessions, however, no amendments to the Convention or to the accompanying arrangements may be adopted except by unanimous vote. Agreement on this point was reached in the first conference of revision and it has been strictly adhered to by all succeeding conferences. At that time, Mr. J. Henry G. Bergne (Great Britain) presented the following questions: " If the result of this conference is to be the modification of the text of the convention, and if the governments are not able to agree to accept unanimously the changes proposed, shall the refusal of a minority to agree involve the withdrawal of all states composing this minority? Or would it be better to consider the convention as the constitution of the Union, a constitution which cannot be modified without the consent of all the contracting states? " [10] The conference adopted the second position.

The convention founding the Union for the Protection of Literary and Artistic Works, the product of successive

[10] *Actes de la Conférence de Rome,* 1886, p. 86.

conferences held at Berne in September, 1884, 1885, and 1886,[11] resembles closely that for the protection of industrial property.[12] Several of the articles are substantially identical in wording. Like the Industrial Property Union the only permanent governing organ provided is an International Bureau placed under the supervision of the Swiss Confederation [13] and the only other organ provided is a Conference of Revision meeting at irregular intervals.[14]

Since 1888, one bureau has served both the Industrial Property and the Copyright Unions and the duties assigned the Bureau by the Berne Convention are much like those given it by the Paris Convention. It collects information of all kinds relative to the protection of the rights of authors in their productions, it undertakes special studies of general questions of interest to the Union, and it furnishes the member states with any special information which they require relative to the protection of literary and artistic works.[15] The provisions for financial main-

[11] The Conference of 1884 was attended by delegates from Germany, Austria-Hungary, Belgium, Costa Rica, France, Great Britain, Haiti, Italy, Paraguay, Netherlands, Salvador, Sweden, Norway, and Switzerland. That of 1885, by delegates from Germany, Argentina, Belgium, Costa Rica, Spain, the United States, France, Great Britain, Haiti, Honduras, Italy, Paraguay, the Netherlands, Sweden and Norway, Switzerland and Tunis. The final conference in 1886 was attended by delegates from Germany, Belgium, Spain, the United States, France, Great Britain, Haiti, Italy, Japan, Liberia, Switzerland, and Tunis. Nine states, Great Britain, Belgium, France, Germany, Haiti, Italy, Spain, Switzerland, and Tunis, signed the Convention September 9, 1886, and exchanged ratifications September 5, 1887. Liberia signed but did not ratify. (*B. & F. State Papers,* LXXVII, 22.) Membership in the union has since increased to thirty-seven: Germany, Belgium, Brazil, Bulgaria, Denmark, Spain, Esthonia, Finland, France, Great Britain and Northern Ireland, Canada, Australia, New Zealand, Irish Free State, India, Greece, Hungary, Italy, Japan, Luxemburg, Morocco, Monaco, Norway, Netherlands, Poland, Free City of Danzig, Portugal, Roumania, Sweden, Switzerland, Syria and Grand Lebanon, Czechoslovakia, Tunis, Liechtenstein, Siam, Vatican City, and Jugoslavia.

[12] The Convention, as revised at Berlin, Nov. 13, 1908, and at Rome, June 2, 1928, will be found in *L. N. T. S.,* CXXIII, 233.

[13] Art. 21.   [14] Art. 24.   [15] Art. 22.

tenance of the Bureau resemble closely those made in the Paris Convention. Provision is made for division into classes, each member declaring at the time of accession the class to which it wishes to belong. One table of classes and units of contribution serves for both unions. The expenses of the office may not exceed 120,000 Swiss francs per annum except upon unanimous decision of one of the conferences provided for by Article 24 of the Convention.[16]

Article 24, which provides for the Conferences of Revision, is very much like Article 14 of the Industrial Property Convention except for the final paragraph containing explicit provision for use of the unanimity rule in adoption of amendments to the Convention. The article is as follows:

1. The present Convention may be submitted to revisions in order to introduce therein amendments calculated to perfect the systems of the union.

2. Questions of this kind, as well as those which are of interest to the Union in other respects, shall be considered in Conferences to be held successively in the countries of the Union by delegates of the said countries. The administration of the country where a Conference is to meet prepares, with the assistance of the International Office, the program of the Conference. The Director of the Office shall attend at the sittings of the Conferences, and shall take part in the discussions without the right to vote.

3. No alteration in the present Convention shall be binding on the Union except by the unanimous consent of the countries composing it.

The explicit provision for use of the unanimity rule in amendment of the Convention was inserted at the Conference of 1885. In the draft convention submitted by the Swiss Government for consideration by the Conference of 1884, the clause is not found, although Article 14 of that tentative plan is substantially the same as the first two

[16] Art. 23.

paragraphs of the present Article 24. In the draft convention adopted by the conference the Swiss Article 14
is carried over as Article 18 without the addition of the
unanimity rule.[17] However, at the Conference of 1885,
the clause was added at the suggestion of the British
delegation.[18] It was urged in support of this proposition
that the legislative authorities of the various countries
would perhaps hesitate to modify their domestic legislation
to bring it into accord with the terms of the Convention
if they had reason to fear that the latter would be revised
at short intervals. Furthermore, the British delegation
believed it should be understood that the Convention
forms the constitution or charter for the Union, and,
consequently, that it should be modified only with the
consent of all contracting parties. Countries desiring
improvements in the Convention, if unable to obtain the
consent of all, would be free to conclude within the limits
of the general convention, special arrangements for this
purpose.[19]

At the time decision was made to use the rule of
unanimous consent in the conferences both unions were
composed of but few members. At the time of the last
conferences of revision, membership had increased to forty
in the Industrial Property Union and to thirty-eight in
the Union for the Protection of Literary and Artistic
Works. Some of the states members of the unions are
highly industrialized, others represented are primarily
agricultural areas. Some possess advanced municipal legis-

[17] Correspondence Respecting the Formation of an International Copyright Union, *British Parliamentary Papers* (cited hereafter as *B. P. P.*),
1886, LXXII, 24.
[18] As Article 17.
[19] L'Union Internationale pour la Protection des Œuvres Littéraires et
Artistique, *Actes de la 2me Conférence Internationale,* Berne, 1885, p. 53.
Mr. J. H. G. Bergne, who in 1886 insisted upon Article 14 of the Industrial Property Convention being interpreted to require unanimity, was a
member of the British delegation at the Conference of 1885.

lation for the protection of property rights in industrial, literary, and artistic works antedating considerably the international efforts in that direction. In others, much of the legislation on the subject is new. Moreover, the conventions necessarily touch many points of self-interest and political prejudice of the member states. Consequently, it is not surprising to find numerous instances in recent conferences of propositions of amendement supported by substantial majorities brought to defeat by minorities that refuse to give way. In some cases, the amendements proposed have been completely blocked by a small minority. In other cases, the minority has yielded to the majority only after the inclusion of a clause virtually nullifying the advance sought by the majority. For example, at the Berlin Conference of 1908 of the Union for the Protection of Literary and Artistic Works an attempt was made to extend the scope of the convention to cover artistic works applied to industry.[20] The amendment was opposed by two states, Great Britain and Switzerland.[21] Instead of abandoning the proposition altogether, the following sentence was added as paragraph 4 of Article 2: " Works of Art applied to industrial purposes shall be protected so far as the domestic legislation of each country allows." [22] At the Hague Conference of 1925 of the Industrial Property Union the British delegation proposed that Article 17 be amended to impose an obligation on member states to submit all disputes relative to the interpretation or application of the Convention, not settled through diplomatic channels, to adjudication by the Permanent Court of International Justice. Although this proposition was supported by 17 votes against 5 (apparently those of the United States, Turkey, Canada, Japan, and Italy) with five abstentions, it had to be abandoned

[20] *Actes de la Conférence de Berlin,* p. 42.
[21] *Ibid.,* pp. 179, 231, 286.
[22] *Ibid.,* p. 315.

4

because of the unanimity rule.[23] In the 1934 conference of the same union at London the delegations of the Netherlands, Switzerland, and Mexico attempted to insert substantially the same provision in the Convention as Article 13 *bis*. Again the United States delegation announced its inability to accept such a provision and the proposal was abandoned after a vote of 9 for, 7 against (Australia, the United States, Finland, Hungary, the Irish Free State, Italy, and Japan) with fourteen abstentions.[24] In the 1925 Industrial Property Conference a majority in one of the sub-commissions conceded with regret that an amendment proposed by the International Bureau to Article 4 of the Convention could not be adopted although supported by 21 votes to 4 against (Cuba, Hungary, Italy, Japan).[25] An amendment to Article 11 went down by 21 votes for, 2 against, with 3 abstaining. The negative votes appear to have been cast by the delegates of Germany and Italy.[26] The opposition of Great Britain and Australia prevented adoption of an amendment to Article 4 *bis* proposed by France forbidding the antedating of patents applied for by foreign patentees within the period of priority fixed in Article 4. The vote was 23 for to 2 against.[27] The opposition of the United States and Great Britain prevented the inclusion of false advertising among the acts of unfair competition, although the Italian and Japanese delegations had likewise raised some objection.[28] The delegates of Great Britain and the United States were also responsible for the defeat of an amendment to Article 4 concerning non-conformity between patent applications.[29]

The Serb-Croat-Slovene State alone defeated an amend-

---

[23] *Actes de la Conférence de La Haye*, p. 424.
[24] *Actes de la Conférence de Londres*, p. 351.
[25] *Actes de la Conférence de La Haye*, p. 428.
[26] *Ibid.*, p. 437.   [28] *Ibid.*, p. 478.
[27] *Ibid.*, p. 431.   [29] *Ibid.*, p. 519.

ment to Article 5 for the abolition of the compulsory working of industrial designs. The Italian delegation supported the view of the Serb-Croat-Slovene delegation but was willing to abstain.[30] Three countries, Italy, Hungary, and the Serb-Croat-Slovene State, objected to an amendment to Article 4 for the suppression of the reservation of rights of third parties.[31] Japan, the Serb-Croat-Slovene State, and Poland prevented an amendment to Article 5 for the suppression of the obligation of working a patent and the substitution of the compulsory license scheme.[32] Finally, an amendment to Article 10, concerning the independence of trade marks, was defeated after receiving 18 votes for, 7 against, with 2 abstentions.[33]

In some cases, the action of the minority can be explained by the fact that the proposition in question has touched an important question of high policy. This is true, of course, of the proposal to refer all disputes arising out of the Industrial Property Convention to the Permanent Court of International Justice. The United States could not be expected to consent, nor could Japan with her known dislike of undertakings involving compulsory adjudication. In some other cases, the proposals appear to strike at what were believed by the states in the minority groups to be important national interests. In other cases, for instance that of the Serb-Croat-Slovene delegation's opposition to amendment of Article 5 of the Industrial Property Convention, opposition may be explained chiefly from the reluctance of certain states to support any change in the Convention which would oblige them to undertake the troublesome task of amending their own municipal regulations.

Assuming the existence of a desire to promote the progressive development of the conventions and assuming

[30] *Ibid.*, p. 519.   [32] *Ibid.*, p. 433.
[31] *Ibid.*, p. 517.   [33] *Ibid.*, p. 444.

some knowledge on the part of the delegates that such is possible only if national interests are on occasion, at least, subordinated to the more general interest, it would seem that delegations representing minority opinions should stand aside and permit adoption of amendments desired by large majorities in cases in which no major national interest or policy is affected. Quite clearly the procedure of both conferences of revision has been shaped somewhat to facilitate this practice. Procedural questions are always settled by majority vote. The commissions and sub-commissions take their decisions by majority. Since all propositions for the amendment of the conventions or arrangements are submitted to consideration by the commissions before being put to a vote in a plenary session, this provides an excellent device for measuring the sentiment for and against. When unanimity is nearly attained in the commission, effort may be made to find a formula which will permit support by the minority as well. If this is not possible, the minority may be urged to give way in the interest of the many. The unanimity requirement is satisfied in the plenary session if no negative votes are cast. Hence, states in opposition in the commission may give way to the majority without being obliged to compromise their views by casting affirmative ballots in the plenary sessions for propositions they opposed in the commission. An abstention is sufficient. Furthermore, the rules of both conferences make it possible for delegations making such a sacrifice to make their sacrifice known, for every delegate has the right to insist upon the insertion of his remarks in the record of the session *in extenso*.[34] Examination of the records of the conferences reveals several instances in which this device made the adoption of a proposition of amendment possible. For example, in the London Industrial Property

[34] Rules of procedure, Literary and Artistic Works, Art. 5; Industrial Property, Art. 7.

Conference of 1934, an amendment was proposed to Article 1, paragraph 3, of the Convention, broadening the definition of industrial property. In the commission the proposition was adopted by 23 votes for, to 2 against (Germany and Italy), with 4 abstaining.[35] Nevertheless, the proposition was adopted without change by unanimous vote in the plenary session, the German delegation yielding without comment and the Italian delegation contenting itself with the announcement that it would have preferred a different text but had given way in view of the contrary opinion generally held.[36] However, this spirit of conciliation does not manifest itself with sufficient regularity to assure the proper development of the conventions.

Another device used by both unions for escape from the rigors of the unanimity rule is the provision made in both conventions for use of restricted unions. Article 15 of the Industrial Property Convention provides that the contracting countries " reserve the right to make as between themselves, special agreements for the protection of industrial property, in so far as such agreements do not contravene the stipulations of the present Convention." In accordance with the terms of this article, three such agreements have been entered into. At the Conference of Madrid in 1891 two such agreements were drawn up, one on the Prevention of False Indications of Origin in Goods [37] and the other on International Registration of Commercial and Industrial Trade Marks.[38] The third was adopted at the Hague Conference of Revision in 1925 and concerns the International Registration of Designs or Models.[39] Article 20 of the Convention on Literary and Artistic Works provides that the " governments of the countries of the Union reserve to themselves the right to enter into special arrangements between each other, pro-

[35] *Actes de la Conférence de Londres*, p. 344.
[36] *Ibid.*, p. 511.   [38] *Ibid.*, p. 559.
[37] As revised, *ibid.*, p. 564.   [39] *Ibid.*, p. 581.

vided always that such arrangements confer upon authors more extended rights than those granted by the Union, or embody other stipulations not contrary to the present Convention." In accordance with the terms of this article, numerous declarations have been drawn up, signed, and ratified by only a part of the membership of the Union.[40] Although use of the restricted union has the advantage of permitting those member states interested to move forward to new commitments in fields not covered by the general conventions, it presents no satisfactory solution to the unanimity problem. If used sparingly, the device would appear valuable; if resorted to with frequency, the result would be confusion.

At the Berlin Conference of 1908 yet another device for mitigation of the unanimity rule was added by the Union for the Protection of Literary and Artistic Works, namely, the right of reservation, a right that the Industrial Property Union has never accepted. The right of reservation was written into the Convention by a provision to the effect that states parties to the convention might, at the time of the exchange of ratifications, declare that on certain points they remain bound only by the provisions of the earlier conventions to which they had subscribed.[41] The report of the commission of the conference to the plenary session throws some light on the factors responsible for the adoption of this regulation. It had not been possible in all cases, the commission declared, to reach agreement on amendments to the Convention, for each country has it own juristic, moral, social, and political conceptions. The majority could not make law for the minority as the conference was not a body representative of a single will but rather an assembly in which distinct wills met, becoming one only on condition of agreement. If agreement could not be obtained, what was to be done?

[40] See B. & F. State Papers, LXXXVIII, 41.
[41] Art. 17, B. & F. State Papers, CII, 627.

It was either necessary to give up completely that which had been attempted or to permit the dissenting states to derogate from the practice of the others. The commission recognized the first solution as simpler, since it meant the maintenance of uniformity in the Union. However, this solution they believed unfair to those states desiring to go forward. They should not be held back until the most cautious were willing to advance. This condition more than anything else justified the existence of restricted unions, reservations, and the inclusion of many propositions in the Convention requiring application only in so far as the domestic legislation of each party would permit. The commission appreciated that many would scoff and declare the result would be that each state would be bound only to the extent it desired. This they recognized, in strict sense, to be true. Nevertheless, they considered the practice of permitting derogations useful because it was the only way in which progressive development of the Convention might be obtained. The new undertakings, though not binding upon all, would at least have the merit of pointing the way in which it was most desirable that the Union should move.[42]

Desirable as development of the Convention may be, the result of seeking it in this way may be to defeat the chief aim of the organization, namely, the achievement of a uniform international regime for the protection of literary and artistic works within which national laws and practices which are in conflict disappear. That the practice of permitting reservations has in fact led to confusion is indicated by the statement of the director of the International Bureau to the effect that the application of the Convention has been greatly complicated as "we have practically as many literary unions as there are groups of countries making reservations." [43]

[42] *Actes de la Conférence de Berlin,* p. 228.
[43] F. Ostertag, "International Unions for the Protection of Industrial, Literary and Artistic Property," *Michigan Law Review*, XXV, 107.

In view of this difficulty, it is not surprising that the last conference of revision, held at Rome in 1928, made strenuous efforts to reduce, if not to eliminate, the practice of reservation. The Convention in its revised form no longer carries a provision authorizing reservations to particular clauses in the text, as did the revised text of 1908. However, Article 27, paragraph 2, prevents the complete elimination of reservations by providing that " the countries on whose behalf the present convention is signed may retain the benefit of the reservations which have been previously formulated on condition that they make declaration to that effect at the time of the deposit of their ratifications." Thus old derogations from uniformity may be retained but no new ones may be introduced.[44]

Examination of the records of the conferences of the Union for the Protection of Literary and Artistic Works reveals that the requirement of unanimity has presented but little difficulty since 1908 for the obvious reason that unanimity can be obtained readily so long as reservations are permitted and so long as articles of the Convention are adopted with the provision that they are " to be applicable only to the extent permitted by the domestic legislation of each party." In the conferences of the Industrial Property Union, however, the rule is coming to be looked upon by many as an impediment fatal to the

[44] The provisions in the Convention for ratification are substantially like those in the Industrial Property Convention. A date (in this case, July 1, 1931) is set by which ratifications should be deposited. One month after that date the Convention comes into force among ratifying powers. However, if as many as six states have ratified before the date set, the Convention comes into force among them one month from the date of the deposit of the sixth ratification. Member states failing to ratify the revised Convention continue to be bound by the earlier text. States outside the Union were permitted to accede to the Union until August 1, 1931, either by acceding to the Convention of 1908 or that of 1928. After that date, only the more recent convention could be accepted as basis for membership in the Union. (Arts. 27, 28, *L. N. T. S.* CXXIII, 233.)   For the practice of the Industrial Property Union see Article 18 of the Convention. (*Actes de la Conférence de Londres,* 1934, p. 535.)

progressive development of the Convention. This conclusion is supported by the frequency with which the desirability of the maintenance of the rule has been brought in question in recent years by those interested in furthering the interests of the Union. In 1930, the British group in the International Association for the Protection of Industrial Property suggested to the Bureau of the Union that in the future revisions of the Convention voted by four-fifths of the states represented at the conferences be obligatory for all.[45] The matter appeared on the agenda of the conference at London in 1934, but the British delegation and the Bureau of the Union, in their joint preparatory work, reported against it.[46] They suggested that if majorities are given authority to adopt amendments without the consent of minorities, the latter will fail to ratify. This would mean that the convention in its old form would remain in force among those states and between them and the states having ratified the amended convention. If this process were repeated by several conferences of revision the result would be a plurality of restricted unions; the unity of the Union would be destroyed and international relations would be complicated and clouded. Another solution, they suggested, would be the introduction of the right of reservation. However, this solution was recognized as open to even greater objection. Reservations sufficiently numerous to achieve the end sought would produce a complicated and confused international regime such as it would be a mistake to invite. Moreover, it was pointed out, the experience of the Union for the Protection of Literary and Artistic Works with the device was not conducive to its adoption elsewhere. In the face of this unfavorable report, the conference naturally took no action.

At the same conference, the delegation of Mexico pro-

---

[45] *Actes de la Conférence de Londres*, p. 164.
[46] *Ibid.*, pp. 164-165.

posed the following amendment to Article 14, paragraph 1, of the Convention:

> Revisions, voted by four-fifths of the states represented will be obligatory for all but without prejudice to the right of the states not participating in the vote to take such measures as they consider necessary for the protection of their industry.[47]

Although the meaning of this proposal appears somewhat doubtful, it seems to suggest revisions voted by four-fifths would be binding neither upon the minority in the conference nor upon the member states failing to send representatives to the particular conference of revision. The first sub-commission of the conference at London dealt with the Mexican proposal. The French delegation promptly objected to the proposal on the ground that it presented a new question of very great importance which was not sufficiently ripe for consideration by the conference. The proposition was then put to a vote and rejected by 23 votes against 1.[48]

A plan of somewhat the same general nature as those suggested by the British group and by the Mexican delegation, but a more elaborate one, has been suggested by Stephen P. Ladas.[49] He suggests that some of the difficulty of achieving unanimity results from the fact that the Union contains states highly industrialized as well as states of primarily an agricultural character. Although he expresses doubt as to whether any real interests would be sacrificed if amendments were in all cases adopted by substantial majorities, it might well appear that the interests of one group or the other were being thrust aside. He suggests, therefore, that the members of the Union be divided into two groups, the one including the highly

---

[47] *Ibid.,* p. 351.
[48] *Ibid.,* p. 352.
[49] Stephen P. Ladas, *The International Protection of Industrial Property,* pp. 811 ff.

industrialized states, and the other those primarily agricultural. Such a grouping might be devised readily from utilization of the six classes into which the member states have already divided themselves for contributing to the financial maintenance of the Union. For the rule of unanimous consent in the Conference of Revision, he would then substitute a rule requiring propositions of revision to be voted by three-fourths of each of the two groups.

In spite of the frequency with which modification of the unanimity rule is being urged in the Industrial Property Union, its early abandonment is not to be expected. The adoption of any of the plans mentioned would itself require unanimity. It may be suggested that since the rule of unanimity is not explicit in the terms of the Convention it would be within the legal competence of any conference to provide in its rules of procedure for some form of majority decision on propositions of amendment. Although this appears true, it seems decidedly improbable that a rule now supported by the practice of more than half a century could be discarded in such fashion. The attempt would lead to dissension. If modification is obtained, it will be obtained with consent. The ideal remedy would appear to be provision in the Convention for amendment by vote of a substantial majority in the Conference of Revision, the amended text to come into force for all at a fixed date, subject, if necessary, to ratification by a fixed proportion of the member states. Although early adoption of such a plan is not anticipated, it is by no means unlikely that the question of modification of the unanimity rule will be discussed at the next conference to be held at Lisbon at a date not yet fixed, and probably at subsequent conferences. Even though the problem is recognized as acute, it is not likely to be settled by the first conference that undertakes serious consideration of it.

The elimination of the principle of reservation in the

conference of the Union for the Protection of Literary and Artistic Works may be expected to make unanimous agreement upon changes in the text of that convention more difficult to achieve. However, no proposal has yet been made from within the Union for modification of the unanimity rule. The question was not raised in the Conference of Rome in 1928 nor is there any present indication it will form part of the agenda of the next conference of revision which was to have been held at Brussels in 1936 but which was postponed *sine die*.

The third union in which the general conference operates under the rule of unanimity is the International Institute of Agriculture. This union was created, in large part, as the result of the efforts of David Lubin, an American, who successfully prevailed upon King Victor Emmanuel of Italy to call an international conference to bring his ideas to fruition. Lubin had visualized an organization with wide powers ranging from the supplying of timely information on crop conditions in the various producing regions to the actual operation of produce exchanges. Indeed, he even described it at one time as a body to possess powers in the international field not unlike those exercised within the United States by the Interstate Commerce Commission.[50] However, when in 1905, the King of Italy issued invitations to a conference to be held at Rome in May of that year, it was made clear to the powers that the proposed international organization was to possess no coercive powers. Rather, it was to be free to study and propose provisions of general agricultural interest, the respective governments being free to adopt them either by national legislation or in the form of international agreements.[51] Available evidence indi-

---

[50] Report of the British Delegates and Minutes of the Proceedings at the International Conference on Agriculture at Rome, 1905, *B. P. P.* (1906), XCVI, 24.

[51] *Ibid.*, p. 7.

cates clearly that the major powers had no intention of going beyond the modest proposal of the King of Italy, and, indeed, suggests that some of them had little enthusiasm for the idea at all. The instructions issued by the British Government to their representatives at the conference state: " His Majesty's Government is disposed to think the field which exists for international action is a small one." [52] In a letter to the French Foreign Minister, the French Minister of Agriculture recommended that the proposed organization confine itself largely to the collection and publication of statistical information of interest to agriculture and to the preparation of memoranda, in the form of resolutions, bringing to the attention of the different governments measures of an undoubtedly general character, the universal adoption of which would appear to be advantageous for agriculture.[53]

By the terms of the Convention prepared by the conference which assembled in Rome, May 28, 1905,[54] the Institute of Agriculture became primarily an agency for collection, collation, and publication of technical, eco-

[52] *Ibid.*, p. 14.

[53] *Conférence Internationale d'Agriculture,* 1905, Procès-verbaux, p. 46.

[54] The conference was composed of 113 delegates representing 41 states. At the present time there are 71 members of the Institute: Group I is composed of Argentina, Brazil, China, France, Germany, Great Britain and Northern Ireland, Italy, Japan, Spain, the United States; Group II is composed of India, Canada, Chile, Egypt, Roumania, Hawaii, Philippine Islands, Porto Rico, Virgin Islands; Group III is composed of Algeria, Australia, Czechoslovakia, French Indo-China, Mexico, Morocco, Netherlands, Turkey, Jugoslavia; Group IV is composed of Belgium, Bulgaria, Denmark, Finland, French West Africa, Greece, Irish Free State, Italian Cyranaica, Italian Eritrea, Italian Somaliland, Italian Tripoli, Netherland East Indies, Norway, Poland, Portugal, New Zealand, Sweden, Switzerland, Tunisia, Union of South Africa, Venezuela; Group V is composed of Belgian Congo, Bolivia, Colombia, Costa Rica, Cuba, Ecuador, Esthonia, Guatemala, Haiti, Hungary, Latvia, Lithuania, Luxemburg, Madagascar, Nicaragua, Panama, Paraguay, Persia, Peru, San Marino, Siam, and Uruguay. Russia withdrew from the Institute in 1938 and on May 10 of the same year Germany gave notice that Austria was no longer a member. *Treaty Information Bulletin,* June, 1938, p. 168.

nomic, and statistical information of interest to agriculturists. To be sure, some provision is made also for the
submission to the various governments of proposals for
the protection of interests common to agriculturists and
for the improvement of their condition. But stipulations
written into the Convention, largely on the initiative of
the British delegates, have successfully curtailed the latter
function. Article 9 of the Convention, which states the
powers of the organization, follows:

The Institute, confining its operations within an international
sphere, shall

(a) Collect, study, and publish as promptly as possible, statistical, technical or economic information concerning farming, both
vegetable and animal products, the commerce in agricultural pro-
duces, and the prices prevailing in the various markets;

(b) Communicate to parties interested, also as promptly as
possible, all the information just referred to;

(c) Indicate the wages paid for farm work;

(d) Make known the new diseases of vegetables which may
appear in any part of the world, showing the territories infected,
the progress of the disease, and if possible, the remedies which
are effected in combatting them;

(e) Study questions concerning agricultural cooperation, insurance, and credit in all their aspects; collect and publish information which might be useful in the various countries in the
organization of works connected with agricultural cooperation,
insurance and credit;

(f) Submit to the approval of the governments, if there is
occasion for it, measures for the improvement of their condition
after having utilized all the necessary sources of information, such
as the wishes expressed by international or other agricultural congresses, or congress of sciences applied to agriculture, agricultural
societies, academies, learned bodies, etc.

All questions concerning the economic interest, the legislation, and the administration of a particular nation shall be excluded from the consideration of the Institute.[55]

The final paragraph in the article was inserted on the motion of T. H. Elliott, a member of the British delegation.[56]

The Conference provided for two governmental organs for the Institute, a General Assembly and a Permanent Committee. The General Assembly was intended to be the supreme organ of the Institute. Article 3 of the Convention provided it should be composed of representatives of the adhering states, each state, whatever the number of delegates sent, being " entitled to a number of votes in the Assembly which shall be determined according to the group to which it belongs, and to which reference will be made in Article 10." [57] Article 4 authorized the General Assembly to elect its own president and vice-presidents, determine the date of its own sessions, and limited it to consideration of " a programme proposed by the Permanent Committee and adopted by the adhering Governments." [58] Article 5 laid down the general proposition that the General Assembly should exercise supreme control over the Institute. To that end it was authorized to " appove the projects prepared by the Permanent Committee regarding the organization and internal workings of the Institute," fix the total amount of expenditures, and audit the accounts. Provision was also made to the effect that the General Assembly " shall submit to the approval of the adhering governments modifications of any nature

---

[55] The convention may be found in B. & F. *State Papers*, C, 595.

[56] Report of British Delegates and Minutes of the Conference, *B. P. P.* (1906), XCVI, 138.

[57] See below, p. 54.

[58] This limitation was inserted on the motion of T. H. Elliott (Great Britain), supported in the debate by the delegates of France and Italy. Only the delegate of Cuba voted against the insertion of this limitation in the Convention. (Report of the British Delegates and Minutes of the Conference, *B. P. P.* (1906), XCVI, 131.)

involving an increase in expenditure or an enlargement of the functions of the Institute." The deliberations of the General Assembly are valid only if delegates are present representing two-thirds of the votes of the adhering states.

The executive power of the Institute was intrusted to the Permanent Committee " which, under the direction and control of the General Assembly, shall carry out the decisions of the latter and prepare propositions to submit to it " (Art. 6). It was to be permitted to elect its own president and vice-president, prepare its internal regulations for approval by the General Assembly, appoint and remove officials and employees of the Office, and vote the budget within the limits of the funds placed at its disposal by the General Assembly (Art. 8). This committee was to be composed of one representative of each adhering state but voting power was assigned on the basis of the group system mentioned in Article 3, votes increasing according to arithmetical progression and financial support according to geometrical progression.[59] Each state was at liberty to select its own group (Art. 10). Adhering states not caring to name representatives on the Permanent Committee were permitted to intrust their votes to the representatives of other powers provided that the actual number of members of the Permanent Committee should not be less than fifteen (Art. 7).[60] By terms of the Statutes drawn up by the Permanent Committee at is first session beginning on May 25, 1908, and approved

[59] The table provided for in Article 10 is as follows:

Groups	Votes	Units of Subscription
I	5	16
II	4	8
III	3	4
IV	2	2
V	1	1

[60] For the difficult problem of state equality raised by the establishment of the Institute, see below, p. 261.

by the General Assembly at its session of November 27, 1908, decisions of the Permanent Committee are in general taken by an absolute majority of votes.[61] Majority vote is interpreted as meaning a majority of the votes cast on the measure in question rather than a majority of the total vote possible if all were present and voting.

The provisions of the Statutes pertaining to procedure to be followed in the General Assembly are quite different. No provision is contained therein for majority decision and, in fact, the resolutions and recommendations of that body are always voted by unanimity. As the representative of Italy in the Conference of 1905, Signor Cappelli, indicated, it was never the intention of the powers that votes be counted in the organ determining the policy of the Institute; each state was to remain in position to veto any attempted deviation from the established policy of the organization.[62] That is, each state remained free to exercise the veto, provided it sent delegates to the meetings of the General Assembly; for Article 5 of the Convention, it will be recalled, made Assembly deliberations valid when delegates representing two-thirds of the total voting power of adhering states were present. While this permitted decisions being taken without express consent of those states failing to send representatives, only in the Permanent Committee, the body designed to deal with " administrative questions," can decisions be taken over the expressed opposition of some of those present.

At each session of the General Assembly committees are named to consider and report upon all items on the agenda. On these committees the equality of member states is maintained, each being permitted a single repre-

[61] Institut International d'Agriculture, Rome, 1934, *Statuts,* Art. 65.
[62] Report of the British Delegates and Minutes of the Conference, *B. P. P.* (1906), XCVI, 122.

sentative and vote on each committee.[63] Each state delegation selects its own representative on each committee.[64] The rules permit the committees to elect their own officers and to establish their own rules of procedure.[65] In contrast to the plenary sessions, decisions in the committees may always be reached by majority vote.

Use of the unanimity rule in the General Assembly has not had consequences of a serious character for the International Institute of Agriculture. In the first place, the Convention itself strips the General Assembly of power to take the initiative in the development of the Institute. Article 4, it will be remembered, provides that the agenda be restricted to consideration of a program prepared by the Permanent Committee and adopted by the governments of the member states. In accordance with the terms of this article, the Statutes provide that, at least three months before the opening of each session, the draft agenda prepared by the Permanent Committee shall be submitted for the approval of each of the parties to the Convention,[66] and then further provides that the General Assembly does not consider itself competent to discuss subjects which are not mentioned in the agenda.[67]

In the second place, contrary to the intentions of those who drafted the Convention, the Permanent Committee has become the more important organ of the Institute. The Assembly was expected to exercise " supreme control " over the Institute. It was to determine the policy to be followed and to stand as judge of the way in which the Permanent Committee secured the enforcement of this policy. In fact, the General Assembly has been in no position to do either of these things. In addition to depending upon the Permanent Committee for preparation of its agenda, it has depended upon it for information

---

[63] *Statuts,* Art. 7.
[64] Art. 6.
[65] Art. 8.

[66] Art. 14.
[67] Art. 5.

concerning the items on the agenda. Composed for the most part of diplomatic officers and meeting at irregular intervals, it has scarcely been feasible for the Assembly to perform this function for itself. Moreover, many of the delegates sent to the General Assembly likewise serve on the Permanent Committee. Consequently, it is not surprising that the Assembly should have developed into a body for approving by unanimous vote resolutions embodying propositions already approved by vote of the Permanent Committee.[68]

Finally, considering the extremely narrow range of activity permitted the General Assembly, its practice of enacting resolutions without departure from unanimity is substantially as efficient as majority procedure would be. Virtually all propositions considered by the General Assembly are first considered in committee where decisions are reached by majority vote. Resolutions thus formulated, as well as most other resolutions considered by the General Assembly, are as a rule put in the form of recommendations having virtually no binding character. The General Assembly " recommends that in so far as possible the Permanent Committee shall give consideration to " or that " the present resolution shall only be given effect so far as the financial resources of the Institute allow." With resolutions worded in this fashion, it is not difficult to persuade delegates who have opposed propositions in the committee to vote for them or to abstain in the plenary session. This practice is facilitated greatly by Article 12 of the Statutes which permits any member to demand the insertion of his speech in the minutes *in extenso*. This offers a satisfactory device for recording one's opposition without necessity of insisting upon voting against a proposition which at best has no obligatory character.[69]

[68] Cf. A. Hobson, *The International Institute of Agriculture*, pp. 92 ff.
[69] For an example of this kind see Institut International d'Agriculture, *Assemblée Générale, Troisième Session*, 1911, pp. 52 ff. The Second

In summary, it may be said that of the three unions whose general conferences use the rule of unanimous consent for the adoption of formal resolutions, one, the Union for Protection of Industrial Property, has had its work definitely obstructed through utilization of the rule. The conferences of revision of that union are charged with keeping the convention up to the needs of the participating powers. This can not be done so long as the negative vote of a single state can prevent the adoption of an amendment sought by all the other members. Although up to the present time, the conferences of revision of the Union for the Protection of Literary and Artistic Works have experienced but little difficulty with the rule of unanimity, the " escape-devices," particularly that of reservation, have caused considerable difficulty. However, the policy of reservation itself was recognized as detrimental to the best interests of the Union and, now that it has been abandoned, the problem of obtaining unanimity will almost certainly emerge to plague future conferences. Finally, the rule of unanimous consent does not appear to have obstructed the activity of the General Assembly of the Institute of Agriculture. But here the problem is very different from that of the other two unions. The Assembly is not charged with the development of an international convention as are the conferences of the other two unions. Indeed, virtually all real power which the participating states have conferred upon the Union is now in the hands of the Permanent Committee, a body which adheres not to the rule of unanimous consent but rather to the principle of majority decision.

Committee had reached a decision by vote of 14 to 3. The delegate of Russia was in the minority and opposed strongly the majority position. However, he was prevailed upon by the delegates of France and the United States not to vote against the proposition in the plenary session, but to indicate his disapproval by inserting his remarks in the *procès-verbal*. This he did.

CHAPTER III

MAJORITY VOTE IN CONFERENCES EXERCISING LEGISLATIVE POWERS

Although the term "international legislation" is used widely in discussion of international affairs, there exists in the international society no organ exercising legislative powers of a general character. That is to say, there exists no international organ with power to impose its will upon member states in respect to matters of international concern in any general sense. States have acknowledged no obligation to acquiesce in changes in the law decreed in such fashion. Where the term "international legislation" is used it is, as a rule, used in the very loose sense of reference to multilateral treaties of a general character. Acts of this kind rest upon the consent of each party thereto rather than upon the will of any external authority, and as a consequence, it seems inappropriate to refer to them as "legislation."

But even though it is inadmissible in the present state of world organization to refer to any international organ as an international legislature and perhaps misleading to refer to multilateral treaties as international legislation, it may be permissible to call attention to the few instances in which international organs are now exercising powers of a legislative character. Attention is to be directed to those organs of an international character which have power to alter the existing legal obligations of participating states as expressed in conventions, annexes to conventions, or agreements without first obtaining the consent of all of those states either through their duly accredited representatives or through the process of ratification. Needless to say, the organs possessing such power are few and they operate within narrowly restricted fields. Those

59

to be considered here are the Congress of the Universal Postal Union, the Congress of the Postal Union of the Americas and Spain, the International Commission for Air Navigation, the Committee of Experts of the International Railway Union, the General Council of the International Relief Union, the Conference of the International Hydrographic Bureau, the Conference of the International Labor Organization, and the General Conference of the Organization for Communications and Transit. Since the procedure of these bodies represents something of an innovation in international practice, it appears worthwhile to examine in some detail the circumstances under which the more important ones were constituted and under which their powers developed. Particular attention will be directed toward the Congress of the Universal Postal Union and toward the International Commission for Air Navigation, as the powers of these organs appear most advanced in respect to the matter here under consideration.

All students of international affairs are aware of the inconvenience and confusion existing in the realm of postal communications prior to the formation of an international postal union.[1] In 1862, in an effort to remedy this situation, Postmaster-General Blair of the United States suggested an international conference for discussion of common postal problems. This conference assembled in Paris, May 11, 1863, and was attended by delegates from fifteen interested states.[2] Although the delegates were without power to adopt any definite agreements of an obligatory character, a number of articles were agreed upon which later facilitated the formation of an international convention.

[1] For description see J. F. Sly, "The Genesis of the Universal Postal Union," *International Conciliation* (1927); P. S. Reinsch, *Public International Unions*, pp. 21 ff.; Woolf, *International Government*, pp. 118-119; Sayre, *Experiments in International Administration*, pp. 19-25.

[2] Austria, Belgium, Costa Rica, Denmark, Spain, the United States, France, Great Britain, Italy, Netherlands, Portugal, Prussia, Sandwich Islands, Switzerland, and the Hanseatic Towns.

In 1874, largely at the instigation of Dr. von Stephan, head of the Prussian Postal Service, a second conference was held, this time in Berne. This conference resulted in the adoption of an international convention signed by the delegates of the twenty-two states which sent representatives.[3] The Convention and the Detailed Regulations as amended by successive congresses remain the basis for the Universal Postal Union. Membership has now increased to include virtually the entire international community.[4]

[3] Great Britain, Germany, Austria, Hungary, Belgium, Denmark, Egypt, Spain, the United States, France, Greece, Italy, Luxemburg, Norway, Netherlands, Portugal, Roumania, Russia, Serbia, Sweden, Switzerland, Turkey. (*B. P. P.,* LXXXII, 529.) The convention was signed October 9, 1874, but the delegate of France withheld his signature until May 3, 1875.

[4] At the time of the Congress, held in Cairo, March, 1934, the following were members of the Union with voting privileges: Afghanistan, Union of South Africa, Albania, Germany, the United States, Island Possessions of the United States other than the Philippine Islands, Philippine Islands, Kingdom of Saudi Arabia, Argentina, Australia, Austria, Belgium, Belgian Congo, Bolivia, Brazil, Bulgaria, Canada, Chile, China, Colombia, Costa Rica, Cuba, Denmark, Danzig, Dominican Republic, Egypt, Ecuador, Spain, Whole of the Spanish Colonies, Esthonia, Ethiopia, Finland, France, Algeria, the French Colonies and Protectorates of Indo-China, the Whole of the Other French Colonies, United Kingdom, Greece, Guatemala, Haiti, Honduras, Hungary, British India, Iraq, Irish Free State, Iceland, Italy, the Whole of the Italian Colonies, Japan, Korea, the Whole of the Other Japanese Dependencies, Latvia, Levant States under French Mandate (Syria and Lebanon), Liberia, Lithuania, Luxemburg, Morocco (except the Spanish zone), Morocco (Spanish zone), Mexico, Nicaragua, Norway, New Zealand, Panama, Paraguay, Netherlands, Curacao and Surinam, Dutch East Indies, Peru, Persia, Poland, Portugal, Portuguese Colonies in West Africa, Portuguese Colonies in East Africa and Asia and Oceania, Roumania, San Marino, El Salvador, Territory of the Saar, Siam, Sweden, Switzerland, Czechoslovakia, Tunis, Turkey, Union of Soviet Socialist Republics, Uruguay, the City of the Vatican, Venezuela, Yemen, Jugoslavia. There are in addition other postal administrations members of the Union but enjoying no separate representation or voting power in the Congresses or Conferences. See Article 9 of the Convention (H. M. Stationery Office, London, 1935). The name of Czechoslovakia was carried in the new convention drawn up in 1939 at the Congress of Buenos Aires. For this reason Germany, Italy, Hungary, Spain and San Marino refused to sign. (*The New York Times,* May 27, 1939, p. 6.) On June 17, 1939, the Slovak State was permitted to adhere and on Nov. 2, 1939, Germany adhered (including Bohemia and Moravia). (*Department of State Bulletin,* Dec. 2, 1939, p. 644.)

The first article of the Convention declares that the countries bound by the Convention form " a single postal territory for the reciprocal exchange of correspondence." The only governing agencies provided are a permanent International Bureau, a periodic Congress, and a Conference which assembles on demand. The provisions of the Convention in respect to the Bureau are in no way remarkable or even novel. It is established at Berne under the supervision of the Swiss Postal Administration. The Bureau is charged with collecting, collating, publishing, and distributing information of every kind which concerns international postal service; with making known proposals for modifying the Acts of the Congresses; with notifying the members of the alterations adopted; with undertaking such work in connection with the editing and arranging of materials in the Convention, Agreements, and their Detailed Regulations as may be assigned to it; with acting as a clearing-house for the settlement of accounts of every description relative to the international postal service; and, finally, with giving, on the request of the parties concerned, an opinion on questions in dispute.[5] It should be emphasized that the Bureau has no power to *decide* in disputes between administrations. Rather the Convention authorizes it to give an advisory opinion on the request of the parties involved. This was made clear when the provision was written into the Convention at the Berne Conference of 1874.[6] The expense of maintaining the Bureau,

---

[5] Art. 24 of the Convention as Revised at Cairo, March 24, 1934, H. M. Stationery Office, London, 1935.

[6] *Documents du Congrès Postal International, réuni à Berne du 15 septembre au 9 octobre 1874,* p. 56. However, Art. 11 of the Convention does provide for arbitration in all disagreements between two or more members of the Union as to the interpretation of the Convention and the Agreements, or as to the responsibility imposed on any administration by the application of these Acts. Should one of the administrations involved fail to appoint an arbiter as provided in the article, the Bureau may do it. Decisions are, of course, by majority vote. The advisory opinion by the Bureau provides a satisfactory method for rapid solution of the rela-

as well as the other organs of the Union, is borne by the member states. To this end, the states are divided into seven classes, each state in the first class contributing twenty-five units, while those in the other six classes contribute twenty, fifteen, ten, five, three, and one, respectively. The class in which a new member is to be placed is determined by agreement between that country and the government of the Swiss Confederation.[7]

If one judges solely by the bare Convention provisions, the character and powers of the Congresses and Conferences of the Postal Union will seem as commonplace as those of the Bureau. The Congress, in which each member of the Union is represented " by one or several plenipotentiary delegates," assembles in regular sessions at intervals of approximately five years for the purpose of revising or completing the acts of the previous Congresses. Extraordinary Congresses may be called on the request of two-thirds of the contracting countries. In the deliberations each country has one vote.[8] The Conference assembles at the request of at least two-thirds of the administrations of the Union for consideration of purely administrative questions.[9] Both the Congresses and the Conferences are authorized to draw up their own standing orders.[10] In recent years the Conferences have been called only at infrequent intervals. The Conference held at the Hague in 1927 was the first since 1890. The Congresses, however, assemble with considerable regularity. Since the World War, sessions have been held at Madrid in 1920, Stockholm in 1924, London in 1929, Cairo in 1934, and at Buenos Aires in 1939.

---

tively minor questions of interpretation which frequently arise when a long and complicated Convention is being applied by so many administrations. It has not prevented some cases from going to arbitration under the provisions of Article 10.

[7] Art. 25.
[8] Arts. 13, 15.
[9] Art. 17.
[10] Arts. 16, 17.

However, closer examination of the Congress will reveal that by reason of the procedure followed and the powers exercised it comes very close to being a true international legislative body within the field of international postal communications, for the Congress possesses the power to amend by majority vote any or all articles of the Convention, Detailed Regulations or the Arrangements.[11] Furthermore, the amendments so voted enter into force on the dates set by the Congress regardless of whether ratifications have been deposited. In large part, this status of the Congress approximating that of a legislative body rests upon practices, some of an extra-legal character, built up by the Congress itself. To a certain extent, however, it may be traced to slight deviations from the normal found in the text of the Convention which forms the basic law of the Union. It appears worthwhile, therefore, to give brief attention to the drafting of the Convention at the Berne Conference of 1874, before passing to a consideration of the practices established by later Congresses.

In the first place, it should be noted, the Convention of 1874 was not the work of diplomats and lawyers drawn from the diplomatic service or foreign offices of the states represented at the conference, but rather the work of postal officials. Of the thirty-six delegates present, twenty held positions analogous to that of Director-General of Posts and ten more held positions of considerable importance within the postal administrations of their own countries.[12]

---

[11] Although Woolf (*International Government*, p. 123) more than twenty years ago pointed out Reinsch's error (*Public International Unions*, p. 26) in asserting that unanimity was necessary in the Congress for amending certain articles of the Convention while a two-thirds vote sufficed for others, the error is being carried on by other writers on the subject. See K. Clark, *International Communications*, p. 38; N. L. Hill, "Unanimous Consent in International Organization," *A. J. I. L.*, XXII, 323. The error undoubtedly results from reading those articles relating to the adoption of amendments in the intervals between Congresses as applying to the Congresses themselves.

[12] Sly, p. 17.

At the first session, rules of procedure submitted by the Swiss Delegation were adopted. Each state and administration was permitted but a single vote regardless of the number of delegates sent.[13] The rules further provided that every proposition placed in deliberation should be submitted to a vote,[14] but were silent on the vote necessary for such propositions to be considered adopted by the conference. Actually, as examination of the records will reveal, a majority vote was in all cases considered sufficient for decision on individual articles of the draft convention and *règlement*. However, both the Convention and the accompanying *règlement* were in the end adopted by unanimous vote, the French delegates abstaining in each case.[15]

Prior to the meeting of the conference a draft convention, which had been prepared by Dr. von Stephan from his experience in organizing the German Postal Confederation, was circulated among the states and administrations invited to send delegates. In accordance with the rules of procedure adopted, this draft convention formed the basis for deliberations in the conference. Article 14 was as follows:

Every three years at least, a Congress of plenipotentiaries of the countries participating in the treaty shall be held with a view of perfecting the system of the Union, of introducing into it improvements found necessary and of discussing common affairs.

Each state shall be represented by one vote. The countries which are not directly represented in the Congress shall have the privilege of transferring their votes to another member of the Union.

They shall choose, at each Congress, the place where the following Congress is proposed to take place.

[13] Art. 5. The Rules of Procedure may be found in *Documents du Congrès* . . . , 1874, p. 15.
[14] Art. 7.
[15] *Documents du Congrès* . . . , 1874, pp. 127, 113.

> *No modification may be proposed to the present convention affecting the rates and the question of transit, unless by the unanimous consent of the countries of the Union represented at the Congress.*[16]

Although the terms of this draft article would have made unanimity requisite only in case of amendments relating to rates or transit, it is undoubtedly fortunate for the legislative efficiency of later Postal Union Congresses that the delegates saw no reason for adopting a provision so restrictive. Consequently, the conference simply accepted the framework of this article and grafted upon it its own rules of procedure. Thus the article, which became Article 18 in the final text, was amended to read as follows:

> Every three years at least, a Congress of plenipotentiaries of the countries participating in the treaty shall be held with a view of perfecting the system of the Union, of introducing into it improvements found necessary, and of discussing common affairs.
>
> Each country has one vote.
>
> Each country may be represented either by one or several delegates, or by the delegation of another country.
>
> Nevertheless, it is understood that the delegates or delegate of one country can be charged with the representation of two countries only, including the one they represent.
>
> The next meeting shall take place in Paris in 1877.
>
> Nevertheless, the meeting may be held sooner, if a request to that effect be made by one-third at least of the members of the Union.[17]

---

[16] *Ibid.*, p. 3. Italics added.

[17] *Ibid.*, p. 139; also *B. P. P.* (1875), LXXII, 529. Some changes have since been made in the article. It now stands as Article 13:

" Delegates of the countries of the Union meet in Congress not later than five years after the date of the entry into force of the Acts of the preceding Congress with the view of revising or of completing them as necessary.

" Each country is represented at the Congress by one or several plenipotentiary delegates furnished by their government with the necessary powers. It may, if it so desires, be represented by the delegation of

The adoption of the article in this form left the Congresses of the Postal Union free to adopt their own rules of procedure.[18] While the terms of the Convention made maintenance of state equality in the awarding of votes mandatory, it left each Congress free to determine for itself the vote necessary for taking decisions. The result has been, as brief description will show, the development of a well-ordered procedure which would do credit to any municipal legislative body.

The chief business of the Congress is to undertake revision of the Convention, the Detailed Regulations, and the Arrangements. Consequently, the procedure has been designed to facilitate this end. At the beginning of each session draft rules of procedure are presented, drawn up in consultation with the International Bureau by the administration of the country entertaining the Congress. These are adopted by majority vote of the Congress, article by article. In general, the rules adopted vary little from Congress to Congress.[19] In conformity with the Convention, Article 1 of the 1934 rules provides that each country shall have a single vote, but other articles make two slight exceptions from this general rule. First, when the Congress is considering the revision of the Arrangements attached to the Convention, the delegates of the countries

---

another country. But it is understood that one delegation can undertake the representation of two countries only, including the country it primarily represents.

"Each Congress settles the place of meeting of the next Congress. The Government of the country in which it is to take place is responsible, in consultation with the International Bureau, for convening the Congress, and also for notifying to all the governments of the countries of the Union the decisions taken by the Congress."

[18] In the Convention, as revised to date, Article 16 carries explicit provision to this effect.

[19] The rules of procedure adopted at the London Congress may be found in *Documents du Congrès Postal de Londres* (1929), II, 33 ff., and those of the Cairo Congress of 1934 in *Documents du Congrès Postal du Caire,* II, 28 ff.

not participating in them may take part in the discussions, but in such cases they have no votes unless they possess instructions from their respective governments to partici- pate in the revision in order that their governments may adhere at an early date.[20]   Second, although all delegates have the privilege of attending and participating in the discussions in all committees, only those designated by the President as members may participate in the vote.[21]   As we shall see, all countries are not given representation on all committees.   Article 9 provides that all propositions submitted to consideration by the Congress must be sub- mitted to a vote.   Ordinarily the vote will be by roll call. In case of equal division of the votes, the President may settle the question by use of his casting vote.[22]   Unless otherwise provided, the rules of procedure adopted for the plenary session of the Congress are also applicable in the commissions.[23]

The agenda of the Congress are built up from proposi- tions for the amendment of the Convention, the Detailed Regulations, and Arrangements submitted in advance by the member administrations.   For recent Congresses, the items submitted have numbered about two thousand.   The propositions submitted are printed by the Bureau at Berne and distributed to all administrations for their considera- tion and comment.   After a sufficient lapse of time for replies to be received, a second edition of the *Cahier des Propositions* is printed containing not only the original propositions but the alternative propositions and objec- tions as well, each printed over the name of the adminis- tration responsible for its inclusion.[24]   Propositions re- ceived after publication of the *Cahier*, but at least five days before the opening of the session of the Congress,

---

[20] Art. 5, *Règlement.*
[21] Art. 10, *Règlement.*
[22] Art. 9, *Règlement.*
[23] Art. 15, *Règlement.*
[24] Cf. H. R. Turkel, " International Postal Congresses," *B. Y. I. L.,* X, 172.

may be considered if supported by at least three administrations in addition to the one presenting it.[25]   After that
date no new propositions may be submitted.   This rule,
of course, is not interpreted to preclude consideration of
amendments and counter propositions resulting directly
from the debates in the plenary session or commissions of
the Congress.   Since 1924, each Congress has elected by
majority vote a preparatory commission composed of delegates appointed by fourteen countries to serve for the
next Congress.   One of the chief functions of this body
has been to sift over the propositions submitted and to
select those which appear most suitable for consideration
by the Congress, this report forming the agenda of the
Congress.[26]   The committee is not empowered to eliminate items from consideration; rather it is to promote
efficiency by eliminating duplication.   This practice greatly
facilitates the work of the Congress, for it is not at all
unusual for a half dozen proposals for amendment of the
same article, differing only slightly one from the other, to
be submitted.   The preparatory committee may select the
one most suitable for consideration.   Any administration
whose proposal has been eliminated by the committee can
bring it before the Congress, if it desires, by offering it in
place of the proposition chosen by the preparatory committee when the matter comes before the Congress.

Early in the sessions of the Congress, the items on the
agenda are distributed among commissions for detailed
examination.   The recommendations made by the commissions may, of course, be ratified, amended or even rejected
in the subsequent consideration by the plenary session.   It
was long the custom of the Congress to establish three
commissions: the first, to consider proposals for amendment of the Convention itself; the second, to consider
proposals relative to the Arrangements dealing with the

---

[25] Art. 4, *Règlement*.   [26] *Ibid.*

exchange of insured letters and packages and parcel posts; the third, with consideration of the Arrangements dealing with such things as money orders, collections, the abandonment of newspapers and periodicals, etc. At the 1934 Congress a fourth committee was added to perform editing functions. The rules provide that the seats on these commissions shall be divided among the administrations in such fashion as to permit the greatest possible number to participate in the preliminary work.[27] Although an effort has been made to keep membership in these commissions down to a point conducive to efficiency in the performance of the work, there has been, for reasons to be noted presently, a marked tendency in recent years for them to increase in size. At the Cairo Congress, they consisted of seventy-four, sixty, thirty-four and six members, respectively.[28] Delegates not designated as members may attend sessions of the commissions and participate freely in the discussions but they possess no votes.[29] Such sub-commissions may be constituted as fit the needs of the Congress and the commissions.[30] Decisions in the commissions and sub-commissions, as in the plenary sessions, are always taken by majority vote, the president of the commission or the chairman of the sub-commission having a casting vote.[31] By long tradition, the presidencies of the first, second, and third commissions are awarded to the British, French, and German delegations, respectively.[32] Following customary diplomatic practice, the President of the Congress is the senior delegate of the country entertaining the Congress.

[27] Art. 10, *Règlement.*
[28] *Documents du Congrès du Caire,* II, 22.
[29] Art. 10, *Règlement.*
[30] *Ibid.*
[31] Arts. 9, 15, *Règlement.*
[32] F. H. Williamson, " The International Postal Service and the Universal Postal Union," *Journal of the Royal Institute of International Affairs,* IX, 77.

One of the great obstacles standing in the way of the adoption of majority vote in international conferences having power to adopt or to amend conventions has always been the question of ratification. Unless unanimous agreement is reached, unanimous ratification is unlikely to follow. In the case of a draft convention, the seriousness of this result depends, of course, both upon the nature of the convention in question and upon which parties fail to ratify. In some cases a convention may be quite useful even though accepted by only a part of those negotiating it. In other cases, it may be useless unless accepted by all or, at least, by certain states. In the former case majority vote would seem to be a useful sort of device. In the latter, use of the unanimity rule might well prevent a waste of effort. In the case of revision of conventions already in force, failure to ratify the changes proposed usually means that the old obligations continue in relations among non-ratifying powers and between them and the states ratifying the new arrangements, while the new enter into force among the ratifying powers only. If this process be repeated by several conferences the result may well be a great confusion of obligations which prevents achievement of the uniformity sought by the convention in the first place.

How has the Postal Union managed to use majority vote for revising the Convention and Detailed Regulations and at the same time prevented the confusion that would result from acceptance of the changes by a part only of the members of the Union? The answer is to be found in part in that clause of the Convention relating to ratification and in part in the character of the service supplied by the Universal Postal Union. Article 14 is as follows:

The Acts of Congresses shall be ratified as soon as possible and the ratifications shall be communicated to the Government of the country in which the Congress was held, and by that Government to the Governments of the contracting countries.

6

If one or more of the contracting parties do not ratify one or other of the Acts signed by them, these Acts are not less binding on the States which have ratified them.

These Acts come into force simultaneously and have the same duration.

From the date fixed for the entry into force of the Acts adopted by a Congress, all the Acts of the preceding Congress are repealed.[33]

It is the final statement, of course, which differs from the clauses found in most conventions and which has tell-

---

[33] Italics added. This article is the direct outgrowth of Articles XIX and XX of the original convention of 1874. They were as follows:

" Article XIX—The present Treaty shall come into force on the 1st July 1875.

" It is concluded for three years from that date. When that term is passed, it shall be considered as definitely prolonged, but each contracting party will have the right to withdraw from the Union on giving notice one year in advance."

" Article XX—After the date on which the present treaty comes into effect, all the stipulations of the special treaties concluded between the various countries and Administrations, in so far as they may be at variance with the terms of the present Treaty, and without prejudice to the stipulations of Article XIV, are abrogated.

" The present Treaty shall be ratified as soon as possible, and, at the latest, three months previous to the date on which it is to come into force. The acts of ratification shall be exchanged at Berne." (*B. P. P.* (1875), LXXXII, 529.)

The Convention of June 1, 1878, revising that of October 9, 1874, carried the following articles:

" XXII—La présente Convention sera mise à exécution le 1er Avril, 1879, et demeurera en vigueur pendant un temps indéterminé; mais chaque Partie Contractante a le droit de se retirer de l'Union, moyennant un avertissement donnée une année à l'avance par son Governement au Governement de la Confédération Suisse."

" Article XXIII—Sont abrogées, à partir du jour de la mise à exécution de la présente Convention, toutes les dispositions des Traités, Conventions, Arrangements, ou autres actes conclus antérieurement entre les divers pays ou Administrations, pour autant que ces dispositions ne seraient pas conciliables avec les termes de la présente Convention, et sans préjudice des droits réservés par l'article XV ci-dessus.

" La présente Convention sera ratifiée aussitôt que faire se pourra. Les actes de ratification seront échangés à Paris." (*B. & F. State Papers,* LXIX, 210.)

ing effect.   Member states are not given the option of
ratifying the new or continuing to be bound by the old.
The revised convention comes into effect on the date fixed
by the Congress, usually twelve or eighteen months after
the date of the Congress, and the conduct of every state
is governed by it after that time or it leaves the Union.
The latter alternative is hardly a possible one for a civi-
lized state as it would mean immediate loss of the benefits
conferred by the convention, chief of which is the freedom of transit for its mails throughout the entire territory
of the Union.   In actual practice, all administrations start
applying the revised convention and regulations on the
date fixed by the Congress for their entering into force
without taking into consideration the extent to which
ratifications have been deposited.[34]   Indeed, although the
Convention and Regulations revised at London entered
into force for all members of the Union July 1, 1930,
twenty-one states, among them Great Britain, Germany,
and Italy, did not deposit ratifications until 1931 and several had not ratified by the time of the Congress in Cairo
in 1934.[35]   The practice of the Union in this respect is
admittedly extra-legal.   Consequently, several attempts
have been made in recent years to legalize it.   At the Congress in Stockholm in 1924, the Mexican delegate proposed fixing a date on which ratifications should be
deposited.[36]   At the London Congress, Ecuador proposed
that since the interval between the adoption of amendments by the Congress and the date for their entering into
force was admittedly short, states be permitted to submit
provisional ratifications within the period, to be followed

[34] Cf. Williamson, *Journal of the Royal Institute of International
Affairs,* p. 74; M. Garbini, "Summary of the Work of the Universal
Postal Union since 1874," *International Conciliation,* 1927, p. 438.
[35] F. O. Wilcox, *The Ratification of International Conventions,* pp.
300-301.
[36] *Documents du Congrès Postal de Stockholm,* I, 465.

by formal ratifications given more or less at leisure.[37] The matter was again under consideration at the Congress at Cairo in 1934,[38] but no action has yet been taken.

In theory, at least, changes may be made in the Convention, its Detailed Regulations, and the Agreements in the interval between meetings of the Congresses or Conferences without the consent of all states in all cases. It is the right of any administration to address to other administrations, through the medium of the International Bureau, proposals concerning the Convention and its Detailed Regulations. But in order for any such proposal to be considered it must be supported by at least two other administrations.[39] The same rule applies to changes in the Agreements except that proposal is restricted to the administrations of those countries participating in the particular agreement concerned. A period of six months is then allowed for the administrations to examine the proposal and to communicate their observations, if any, to the Bureau. No amendments are permitted. The communications are then assembled by the Bureau and sent to the administrations with an invitation to vote for or against the proposals. Those not sending their votes within six months are considered to have abstained.[40] Propositions involving the addition of new provisions or the modification of Parts I and II, or of Articles 32 to 36, 52 to 57, 59 to 61, 63 to 66, or 68 to 81 of the Convention, or any of the articles of its Final Protocol or of Articles 1, 5, 16, 60, 72, or 93 of its Detailed Regulations or any article of their Final Protocol are considered adopted only if a unanimous vote is given. Proposals for modification of any other article need receive but a two-thirds vote. A simple majority suffices for the adoption of an interpretation of any

<hr>

[37] *Documents du Congrès Postal de Londres,* II, 64.
[38] *Documents du Congrès Postal du Caire,* I, 23.
[39] Art. 19 of the Convention.
[40] Art. 20.

of the articles, provided it does not involve a case of disagreement between two or more administrations which must be submitted to arbitration under the terms of Article 11 of the Convention.[41]

In actual practice this machinery for making changes in the Postal Convention and Regulations in the intervals between Congresses is rarely used.[42]   The reasons for this are not difficult to discover.   In the first place, unanimity is required for most changes of real importance,[43] and it

[41] Art. 21.

[42] Cf. Williamson, p. 74, who says " revisions are in practice limited to periodical Congresses."

[43] Unanimity is required if the proposal involves the addition of new provisions or the modification of the provisions of Part I and II, or of Articles 32 to 36, 52 to 57, 59 to 61, 63 to 66, 68 to 81 of the Convention, or of any of the Articles of its Final Protocol or of the Articles 1, 5, 16, 60, 72, and 93 of its Detailed Regulations or any of the articles of their Final Protocol. Part I relates to the organization and extent of the Union, its Congresses, Conferences, committees, proposals for change between Congresses, and the International Bureau. Part II is largely given over to fundamental principles of the Union—freedom of transit, prohibition of authorized charges, temporary suspension of services, monetary standard, equivalents, forms, language, and identity cards. Articles 32 to 36 contain general provisions relating to the definition of correspondence, rates of postage, prepayment, charge on unpaid or insufficiently prepaid correspondence, and surtaxes. Articles 52 to 57 relate to registered articles—charges, advice of delivery, responsibility, exceptions in respect of responsibility, cessation of responsibility, and payment of compensation. Articles 59 to 60 also relate to registered articles—fixing of responsibility and repayment of compensation to the dispatching office. Articles 61, and 63 to 66, and 68 to 71 deal with cash on delivery packets. Articles 72 to 78 relate to the allocation of postage collections. Article 79 relates to non-observance of freedom of transit, while Article 80 contains an undertaking on the part of all to prevent counterfeiting of stamps of other countries. Article 81 fixes the date on which the Convention will enter into force and fixes its duration. The Final Protocol contains provisions in respect to the withdrawal of correspondence, fixes basic postage rates with the proviso that any administration may increase fifty percent or reduce twenty percent from them and regulates the posting of correspondence abroad. It also permits some countries to substitute the ounce avoirdupois for the decimal-metric system and contains regulations on reply coupons, registration fees, and air services. The same document fixes warehousing charges and fixes special rates for the Trans-Siberian Railway and for Uruguay. Article 1 of the Detailed Regulations relates to

must be recognized that the unanimity here required is exceedingly difficult to obtain. Small minorities are much more inclined to give way in conferences when confronted by the arguments and appeals of their fellow delegates than when acting independently from their own capitals. Unless the proposal relates to one of the matters subject to change by two-thirds vote and unless it appears certain to command quite general support, it is more feasible to await one of the regular Congresses so that the question may be dealt with by majority vote than to attempt interim change. Moreover, for matters considered urgent, resort may be had to a Conference or an extraordinary Congress, either of which may be called by request of two-thirds of the contracting countries.[44] This method is likely to produce the desired changes almost as rapidly as the interim procedure, granting that the latter be successfully employed. The interim procedure, it will be recalled, is not rapid. Six months are required for consideration of the proposal and another six months for the vote. Moreover, no addition or modification so adopted may be brought into force until at least three months after its ratification.[45] Suggestion has been made from time to time to reduce the periods permitted for consideration and vote, but states far removed from Berne have always objected and the Congress has never taken action.

The Convention of the Postal Union of the Americas

---

transit in closed mails and *à découvert*, Article 5 to the fixing of postage rates, Article 16 to a definition of printed matter, Article 60 to transit statistics, Article 72 to the settlement of transit charges, and Article 93 fixes the date on which the Regulations come into force and their duration. The Final Protocol of the Detailed Regulations contains a provision in respect to the payment of balances resulting from transit charges and permits the United States Post Office to enclose the letter bill in a bag containing ordinary letters, provided that the letter F is clearly shown on the label of the bag.

[44] Arts. 15, 17.
[45] Art. 23.

and Spain [46] is subject to modification by Congresses which normally meet at five year intervals.[47] In the Congress all decisions are taken by majority vote.[48] In the intervals between Congresses nineteen of the thirty-two articles of the Convention may be modified only with unanimous consent, three may be modified by a two-thirds vote, and the remaining ten by majority vote.[49] Modifications so adopted become effective for all parties four months after the date of communication to the International Office at Montevideo.[50] Revisions adopted by the Congress become effective for ratifying powers, however, on the date set by the Congress, and, like the Universal Postal Union Convention, entrance into force of the new means abrogation of the old. The failure of one or more of participating countries to ratify the new convention does not destroy its validity for those states that have ratified.[51] Thus, the procedure for change in the intervals between Congresses is such as to make possible imposition of a legal obligation upon member states without their consent since modifications so made enter into force at the end of four months. To be sure, member states opposed to the changes may exercise their privilege of withdrawal from the Union, but this requires one year's notice given to the Government of Uruguay.[52] In fact, if not in legal theory, modifications made by the Congress may likewise enter

[46] The Postal Union of the Americas and Spain, formerly the Pan American Postal Union, was created under the convention signed at Buenos Aires on September 15, 1921 (*L. N. T. S.*, XXX, 141; M. O. Hudson, *International Legislation*, I, 702). It has been revised at Mexico City (1926), Madrid (1931), and Panama (1937). For the latest revision see Union Postal de los Americas y España, *Congreso de Panamá*, 1937. The twenty-one American republics and Canada and Spain are members of the Union.

[47] Art. 24 of the Convention.

[48] Statement of the Director of the International Office to the writer, August 19, 1937.

[49] Art. 25.

[50] Art. 26.

[51] Art. 32.

[52] *Ibid.*

into force without all states consenting inasmuch as the alternatives placed before states which have found themselves in a minority is acceptance of the revised convention or withdrawal from the Union.

Another international organ which may be said to exercise powers of a legislative character, the International Commission for Air Navigation, came into existence at Paris, July 11, 1922, in accordance with the provisions of Article 34 of the Air Navigation Convention of October 13, 1919, drafted at the Peace Conference.[53] The Convention had been signed, within the fixed period, by twenty-six states, and came into force when ratifications were deposited with the Government of France by fourteen.[54] Since that time twenty-one more states have become parties to the Convention,[55] three have denounced it,[56] and one has ceased to be a party by reason of its loss of international personality.[57]

By the terms of the Convention in the form adopted in 1919, the International Commission was permitted to amend the Annexes A to G attached to the Convention by a vote of three-fourths of the total vote possible if all representatives were present. By an amendment which entered into force December 14, 1926, it was provided that this majority must include the votes of at least three of the following powers: the United States, the British

[53] The convention may be found in *L. N. T. S.*, XI, 173; *B. & F. State Papers*, CXII, 931.

[54] Belgium, Bolivia, France, Greece, Japan, Portugal, Siam, the Serb-Croat-Slovene State, the United Kingdom (and Canada, Australia, Union of South Africa, New Zealand, and India).

[55] Persia (1922), the Irish Free State (1922), Bulgaria (1923), Czechoslovakia (1923), Italy (1923), Poland (1924), Roumania (1924), Uruguay (1924), Chile (1926), Denmark (1927), Sweden (1927), the Saar Territory (1927), Netherlands (1928), Panama (1929), Iraq (1931), Norway (1931), Finland (1932), Switzerland (1934), Spain (1935), Argentine Republic (1935), Peru (1937).

[56] Bolivia (1924), Panama (1931), Persia (1933).

[57] The Saar Territory (1935).

Empire, France, Italy, Japan.[58] By a second amendment, effective May 17, 1933, amendment of the Annexes A to G may now be accomplished by a three-fourths vote of the Commission, the vote including at least two-thirds of the total vote possible if the delegates of all members were present.[59] These annexes provide rules binding upon all contracting parties in respect to the following subjects: the making of aircraft and call signs, certificates of airworthiness, log books, rules as to lights and signals and for air traffic, minimum qualifications for obtaining certificates and licenses as pilots and navigators, international aeronautical maps and ground marking, and the collection and dissemination of meteorological information. No subsequent ratification by the contracting states is required. The Commission is also charged with the duty of proposing all amendments to the convention proper by vote of at least two-thirds of the total possible vote, but ratification by all contracting states is prerequisite to their becoming effective.[60] Disputes between two or more member states arising out of interpretation of the technical regulations in the annexes are settled by majority vote of the Commission.[61]

In view of these departures from the general rule of unanimous consent, some of which represent innovations in international practice, it seems desirable to examine the circumstances under which these articles were written into the Convention and the experience of the International Commission operating under them.

The Air Convention of 1919 was the direct outgrowth of war-time experience. The pre-war controversy between those jurists who held the air free and those who held it subject to national sovereignty had been settled conclusively by both belligerents and neutrals alike asserting

[58] International Commission for Air Navigation, *Official Bulletin,* XII, 17.
[59] *O. B.,* XXII, 56.   [60] Art. 34.   [61] Art. 37.

jurisdiction over the air space above their territories and territorial waters. Moreover, the war made apparent the urgent need for agreement concerning air navigation, for not only had the great military importance of the aeroplane been demonstrated, but its commercial possibilities as well could now be perceived. Development would be retarded unless agreement could be reached upon regulations to govern communications by air. Some even appreciated that, owing to the rapidity with which technical changes were being made in aviation, these regulations would have to be subjected to frequent change. Undoubtedly agreement was facilitated by reason of the experience of the Allied and Associated Powers with international collaboration in this field through their Inter-Allied Aviation Committee. It was the officers of this committee who first called the attention of the Peace Conference to the desirability of perpetuating the war-time organization in a permanent instrument of international regulation.[62] Their suggestion presumably met with approval for on March 12, 1919, the Supreme War Council adopted a resolution providing that the Aviation Commission of the Peace Conference, consisting of two representatives each of the United States, the British Empire, France, Italy, and Japan, with five representatives of other states at the Conference, should consider " a convention in regard to international aerial navigation in time of peace." [63] On March 15, the Supreme Council decided the representation of the smaller states should be increased from five to seven, Belgium, Brazil, Cuba, Greece, Portugal, Roumania, and Serbia being permitted to name one each.[64] The personnel of the commission named was almost exclusively military so far as the chief delegates were concerned, although Cuba was

[62] Cf. Roper's statement in International Commission for Navigation, *Extraordinary Session, June, 1929, Draft Minutes,* p. 145.

[63] D. H. Miller, *My Diary at the Conference of Paris,* XV, 352.

[64] *La Documentation Internationale, La paix de Versailles,* VIII, 7.

represented by the jurist, Bustamante, and Japan and Italy drew one each of their chief delegates from non-military circles. Three of the chief delegates, Colonel Dhé (France), General Patrick (United States), and Signor Chiesa (Italy) had served on the Inter-Allied Aviation Committee which had been composed of two representatives each from France, Great Britain, the United States, and Italy. The Commission met under the presidency of Colonel Dhé, and later of General Duval (France).

The method followed by the Commission in the performance of its work was, first, to formulate general principles which should govern the drafting of a code for international aerial navigation in time of peace, and then to turn over to sub-commissions the actual formulation of the drafts, the drafts to be amended and adopted in plenary session. The tenth of the twelve general principles agreed upon was " the recognition of the necessity of a permanent International Aeronautical Commission." [65] It will be noted that the terms of the resolution adopted by the Supreme Council had not made this explicit. The sub-commissions provided no representation for the smaller powers except that Belgium was assigned one place on the Legal Sub-Commission.

To the Legal Sub-Commission was given the task of formulating the provisions of the Convention itself and of the Annex dealing with customs regulations. Although some of its personnel were drawn from military and naval circles (all three representatives of the United States), lawyers predominated. Included were White Smith (British Empire), M. d'Aubigney and M. de la Pradelle (France), Signor Buzzati (Italy), M. Yamakawa (Japan), and M. Rolin-Jaequemyns (Belgium). In addition to the general principles formulated by the Commission, the Sub-Commission had for its guidance draft conventions submitted by the British Government and by the

[65] *Ibid.,* p. 129.

French Interministeral Commission on Civil Aviation.[66]
In the French draft no provision was made for the creation of a permanent international commission. Instead,
they believed the necessary changes in the technical provisions which were to be placed in annexes to the Convention could be achieved by calling special conferences at the
request of not less than two-thirds of the contracting
states. In the absence of any statement to the contrary, it
seems reasonable to presume it was their intention that
decisions in such conferences be reached by the customary
rule of unanimous consent.

The British draft convention was much more elaborate
and in its Article 23 may be seen the basis for what came
to be Article 34 of the Convention of October 13, 1919.
The British Article 23 was as follows:

I) There shall be established at ——————— under the name
of " The International Commission for Aerial Navigation," a permanent commission consisting of two representatives each of the
United States of America, the British Empire, France, Italy and
Japan, with five representatives elected by the other contracting
States (with delegates representing technical and local interest as
required) which shall be empowered:—

a) To receive proposals from and to make proposals to any of
the contracting States for the modification or amendment of, or
for additions to, the provisions of the present Convention, and
to notify alterations adopted.

b) To notify, amend or add to any detailed provisions of a
technical character contained in Articles 6 to 9 inclusive of the
present Convention or in the annexes thereto.

c) To collect, collate, publish and distribute for and to the
contracting States information of every kind which concerns aerial
navigation from an international standpoint.

d) To advise upon and assist in the negotiation of the international arrangements contemplated in Article 13 of the present
Convention.

[66] For texts of these two plans, see pp. 219 ff.

e) To give at the request of contracting States concerned an opinion on questions in dispute arising out of the present Convention.

II) The proposals mentioned in sub-paragraph (a) above must receive the unanimous assent of the contracting States before they are adopted as alterations to the present Convention. The procedure for receiving the proposals, for obtaining the views of the contracting States and for ratifying alterations adopted in pursuance of sub-paragraph (a) above shall in all respects be similar to that of the International Bureau of the Postal Union.

III) Any modifications, amendments or additions, made by the I. C. A. N. in pursuance of sub-paragraph (b) above must receive the unanimous assent of the representatives of the contracting States constituting the I. C. A. N. before they are adopted as alterations of the present Convention. Any alterations made in pursuance of sub-paragraph (b) above shall take effect three months after the date of its notification to the contracting States.

IV) Any alterations to the present Convention made in pursuance of sub-paragraph (ii) and (iii) above shall be treated as though they formed part of the present Convention.

V) The expenses of the I. C. A. N. together with those of its permanent Secretariat shall be borne by and between the contracting States in the following proportions. . . .

Several features of this proposal should be noted. In the first place, the British were proposing that the Permanent Commission be empowered to alter the technical portions of the Convention and Annexes without necessity of securing ratification by the contracting states, indicating appreciation on their part of the rapidity with which such technical changes would have to be made. Second, they proposed that this Commission should use the unanimity rule but planned to make that less of an obstacle to action by the device of excluding all but five of the smaller powers from representation. Third, any alteration in the principles formulated in the Convention was to be made in the customary fashion, unanimity in the Commission in proposal followed by acceptance by all contracting states.

Most of the features of this plan met the approval of the Legal Sub-Commission composed of the lawyers and diplomats representing almost exclusively the larger powers. However, the British proposal undoubtedly was felt to be too flagrant a violation of state equality. Therefore, the Sub-Commission substituted a poorly devised plan of its own whereby each of the five states named in the British plan was to retain its two representatives and two votes, the remaining states having one representative each with half votes up to a total of nine.[67] At no time did the Sub-Commission consider allowing modification of the Annexes by less than a unanimous vote.[68] They even hesitated to approve the British suggestion for dispensing with ratification for such changes but included it in their draft after White Smith (Great Britain)[69] and Buzzati (Italy)[70] had emphasized the dispatch with which such changes must be made if air law was to be kept abreast of technological change. The lawyers and diplomats apparently lacked the necessary breadth of vision to propose to the plenary session a Permanent Commission which in its procedures would represent a break with the past.

When the draft of the Legal Sub-Commission came before the plenary session it was immediately attacked by the representatives of the minor powers for its marked departures from state equality.[71] As a compromise solution, Admiral Knapp (United States) offered the following text:

Each of the five powers first named shall have the smallest whole number of votes which when multiplied by five will give a product exceeding by at least one vote the total number of the

---

[67] Art. 34 of the draft submitted by the Legal Sub-Committee, *ibid.*, p. 508.

[68] *Ibid.*, pp. 336 ff.   [69] *Ibid.*, p. 337.   [70] *Ibid.*, p. 338.

[71] See particularly the remarks of the representatives of Brazil, Serbia, and Portugal (*ibid.*, p. 56) and those of Bustamante (*ibid.*, p. 102).

votes of all the other contracting states. Each of the powers except the first five shall have one vote.[72]

Although this could have been little more palatable for the minor powers than had been the original proposal it was unanimously adopted except for Cuba,[73] and became, with only slight change, part of Article 34 of the final Convention.[74]

Having disposed of the question of representation the Commission turned to that of the powers to be exercised by the International Commission. It will be recalled that the Legal Sub-Commission had carried over from the British Draft the provisions permitting the alteration of the Annexes without the necessity of securing ratification. This feature had been included by the Sub-Commission without enthusiasm, M. d'Aubigny (France) declaring it to be a very dangerous article.[75] In the Commission, the Marquis of Londonderry (British Empire), the spokesman for the state responsible for its inclusion in the draft, now proposed its deletion, as he believed it lodging too great power in an international organ. When this awoke no response, British opposition to the clause was shifted to the fact that changes in the Annexes could then be made without the consent of the British Dominions which possessed voting power only indirectly through the vote of the British Empire. M. Chauvin (France) remarked, a little unfairly, that France and Italy were accepting the paragraph although their colonies were without direct representation. The paragraph was adopted without amendment by unanimous vote except for Great Britain which entered a reservation for the Dominions.[76]

[72] *Ibid.*, p. 59.
[73] *Ibid.*
[74] For more complete consideration of the problem of equality in the International Commission for Air Navigation, see below, p. 267.
[75] *La Documentation Internationale,* VIII, 581.
[76] *Ibid.*, p. 60.

The Commission next considered the question of the vote necessary for taking decisions in the International Commission. The draft as it came from the Sub-Commission required unanimity in amendments to the Annexes but was silent on the vote necessary for proposing amendments to the Convention itself. Presumably, unanimity was intended in both cases although it would obviously be much less important in the latter case than in the former since action of the Commission was to be final in amendment of the Annexes and dependent upon ratification by all in amendment of the Convention. When the article was read the delegation of the United States immediately proposed replacing the word " unanimity " with " a vote of two-thirds of the total possible number of votes," and their amendment was so worded as to permit decision by two-thirds both in the amendment of the Annexes and in the proposal of amendments to the Convention.[77] It follows (translation):

> Any modification of the provisions of any of the Annexes may be made by the I. C. A. N. when such change is authorized by the votes of two-thirds of the total possible vote and shall become effective as soon as the notice is given thereof by the I. C. A. N. whether it originates with one of the contracting states or with the I. C. A. N. itself. No such modification shall be proposed for acceptance by the contracting states unless it shall have received the sanction of at least two-thirds of all the possible votes which may be cast in the I. C. A. N.
>
> All such modifications of the articles of the Convention (not of the provisions of the Annexes) must be formally adopted by the contracting states before they become effective.

This text was adopted by the Commission, two states, Japan and the British Empire, voting against it, the latter again resting her opposition upon the failure of the Convention to provide direct voting power for the Domin-

[77] *Ibid.*

ions.[78] At a later meeting, the Marquis of Londonderry (British Empire) asked that, in the paragraph dealing with the manner of changing the Annexes, the words "two-thirds" be changed to "three-fourths." This was adopted by unanimous vote.[79]

Finally, the provision in Article 37 of the Convention which permits the Commission to make decision by majority vote in disputes between contracting states arising out of interpretation of the Annexes was inserted at the suggestion of the Legal Sub-Commission. Neither the French nor the British draft conventions had contained any provision of this character. The suggestion of the Sub-Commission resulted directly from its consideration of a provision for arbitration of disputes growing out of interpretation of the Convention. It did not seem appropriate that disputes arising out of the Annexes be submitted to formal arbitration, yet clearly some method of resolving such differences was essential. It was suggested, therefore, that these be settled by the Commission. From this point, the Sub-Commission maneuvered itself into making provision in such cases for decision by majority vote, although clearly it had no enthusiasm for it. But if arbitral bodies properly decide disputes concerning the Convention by majority vote, logically, the Commission should follow a similar rule when performing a like function in disputes arising out of the Annexes. La Pradelle observed that if the Commission were empowered to exercise such a power by majority vote it would, in fact, have power to amend the Annexes without consent of all, a power which was not provided for in the draft convention before the Legal Sub-Commission. Inasmuch as this argument could have been applied with almost equal force against majority decision by arbitral tribunals in respect to the meaning of the Convention, it was not pressed, the Legal Sub-Commission

---

[78] *Ibid.*, p. 61.   [79] *Ibid.*, p. 75.

7

suggesting and the plenary session adopting the provision for majority decision by the Commission in disputes growing out of interpretation of the Annexes.[80] Only the British delegation voted against it in the plenary session.[81]

Thus it will be seen, the more important departures from the rule of unanimity provided for in the Aerial Convention of 1919 originated in large part with the military and naval aerial technicians and were adopted by a commission in which this type of delegate predominated over those with legal or diplomatic backgrounds. The departures from the rule of equality in assigning representation and voting power, however, find their origins in the draft convention submitted by the British Government, were approved by the legal group from which the representatives of the smaller states were almost completely excluded, and then adopted by the larger body, not without protest from the representatives of the powers discriminated against.

How have these provisions stood the test of practice? In the first place, those establishing inequality in representation and in voting power have undergone complete change through the process of amendment. This has resulted from a desire to make acceptance of the Convention more general.[82] However, those clauses providing for deviations from the rule of unanimous consent have been retained. Moreover, there has been some tendency in the practice of the Commission to approximate the majority principle more closely than the original Convention provided.

In the first place, the Commission in drafting its own Articles of Administration at its first session, in accordance with Article 34 of the Convention, made full use of its opportunity to fashion a workable procedure.[83] Article 12 provides all decisions for which a special quorum is not

---

[80] Cf. *ibid.*, pp. 357-364, 505.
[81] *Ibid.*, p. 63.
[82] See below, p. 270.
[83] *O. B.*, I, 8.

required either by the Convention or by the present regulations must be passed by a majority of the votes of the members present. Articles 10 and 11 adopt the Convention restrictions upon alterations of Annexes A to G and upon proposal of amendments to the Convention. The other restrictions upon decision by simple majority are not numerous. A decision to proceed immediately to the consideration of a question not submitted to the representatives by the Secretary-General as part of the agenda at least seventy-five days in advance of the session, requires a unanimous vote of the delegates present, including at least two-thirds of the total membership.[84] The budget must be adopted by two-thirds of the total possible number of votes,[85] and a vote of three-fourths of the total is required to amend the rules of procedure.[86]

There remain many decisions the International Commission may take by simple majority vote.[87] It may select its own officers, decide all procedural questions not involving amendment of the rules, make recommendations to the member states, offer opinions on the meaning of the Convention or on questions submitted by member states, or perform any of the numerous functions imposed on the Commission by Articles 9, 13, 14, 15, 16, 27, 28, and 36 for which no special majority is specified. For instance, Article 14 provides that every aircraft used in public transport and capable of carrying ten or more persons shall be equipped with sending and receiving wireless apparatus

[84] Art. 5, Administration of the International Commission for Air Navigation. Originally the rule provided for 45 days' notice. This was changed to 75 on motion of Japan. *O. B.*, XVII, 21.

[85] Art. 21.

[86] Art. 26.

[87] No quorum is provided for in the rules but since much of the work of the Commission relates to modifying the Annexes it is doubtful if a session would be undertaken with less than two-thirds of the members present—the minimum vote required for that purpose. The Commission rejected a proposal to amend the rules to permit absent delegates to cast their votes by subsequent declaration. *O. B.*, XIX, 72.

when the methods of employing such apparatus shall have been determined by the International Commission. The Commission may later extend the obligation of carrying wireless apparatus to all other classes of aircraft under the conditions and according to the methods which it may determine. The Commission decided over the negative vote of Belgium to require all aircraft engaged in public international transport to be fitted with wireless apparatus [88] and later extended these regulations to other classes of aircraft.[89]

Although the Commission has provided through a special set of rules for a simple procedure governing the settlement of disputes relative to the Annexes,[90] this procedure has never been utilized. However, its existence has no doubt had an important part in the development of a far less formal and a much more rapid technique of settlement. When difficulties arise concerning the interpretation of the Annexes or even of the Convention, a contracting state applies informally to the Secretary-General or to some of the experts for an opinion or the Commission itself may be asked to give its opinion. This they have done on numerous occasions,[91] and by majority vote if necessary, although when a dispute concerning interpretation of the Convention actually takes form between two or more states the Commission necessarily denies its competence to deal with the matter.[92]

Likewise, the development of a committee system has been an important factor in the Commission's tendency to approximate rather completely the majority principle. Article 15 of the Commission's rules of procedure provides that certain questions may be referred to sub-commissions of experts, the number, constitution, and func-

---

[88] *O. B.,* I, 17.   [89] *Ibid.,* XV, 45.   [90] *Ibid.,* XII, 35.
[91] See, for example, *ibid.,* V, 38; *ibid.,* VI, 21; *ibid.,* VIII, 34; *ibid.,* XXIII, 88.
[92] See, for example, *ibid.,* XIV, 30.

tions of which will be decided annually. At the first session of the Commission sub-commissions were established and have been reconstituted annually in substantially the same form. Thus at the twenty-third session the following were established: operational, legal, wireless, meteorological, medical, maps, materials.[93] These committees are composed of experts selected by the member states, no state having more than three on the operational sub-commission nor more than two on any of the others. Each state delegation, regardless of its size, possesses a single vote,[94] and decisions are reached by majority. Many of the questions placed on the agenda of the International Commission are referred by it to one or more of these sub-commissions. The Commission members have such respect for the talent of the experts constituting these sub-commissions that it is by no means uncommon for draft resolutions formulated by them on the basis of their investigations to be adopted by the Commission by unanimous vote and without debate. Thus a decision reached in the first place by a simple majority becomes one reached by unanimous vote in the Commission. However, this is by no means the case on all occasions. Quite frequently divisions arising in sub-commissions are reflected in the final vote in the Commission.[95]

[93] *Ibid.,* XXIII, 96.

[94] Prior to the establishment of equality in voting power in the Commission, each state delegation possessed in the sub-commission the same number of votes it had in the Commission.

[95] See, for example, the vote on the resolution applying the provisions of Article 14 to all aircraft engaged in public international transport (*O. B.,* I, 16) ; on the report of the operational and materials sub-commissions (*ibid.,* XII, 26) ; on the recommendation to the states of a procedure in case of accidents (*ibid.,* XI, 23) ; on the report on the unification of terms in aeronautical technic (*ibid.,* XIII, 46) ; on the amendment of Annex D (*ibid.,* X, 20) ; on the amendments to Annex E (*ibid.,* XIII, 53; *ibid.,* XVIII, 39) ; on amendments to Annex G (*ibid.,* XI, 20; *ibid.,* XIV, 20) ; on the proposal to amend the convention (*ibid.,* XVII, 25).

Moreover, in its interpretation of the Convention the Commission has been inclined to read into it authorization for what has appeared to them as a reasonable procedure and to expand somewhat the scope of what may be done by majority vote. In formulating the document, the drafters made no provision for the amendment of Annex H. The explanation is apparent when the history of the drafting of the Convention is considered. In the early drafts the Commission had been empowered to alter the technical portions of the Convention which were included, for the most part, in the Annexes. Alteration in matters of principle was to be left to the states. However, the delegates constituting the drafting committee were not prepared to concede that change might be made in the technical regulations pertaining to customs without explicit consent by all parties. Therefore, when the draft convention was amended to permit modification of the Annexes by less than unanimous vote, something had to be done to remove Annex H from that category. An American delegate suggested that instead of the Commission having power to amend the Annexes or the technical portions of the Convention, the Commission's power be restricted to amending Annexes A to G. This suggestion was accepted with the result that the Convention included a procedure for amending Annexes A to G and the articles of the Convention proper but no procedure for amending Annex H.[96]

At its first session the International Commission took the narrow view that the annex in question could be amended only through a special convention necessitating agreement by all states, followed by ratification.[97] However, by the twenty-third session the Commission had reached the conclusion that amendments to Annex H might be treated as amendments to the Convention, i. e.,

[96] Cf. *La Documentation Internationale*, VIII, 580 ff.
[97] *O. B.*, I, 21.

proposed by two-thirds vote of the Commission subject to ratification by all contracting states.[98]

But much more important has been the Commission's interpretation on the extent of its competence in respect to the amendment of Annexes A to G. Did Article 34 of the Convention, providing for "modification" of the Annexes by majority vote, mean that the Commission was restricted to making changes in the original text of the Annexes or could new material be added? The Commission considered this question at its fifteenth session and answered it in the following fashion:

> The Commission considers that the terms of Article 34 of the Convention . . . give to the Commission the power not only to modify the original text of Annexes A to G, but also to complete it, taking into account the progress made in aeronautical technics and the development of air navigation; the Commission being required, however, in this work, which forms one of its most important duties, to remain always within the general framework of the Convention.[99]

Formal amendment of the Convention also has been used to make alteration of the Annexes A to G a somewhat less formidable task. It will be recalled that the Convention as adopted provided that this might be done by a three-fourths majority vote in the Commission, including three-fourths of the total possible votes. Later this was amended to provide that the votes of at least three of the five enumerated powers must be included. The rule had the effect, of course, of counting those states absent with those opposed. The result has been a severe limitation upon the power of the Commission to amend the Annexes by three-fourths vote.[100] In six of the first

[98] *Ibid.*, XXIII, 82.

[99] *Ibid.*, XV, 37.

[100] Publicists who have described the working of the International Commission for Air Navigation generally have assumed that because the Convention permits amendment of the Annexes by three-fourths majority it

twenty-three sessions this could be done only by absolute unanimity of those present. In three other sessions the

has always been possible in practice to adopt changes when not more than one-fourth oppose the proposition brought forward. In actual practice, as the table which follows shows, a much smaller vote generally has been sufficient to prevent adoption of such amendments.

Session		States Present	Absent	Total Votes	Votes to Defeat Amendment to Annex in Commission	Negative vote in Commission Needed to Defeat An Amendment
1. (July	1922)	10	0	13	4	4
2. (Oct.	1922)	7	3	13	4	1
3. (March	1923)	7	3	13	4	1
4. (June	1923)	9	2	15	4	2 (or one great power)
5. (Oct.	1923)	8	4	16	5	1
6. (March	1924)	11	2	17	5	3
7. (Oct.	1924)	12	3	19	5	2 (or one great power)
8. (April	1925)	10	5	23*	5	1
9. (Oct.	1925)	12	3	23	6	3 (or one great power)
10. (May	1926)	15	1	24	7	5
11. (Nov.	1926)	14	2	24	7	5
12. (April	1927)	12	4	16†	5	1
13. (Oct.	1927)	17	2	19	5	3
14. (June	1928)	17	2	19	5	3
15. (March	1929)	17	3	20	6	3
16. (June	1929)	18‡	2	20	6	4
17. (Dec.	1929)	19§	2	21	6	4
18. (June	1930)	17‖	3	21	6	3
19. (June	1931)	17‖	4	21	6	2
20. (May	1932)	20§	3	23	6	3
21. (May	1933)	20‖	3	23	6	3
22. (May	1934)	23	5	28	10¶	5
23. (May	1935)	24	6	30	11	5

* Vote of 4 great powers increased from two to three by operation of provision of Article 34.

† Each state now 1 vote. (Amendment to Article 34 effective Dec. 14, 1926.)

‡ Four additional without votes.

§ Six additional without votes.

‖ Five additional without votes.

¶ Quota changed by amendment to Article 34, effective May 17, 1933.

vote of a single great power was sufficient to prevent an amendment being carried. At its best the rule in operation merely gave the Commission power to amend the Annexes over the negative votes of a very few delegations.

If the three-fourths rule was to be as effective as the authors of the Convention desired and as publicists have believed it to be, changes had to be made to meet the situation which had developed. First, it was suggested that the Commission amend its own rules of procedure to permit states not represented to send in their votes. Absence, it was known, did not in general indicate disapproval of work being undertaken by the Commission. Rather it was likely to be indicative of indifference. In many cases it resulted from the difficulty of supplying a suitable delegate at a session held in some European city far from the home capital. However, when this proposal came before the Commission it was immediately foreseen that here was a rule capable of cutting in both directions. Consequently, the body wisely declined to amend its rules of procedure to make absentee voting possible.[101]

In the meantime, the Commission had undertaken to meet the difficulty by process of amending the Convention. The entering into force of the first amendment to Article 34 in December, 1926, had made the matter more urgent. It had deprived the great powers of their extra votes, thus making it possible for an even smaller number of absent delegations to thrust the Commission back on a unanimity rule. Consequently, at the extraordinary session of June, 1929, when Article 34 was being amended to remove the last vestiges of inequality between contracting states, it was proposed that in the future the three-fourths vote for amending the Annexes need include only two-thirds of the total vote possible instead of three-fourths. This amendment entered into force May 17,

[101] *O. B.*, XIX, 72.

1933, just too late to be operative in the twenty-first session. Although at first glance a change from three-fourths to two-thirds may appear to be of an almost insignificant character, this is not in fact the case. As shown above, it has been possible in recent sessions to overcome a larger number of negative votes in the Commission than at any time since 1926, in spite of the fact that absence has been higher than at any other time in recent years.

The three-fourths rule for amendment of the Annexes should serve the needs of the International Commission for Air Navigation very well, now that the vote need no longer include such a high percentage of the total possible vote. To be sure, this procedure falls considerably short of the majority rule considered appropriate for well ordered legislative bodies. However, there are two factors which make this situation acceptable. First, there is the strong tendency, already noted, for the Commission to approve decisions reached by majority rule in the sub-commissions. It was this practice which made possible some amendment of the Annexes during the sessions in which the Commission was obliged to obtain the consent of all present to take such action. In the second place, procedure appropriate for a national legislative body may not be appropriate for an international one. In the former we are accustomed to have majorities pushing ahead and taking decisions over large minority groups. The minority groups expect to acquiesce. International government has not yet progressed to the point where minorities are so willing to give way when the majority position is opposed strongly. Quite possibly the attempt of a small majority to lead a minority of almost equal size faster than it desired to go would result in a wholesale renunciation of the Convention. Instead, it is desirable that there be a method by which large majorities may overcome obstruction or opposition by small minority groups, and that without being obliged to resort to the platitudes or evasive phraseology so characteristic of resolutions drafted by bodies adhering strictly to the rule of unanimous consent.   The three-fourths rule seems suitable for this purpose.

Of the other international organs which exercise powers of a legislative character little need be said.   The Committee of Experts of the Railway Union was established by virtue of the provisions of the Convention on the Transport of Goods by Rail, signed at Berne, October 23, 1924, the Convention entering into force October 1, 1928.[102] The Committee is authorized to make changes by majority vote in the terms of Annex I to the Convention, Regulations Concerning Articles Accepted for Carriage, Subject to Certain Conditions.   The decisions of the Committee are reported to the participating governments through the Central Office of the Union at Berne and come into force on the first day of the third month thereafter unless at least two governments have made objection.[103]   Thus the Committee is competent to alter the technical regulations over the opposition of one member state.   Germany, France, and Italy are represented permanently on the Committee of Experts and all other contracting states may be represented when they desire.[104]

The General Council of the International Relief Union established by the Convention signed at Geneva, July 12, 1927, in force, December 27, 1932,[105] may amend the Statute annexed to the Convention by two-thirds vote, provided that at least three-fourths of the General Council are present.[106]   The Statute contains provisions relating

[102] *L. N. T. S.*, LXXVII, 367; Hudson, *International Legislation*, II, 1393.
[103] Art. 60.
[104] Art. 1, Annex VII.   The following states are parties to the Convention: Germany, Belgium, Bulgaria, Denmark, Danzig, Spain, Esthonia, Finland, France, Greece, Hungary, Italy, Latvia, Lithuania, Luxemburg, Norway, Netherlands, Poland, Portugal, Roumania, Jugoslavia, Sweden, Switzerland, and Czechoslovakia.
[105] *L. N. T. S.*, CXXXV, 247.
[106] Art. 21 of the Convention.

to the internal organization of the Union, including the control of the funds of the organization. The General Council is composed of one delegate from each member state.[107]

The Statutes of the International Hydrographic Bureau may be amended by a vote of two-thirds of the members of the Supplementary or Periodic Conference.[108] When voting on changes in the Statutes, each state has one vote, although when electing Directors or the Secretary-General a system of voting weighted by tonnage is used.[109] The Statutes, it should be noted, provide that the Bureau " be a consultative body only " with " no authority whatsoever over the Hydrographic Offices of the Members " and that the Bureau " shall never deal with any subject which involves questions of international policy." [110]

The Constitution of the International Labor Organization which forms Part XIII of the Treaty of Versailles,[111] may be amended by a vote of two-thirds of the delegates present in a meeting of the Conference, amendments taking effect when ratified by the states whose representatives compose the Council of the League of Nations and by three-fourths of the members.[112] The Conference is composed of four representatives of each member state, two representing the government and two others, nominated in agreement with the most representative employers' and workers' organizations, representing respectively the employers and workers within each state.[113] The

[107] Art. 6.
[108] Art. 61, *Statutes of the International Hydrographic Bureau,* Third International Hydrographic Conference, Monaco, 1932.
[109] Art. 35 and Appendix D.
[110] Art. 7.
[111] The Constitution of the International Labor Organization is embodied also in Part XII of the Treaty of Saint-Germain, Part XII of the Treaty of Neuilly, and Part XIII of the Treaty of Trianon.
[112] Art. 422 of the Treaty of Versailles.
[113] Art. 389.

amending clause was but one of several somewhat novel provisions written into the terms of the treaty by the Commission charged by the Peace Conference with preparation of the Constitution of the organization.[114] The British draft convention of February 2, 1919, which was taken by the Commission as a basis for work, provided in Article 36 that " amendments shall only come into effect if they are unanimously agreed to and ratified by all the High Contracting Parties." [115] When the article came before the Commission, Delevingne (Great Britain) suggested substitution of the amending clause which was actually adopted, explaining that this was modeled upon the provisions of Article 26 of the League Covenant.[116] The proposal of Delevingne was accepted by the Commission almost without discussion although Vandervelde (Belgium) did declare it " was still too rigid." [117]

The procedure for amending the Constitution of the International Labor Organization has been used on one occasion only. On November 2, 1922, the Conference adopted by vote of 82 to 2 with 6 abstentions an amendment increasing the number of members of the Governing Body from twenty-four to thirty-two.[118] The amendment did not become effective until June 4, 1934.[119]

[114] The Commission was composed of two representatives from each of the five great powers and in addition five persons to be selected by the other powers at the conference. The latter decided to be represented by two delegates selected by Belgium with Czechoslovakia, Cuba, and Poland selecting one each. The personnel included such champions of labor as Samuel Gompers, G. N. Barnes, and M. Vandervelde. For a full list of the members of the Commission and substitutes used see International Labor Office, *Official Bulletin,* I, 1.

[115] Minutes in *Official Bulletin,* I, 77. For the full text of the British draft of Feb. 2, 1919, see *Origins of the International Labor Organization,* ed. J. T. Shotwell, I, Part IV, Sec. A. The proposals of the French, Italian, and American delegates appear as Documents 35, 36, and 37 in Vol. II.

[116] *Official Bulletin,* I, 76.

[117] *Ibid.,* p. 77.

[118] *International Labor Conference,* 4th Session (1922), I, 389.

[119] *L. N. T. S.,* CXLIX, 35.

Fully as significant as the power to amend the Constitution of the International Labor Organization without the consent of all states is the power of the Governing Body to interpret and apply by majority vote the formula "states of chief industrial importance." In the constitution proposed to the drafting Commission by the British delegation it was suggested that the Governing Body be composed of twenty-four members as follows: twelve to be government members of whom five shall be nominated by the Governments of Great Britain, the United States, France, Italy, and Japan and the remainder to be elected by the Conference from the representatives of the other states; six to be elected by the delegates to the Conference representing employers; and six to be elected by the delegates to the Conference representing workpeople.[120] Vandervelde (Belgium) objected to this plan on the ground that it would be offensive to the small powers [121] and the British delegation proposed the following which was accepted and became part of Article 393 of the Treaty:

Of the twelve members representing the Governments, eight shall be nominated by the High Contracting Parties which are of the chief industrial importance, and four shall be elected by the Government delegates to the Conference.

The question as to which are the High Contracting Parties of the chief industrial importance shall be decided by the Executive Council of the League of Nations.[122]

As previously noted, Article 393 has since been amended to increase the total membership to thirty-two, sixteen representing governments. Eight continue to be selected by the states of chief industrial importance.[123]

[120] Art. 7 of Draft of Feb. 2, 1919, and attached Protocol, in Shotwell, *Origins,* I, Part IV, Sec. A.

[121] Minutes in *Official Bulletin,* I, 82.

[122] *Ibid.,* p. 84.

[123] Art. 393 as amended June 4, 1934, is as follows:

"The International Labor Office shall be under the control of a Governing Body consisting of thirty-two persons:

In June, 1934, when the elective members of the Governing Body were being selected, the eight states of chief industrial importance were Belgium, Canada, France, Germany, Great Britain, India, Italy, and Japan. But soon thereafter the United States accepted membership in the International Labor Organization and Soviet Russia acquired it by reason of becoming a member of the League of Nations. In January, 1935, on the basis of a report submitted by the officers of the International Labor Office, the Governing Body declared the following should, as states of chief industrial importance, be entitled to nominate members of the Governing Body: France, Germany, Great Britain, India, Italy, Japan, the United States, and the Union of Soviet Socialist Republics.[124] Thus the Gov-

---

" Sixteen representing Governments, eight representing the employers, and eight representing the workers.

" Of the sixteen persons representing Governments, eight shall be appointed by the Members of chief industrial importance, and eight shall be appointed by the Members selected for that purpose by the government delegates to the Conference, excluding the Delegates of the eight Members mentioned above. Of the sixteen Members six shall be non-European States.

" Any question as to which are the Members of chief industrial importance shall be decided by the Council of the League of Nations.

" The persons representing employers and the persons representing the workers shall be elected respectively by the employers' Delegates and the workers' Delegates to the Conference. Two employers' representatives and two worker's representatives shall belong to non-European states.

" The period of office of the Governing Body shall be three years.

" The method of filling vacancies and of appointing substitutes and other similar questions may be decided by the Governing Body subject to the approval of the Conference.

" The Governing Body shall, from time to time, elect one of its number as its Chairman, shall regulate its own procedure, and shall fix its own time of meeting. A special meeting shall be held if a written request to that effect is made by at least twelve of the representatives on the Governing Body."

[124] International Labor Office, *Minutes of the Sixty-Ninth Session of the Governing Body* (January, 1935), p. 45. The resolution was adopted by 24 votes to 1. By vote of 29 to 0, " the states which no longer figure on the list and which at present sit with the Governing Body " were invited to be associated with its work as deputy members until the next elections.

erning Body not only changed the list of states of chief industrial importance but it exercised this power by majority vote in the midst of the term of those serving, depriving the displaced states, Belgium and Canada, of opportunity to seek places on the Governing Body by election.   Appeal from the finding of the Governing Body would lie, of course, to the Council of the League of Nations.   However, Belgium accepted the decision of the Governing Body, and Canada, although asserting that the Governing Body was not competent to make changes in the list and that in no case should changes be made within the three year period of election, did not carry the matter to the Council.   Canada's failure to protest is probably not unrelated to the fact that when a vacancy occurred in the list of states of chief industrial importance by reason of Germany's notice of withdrawal becoming effective October 21, 1935, Canada was selected by the Governing Body to fill the vacancy.   Hence, precedent now has been established both for changing the list and for making those changes whenever circumstances dictate.[125]   Such action is taken by the Governing Body by a simple majority vote.[126]

The old Statute of the Organization for Communications and Transit, adopted by the third General Conference of the Organization, at Geneva, September 2, 1927,[127] was subject to modification by a two-thirds majority of the delegates voting in any General Conference.[128]   In the General Conference each member state had one vote.[129] The member states included all members of the League and such other states as were admitted to participation in

[125] Cf. C. W. Jenks in *B. Y. I.L.*, XVII, 178.

[126] Art. 9, Standing Orders of the Governing Body of the International Labor Office.

[127] League Doc. C. 558(c). M. 200(c). 1927. VIII; Hudson, *International Legislation*, III, 2106.

[128] Art. 19 of the Statute.

[129] Art. 6.

the Organization by resolution of the Assembly. The new Statute of the Organization, adopted by the Council of the League of Nations, January 29, 1938,[130] provides for revision of Articles 1 to 4 by the Assembly of the League, the remaining articles being subject to amendment by two-thirds vote of the Assembly enlarged by representation of such non-League states as have been admitted to participation in the Communications and Transit Organization.[131]

It may be asked why it is possible to take decisions by some form of majority vote in the organs which have been described inasmuch as these decisions become binding upon all parties to the conventions or agreements without their individual consent. In some cases, notably those of the Hydrographic Bureau, the Relief Union, and the Communications and Transit Organization, the instruments which may be revised without the consent of all impose such slight obligations upon the participating states that it is not surprising that the customary procedure is permitted to yield to a procedure based upon the demands of convenience. In the case of the International Commission for Air Navigation and the Railway Union, the instruments which may be changed are annexes to treaties, annexes which contain regulations of a technical character. However, the Annexes to the Convention on Air Navigation can not be considered unimportant. Two of the organizations, the International Labor Organization and the International Commission for Air Navigation, were the creation of the Peace Conference period, a period in which appreciation of the need for effective international government was perhaps at its maximum. The extraordinary powers of the Congress of the Universal Postal Union appear to need more extended explanation.

In the first place, the Postal Union is supplying an

[130] League Doc. C. 95. M. 48. 1938. VIII.
[131] League of Nations, *Statute of the Organization for Communications and Transit*, 1938, Art. 28.

8

essential service, a service which the government of every
state and most of the citizens of those states find indispensable.   Furthermore, it is recognized as indispensable.
All are interested in promoting a system of rapid and
inexpensive postal communications operating without serious inconveniences or interruptions.   Agreement upon the
fundamental principles to be followed in supplying this
service was reached at Berne in 1874, and it has been
further recognized that these principles and the detailed
regulations must be permitted to develop to meet changed
conditions.   Too great a lag would exist between the
needs of postal communications and the law governing it
if changes must await the consent of more than eighty
administrations.   Much the same thing is true, though
perhaps less markedly so, in air and rail transport.   The
theoretical demands of state sovereignty are met in the
Postal Union by maintenance of the form of ratification
and the right of withdrawal from the Union, but, as we
have noted, ratification has become in this case an empty
form and withdrawal is a step no state is prepared to take.
In the Railway Union and in the International Commission for Air Navigation the theoretical demands are met
by restricting change without consent to annexes to the
conventions proper.

In the second place, the conduct of the Postal Union
and its Congress has from the first been in the hands of
persons drawn almost exclusively from the postal administrations of the respective members of the Union.   As we
have noted, technical delegates also had a large share in
the drafting and development of the Convention on Air
Navigation and in the preparation of the Constitution of
the Labor Organization.   Such delegates are far less inclined than are lawyers and meticulous diplomats to be
concerned with building and preserving a system in which
each state is armed with the *liberum veto* in order to pro-
tect its " interests."   On the contrary, they generally are

inclined to approach the problem in a very practical manner, being concerned chiefly with building a system which will best promote the end in view. For example, to a postal official, intent on promoting the interest of his country, the advantages of the maintenance of a veto for each government are likely to seem rather illusory compared with the construction of an organization suitable for allowing the postal law to keep pace with postal needs. Hence, it does not appear unnatural that the postal technicians should have used the majority rule in their drafting conference and should have continued that rule in all subsequent Congresses and Conferences of the Union.

Finally, in the case of the Postal Union it should be recognized that while the Congress possesses power to make any change in the Convention, its Detailed Regulations, and the Agreements, by majority vote—and some are made by very small majorities [132]—the Convention also provides one very important safety valve. Since the formation of the Union, it always has been possible for members to enter into subsidiary agreements accession to which is optional.[133] No restriction is placed upon the

---

[132] Propositions are adopted when supported by a majority of the delegations participating in the vote. Because the number abstaining is sometimes large, it frequently happens that propositions are carried by a minority of the Congress. Indeed, this has occurred so frequently that the delegation of Ecuador, supported by Bolivia and the U. S. S. R., at one time sought to introduce compulsory voting. This was defeated by a large majority. (*Documents de Congrès Postal de Londres*, II, 20.) It is significant that no attempts have been made to require extraordinary majorities or even majorities of the entire Congress for adoption of propositions. As the delegate of Belgium put it, if important propositions not supported by actual majority of the Congress are carried because many abstain, the abstaining delegates are accountable to their own governments for it. (*Ibid.*, p. 21.)

[133] Art. 5 of the Convention is as follows: " Countries of the Union have the right to maintain and to conclude treaties, as well as to maintain and to establish restricted Unions, with a view to the reduction of postage rates or to any other improvement of postal relations.

" Moreover, Administrations are authorized to make with one another any necessary agreements on the subject of questions which do not con-

nature of these agreements except that their terms must never be less favorable than those laid down by the Acts of the Union. This, of course, permits small groups of members to forge ahead with agreements among themselves covering in some cases services not regulated by the Convention. Equally important, it permits majority groups to do so without necessity of forcing a large and unwilling minority to accept fundamental changes. Thus, when faced with determined opposition, even majority groups may choose to resort to supplementary agreement rather than risk serious internal strife in the Union. For example, while it is clearly within the power of a majority in the Congress to adopt the principle of gratuity of transit as binding upon all, it seems reasonable to doubt whether a bare majority in any Congress would seek to force adoption of this principle. Harmony can be maintained, and at least some of the advantages reaped, by permitting the restricted union formed for the Americas and Spain to continue to provide it among adhering members. At the present time, numerous subsidiary agreements are in force covering such things as the insurance of letters, parcel-post, money orders, and reduced rates of letter postage.

---

cern the Union generally, provided that conditions less favorable than those laid down by the Acts of the Union are not introduced. In the letter post, for example, they may conclude mutual arrangements for the adoption of lower postage within a zone on either side of their frontiers.'' Substantially the same provisions appear as Article 20 of the original convention of 1874. (*B. P. P.,* 1875, LXXXII.)

CHAPTER IV

MAJORITY VOTE IN CONFERENCES ACTING
Ad Referendum

In the preceding chapter consideration has been given to organs having authority to adopt rules which become legally binding upon all member states without the consent of all being expressed either in the conference which formulates the rules or through the process of ratification. Such powers, it is believed, may properly be described as legislative. There remains to be described a large number of permanent international organs which possess power to propose new international conventions or the revision of existing ones by some form of majority rule, the obligation to apply the new or revised text, however, extending only to those states expressing their consent through formal ratification. In yet another case, amendment of the basic convention of a union may be proposed by a vote short of unanimity but amendments so brought forward become effective only when ratified by all.

Included in the first group are the Conference of the International Labor Organization, the General Conference for Communications and Transit, the International Committee of the International Office of Public Health, the International Conference of American States, the Conferences of the Telecommunications Union, and the General Conference of the Metric Union. Of these organizations, the International Labor Conferences probably exercise powers of the most significant character.

The competence of the International Labor Organization is wide, extending to the fulfillment of the purposes of the organization as set forth in the Preamble to Part XIII of the Treaty of Versailles, perhaps best described as authority to promote the protection of workers.[1] Authority to act, however, is strictly limited. By Article 405 the General Conference is given authority to adopt propositions in either of two forms. First, it may adopt recommendations to be submitted to the members for consideration with a view to effect being given by national legislation. Second, the Conference may adopt draft conventions. Each member of the International Labor Organization undertakes to bring the recommendation or draft convention before the authority within whose competence the matter lies, within a period of one year, or in exceptional circumstances, eighteen months. In the case of a federal state, the power of which to enter into labor conventions is subject to limitations, it shall be in the discretion of the government to treat a draft convention as a recommendation. Consequently, it may be asserted that the adoption by the Conference of a recommendation or of a draft convention imposes a legal obligation upon every member state to submit the matter to the competent authority or authorities [2] for action. In the case of draft conventions, ratification by two or more members transforms them into conventions which place upon the ratifying powers obligation to comply with their terms. Furthermore, in Article 408 each member agrees to make an annual report to the International Labor Office on the measures taken to give effect to conventions to which it is a party, and in Articles

[1] The Permanent Court of International Justice has declared the competence of the International Labor Organization is founded upon the Preamble. Article 387 which follows immediately provides that " a permanent organization is hereby established for the objects set forth in the Preamble." In the opinion of the Court, Art. 427 with its enumeration of general principles " does not define or limit the powers of the organization." *Publications of the P. C. I. J.,* Series B, Advisory Opinion No. 13, p. 15.

[2] In the case of draft conventions, this is understood to mean the legislative authorities even in those states in which the government may ratify without their consent. Cf. J. Morrellet, " Legal Competence of the International Labor Organization," *Annals,* March, 1933, p. 51.

409 to 420 sanctions are provided in accordance with two procedures, one growing out of " representations " and the other from " complaints." The application of the sanctions clauses is under the control of the Governing Body.[3]

As previously noted, the principle of state representation through plenipotentiaries has been discarded in the General Conference of the Labor Organization in favor of representation on a functional basis, each member state having four representatives, two for the government and one each for the most representative labor and employer groups. The principle of unanimity has naturally been completely rejected. The Conference, by provision of Article 403, decides all questions by a simple majority of the votes cast by the delegates present except when the treaty has expressly stipulated the contrary. The voting is valid only if the number of votes cast is equal to half the number of delegates attending the Conference. But a special majority of two-thirds of the votes cast by the delegates present is required for most of the important functions of the Conference. Such a vote is required for the final vote on a recommendation or draft convention;[4] a decision to reject the credentials of a delegate;[5] a decision to hold a Conference away from the seat of the League;[6] a decision to include in the agenda of the next Conference a matter which has not been approved by the Governing Body or to include for immediate examination a matter which has been placed on the agenda by the Governing Body but to which a member state has made objection;[7] and for the proposal of amendments to Part XIII of the Treaty, such becoming binding when ratified by the states whose representatives compose the Council of the League of Nations and by three-fourths of the members.[8]

[3] For consideration of this, see below, p. 141.
[4] Art. 405.
[5] Art. 398.
[6] Art. 391.
[7] Art. 402.
[8] Art. 422.

But for the opposition of one state, the United States, the Commission which formulated the fundamental laws of the Labor Organization would have proposed to the Peace Conference a constitution in which the General Conference was armed with even more extensive powers. It will be recalled that the statesmen in the Allied countries in 1919 were alarmed sufficiently by rising industrial unrest and the challenge of socialism and communism to give time in the Peace Conference to the creation of an organization which might prove to the workers throughout the world that progress toward social justice could be achieved without abolition of the capitalist system.[9] Moreover, this alarm appears to have been reflected in the choice of the personnel of the drafting commission inasmuch as the representatives of the labor movement predominated markedly over the diplomats. The situation called for the construction of an organization constituted in such fashion that the duty of states to promote labor welfare might be transformed into a legal obligation on their part to do so. This appeared to necessitate an organization in which labor shared in the control, an organization which could do something more than make recommendations to the states of the world. The draft plan submitted by the British delegation, and taken by the Commission as a basis for discussion, was well suited for accomplishing these ends.[10] Provision was made for functional representation (Art. 3),[11] for adop-

[9] Cf. J. T. Shotwell, " The International Labor Organization as an Alternative to Violent Revolution," *Annals,* March, 1933, p. 18; E. J. Phelan in *Origins of the International Labor Organization,* ed. J. T. Shotwell, I, 207; F. G. Wilson, *Labor in the League System,* p. 34; L. L. Lorwin, *Labor and Internationalism,* p. 189.

[10] The full text is in Shotwell, *Origins,* I, Part IV, Sec. A.

[11] The British draft proposed a Conference in which each power would be represented by three delegates, one representing the government, and the other two the employers and workers, respectively. They further proposed that the government representative have two votes, the others one each. Gompers (U. S.) and Colliard (France) objected to the plural voting for the government representative and Vandervelde (Belgium)

tion of conventions by two-thirds majority vote, with state signature omitted by implication (Art. 18), and for sanctions through "representation" (Art. 22) and "complaint" (Art. 24). But the British draft article on conventions was weakened definitely in the Commission in order to gain the assent of the delegation of the United States. The plan as submitted was remarkable in that it proposed that the Conference, made up of delegates voting as individuals, *half of whom would be uncontrolled by governments,* should adopt by two-thirds vote conventions which would become binding upon each member state unless such conventions were disapproved by the legislative body of the member state within a period of one year. The draft article was as follows:

When the Conference has approved any proposals as to an item on the agenda, these proposals shall be embodied in the form of an international convention.

The convention shall then forthwith be laid for final consideration and decision before the Conference.

If the convention receives the support of two-thirds of the votes cast, it shall be held adopted by the Conference, and a copy of the convention authenticated by the signatures of the President of the Conference and of the Director shall be deposited with the Chancellor of the League of Nations.

Each of the High Contracting Parties undertakes that it will within the period of one year from the end of the meeting of the Conference communicate its formal ratification of the convention to the Director, and will forthwith take all steps necessary to put the convention into operation unless such convention is disapproved by its legislature.[12]

Opinion in the Commission on this article may be said to have divided along three lines. The British, apparently with considerable support, were proposing wide deviation

suggested the system of representation and voting strength which was actually adopted by the narrow margin of 8 votes to 6. *Official Bulletin,* I, 18, 26, 27, 186.

[12] *Official Bulletin,* I, 12.

from the procedure usually followed by states in adopting
international conventions, in the composition of the conference, in the vote for proposal and in assuming consent
of each state, unless disapproval were expressed by the
legislature.   But in no sense were they proposing that the
Labor Conference have power to impose labor legislation
upon an unwilling state.   The Italian delegation, supported by the French, did not believe the plan went far
enough in the direction of creating an international legislative body with precisely such powers to bind member
states, while the American delegation believed the plan
went too far in this direction.   As a counter proposal to
the British, Baron Mayor des Planches (Italy) suggested
the following:

> The Commission resolves that all States participating in the
> Conference shall be obliged to carry out within one year Conven-
> tions approved by a two-thirds majority of the Conference. Gov-
> ernments have the right of appealing against the decisions of the
> Conference to the Executive Council of the League of Nations,
> which may order the question to be reconsidered by the Confer-
> ence. Against the second decision of the Conference there is no
> appeal.[13]

In defense of his resolution, the Italian delegate declared the needs of workpeople and employers were better
understood by industrial bodies than by political assemblies.   Should national parliaments possess veto rights the
effectiveness of decisions of the Conference would be reduced considerably.   Appeal to the League Council would
be ample protection against mistakes in the Conference.
After opposition to the plan both on grounds of principle
and expediency had been expressed by the delegates of
Belgium, the United States, Japan, Great Britain, Cuba,
and Poland, it was withdrawn,[14] only to be revived later
by the French delegation in the form of a recommendation

[13] *Ibid.,* p. 51.   [14] *Ibid.,* pp. 52-53.

that as soon as possible " a deliberative international assembly will be constituted . . . endowed with the powers proposed by the Italian delegation." [15] However, when it became apparent that the delegation of one of the great industrial states, the United States, was unprepared to take even the short step proposed by the British in the direction of an international legislature for labor, the French resolution was not pushed to a vote.

American opposition to the British plan was placed upon constitutional grounds, Robinson (United States) declaring that Article 1 of the United States Constitution confers upon Congress the sole right of legislating, a right which in his opinion could not be delegated to the executive power even with the reservation of a right of veto by Congress.[16] As a substitute, the American delegation proposed, in essence, that Conference decisions be embodied in recommendations rather than in conventions and that the only obligation on member states be to lay " the recommendation before the national authority or authorities within whose competence the matter lies." [17] Vandervelde declared acceptance of the American proposal meant the removal of all real obligation, a step which would render the work of the Commission abortive.[18] Barnes suggested a compromise formula be sought and to that end a sub-committee composed of Delevingne (Great Britain), Robinson (United States), and Mahaim (Belgium) was appointed.[19] The compromise suggested by this sub-committee providing first, that the Conference be given power to submit propositions either in the form of recommendations or conventions, and second, that federal states whose power to enter conventions on labor matters is subject to limitations may elect to treat any draft convention as a recommendation, was accepted by a

[15] *Ibid.*, p. 54.
[16] *Ibid.*, p. 57.
[17] *Ibid.*, pp. 150-151.
[18] *Ibid.*, p. 156.
[19] *Ibid.*, pp. 157-158.

vote of 10 for with 4 abstaining.[20]   In the Peace Conference, largely as a result of Japanese insistence, the article
was further weakened by insertion of the clause instructing the Conference when framing a recommendation or
draft convention to " have due regard " for difference in
climatic conditions, industrial developments, and other
special circumstances, as well as by the provision that in
" exceptional circumstances " members may have eighteen
months rather than one year to bring recommendations or
draft conventions before the appropriate authorities.[21]

Although the competence of the International Labor
Conferences as finally fixed by the Treaty was not as great
as the majority of the drafting commission desired that it
should be, full use has been made of the powers that were
conferred. In the first twenty-three sessions of the Conferences sixty-two draft conventions and fifty-six recommendations have been adopted under the rules which permit such
action by two-thirds vote. Forty-five of the conventions
are in force by reason of having been ratified by two or
more states. A total of 782 ratifications have been registered. Ten conventions have been ratified by thirty or
more states and twenty-one by twenty or more.[22] Undoubtedly, much of the success of the International Labor
Organization in extending state obligations in respect to
the adoption and maintenance of reasonable labor legislation can be attributed quite properly to the discarding of
the unanimity rule in the proposal of conventions. Of
the first fifty-eight draft conventions adopted, only fourteen received a unanimous vote in the Conference, the
remaining forty-four being proposed over the negative
votes of from one to thirty-eight delegates. Although the

---

[20] *Ibid.,* p. 183. The Japanese delegation abstained because the position
of the parties would not be identical and the Italian " because it diminished too greatly the powers of the Conference."

[21] Cf. Phelan in *Origins,* I, 203.

[22] The figures on ratifications are from International Labor Office, *Report
of the Director,* 24th Session, Geneva, 1938.

records suggest that where an approach to unanimity in the Conference can be obtained, ratification is likely to be more general, they by no means show unanimity or even approximate unanimity necessary for wide ratification in all cases. Of the ten conventions most widely ratified, five were opposed in the Conference, and two of these were opposed by as many as twenty-four delegates.[23] On the other hand, a few draft conventions proposed by unanimous or near unanimous vote remain among the most poorly ratified.[24] However, there appears to be sufficient correlation between an approach to unanimity in the proposal of conventions and wide ratification to justify the assertion that the framers of the Constitution of the International Labor Organization were wise in adopting the two-thirds rule for the proposal of conventions rather than a simple majority rule, even though this rule has prevented the proposal of several conventions desired by a substantial majority of the Conference.[25]

[23] The draft convention on Weekly Rest in Industry was adopted by vote of 73 to 24 (*Int. Lab. Conf.,* 3d Session, I, 488) and has now been ratified by 30 states. That on the Marking of Weight of Packages Transported by Vessel was adopted by vote of 98 to 24 (*Int. Lab. Conf.,* 12th Session, I, 599) and has now been ratified by 34 states.

[24] For example, the draft convention on Sickness Insurance (Agriculture) was adopted by vote of 101 to 0 (*Int. Lab. Conf.,* 12th Session, I, 417) but has been ratified by only 11 states.

[25] The following have received a majority vote in the Conference but have failed of adoption by reason of the two-thirds requirement: A draft convention concerning weekly suspension of work for 24 hours in glass manufacturing processes where tank furnaces are used, 68 to 37 (*Int. Lab. Conf.,* 7th Session, I, 414); draft convention concerning the employment of women at night, 74 to 40 (15th Session, I, 477); draft convention on hours of work in public works, 67 to 38 and 71 to 42 (19th Session, I, 693, and 20th Session, I, 446); draft convention concerning the reduction of hours of work in the building and civil engineering industry, 57 to 40 (19th Session, I, 696); draft convention on reduction of hours in iron and steel works, 67 to 40 (20th Session, I, 448); draft convention on reduction of hours in coal mines, 66 to 37 (20th Session, I, 450). It should be noted that the Constitution of the International Labor Organization provides that where two-thirds vote for proposal is not achieved in the Conference, it is nevertheless within the right of any

Not only have the Labor Conferences made full use of their powers to act under two-thirds vote, but they may even be said to have extended them somewhat through interpretation. The Constitution of the organization is silent on the method by which conventions once adopted may be revised. Yet the Conference has found revision by two-thirds vote within the scope of its powers. Beginning with the first session, it was the practice to include within each convention an article providing that at least once in ten years the Governing Body present to the General Conference a report on the working of the convention and that it decide whether or not the question of revision be placed on the agenda of the Conference. In 1928, the Governing Body instructed the Standing Orders Committee to make a study of the procedure to be followed in the revision of conventions. In accordance with the recommendations made by that body, revision of conventions is to be considered only upon the proposal of the Governing Body and may be made by the same vote required for the proposal of a draft convention. In general, it may be said that adoption of a revision does not abrogate the old convention, but its coming into force does close the old text to ratification. Further, those states ratifying the new text are freed from their obligations under the old.[26] By the end of the twenty-third session (1937), six conventions had been revised.[27]

Like the International Labor Conferences, the General Conferences of the Organization for Communications and

---

of the Members to agree to such a convention among themselves (Art. 407).

[26] C. W. Jenks, "The Revision of International Labor Conventions," *B. Y. I. L.,* XIV, 43.

[27] The Protection Against Accidents (Dockers) (*Int. Lab. Conf.,* 16th Session, I, 328); Night Work (Women) (18th Session, I, 318); Hours of work in Coal Mines (19th Session, I, 583); Minimum Age at Sea (22d Session, I, 395); Minimum Age in Industry (23rd Session); Minimum Age (Non-Industrial Employment) (23rd Session).

Transit have power to propose draft conventions by two-thirds majority vote.[28] Recommendations for submission to the governments or to the Assembly of the League of Nations may be proposed by a similar vote.[29] General Conferences may be called at any time by the Council of the League or by the Secretary-General of the League upon request of one-half of the Members of the Organization.[30] Membership in such Conferences is open to delegations from all members of the League, from all states non-members of the League admitted to participation in the Communications and Transit Organization by resolution of the Assembly, and from such other states as may be invited by the Council of the League to take part.[31] Each delegation possesses one vote. The agenda of every Conference are drawn up by the Committee for Communications and Transit, communicated to the Council, and forwarded by the Secretary-General of the League to every member state at least four months before the Conference opens.[32] Draft conventions adopted impose obligation only upon those states electing to ratify. Several of the draft conventions adopted by Conferences of the Communications and Transit Organization have been ratified rather widely. The Convention and Statute on Freedom of Transit, and the Declaration Recognizing the Right to a Flag of States Having no Sea Coast, adopted at Barcelona, April 20, 1921, have been ratified by thirty-one and thirty-six states, respectively. The Convention and Statute of the International Regime of Railways and the Convention and Statute of the International Regime of

---

[28] League of Nations, *Statute for the Organization for Communications and Transit,* 1938 (League Doc. C. 95. M. 48. 1938. VIII), Art. 22. The earlier Statutes of the Organization also made provision for adoption of draft conventions by two-thirds vote. See Art. 12 of the Statute adopted at Barcelona in 1921 (League Doc. C. 662. M. 265. 1923. VIII) and Art. 9 of 1927 Statute (League Doc. C. 558(c). M. 200(c). 1927. VIII).

[29] *Ibid.*   [30] Art. 17.   [31] *Ibid.*   [32] Art. 20.

Maritime Ports, adopted at Geneva, December 9, 1923, have been ratified by twenty-six and twenty-four states each.[33]

The International Conferences of American States, meeting at intervals of approximately five years, now adopt draft conventions and other less formal instruments by majority vote. Each conference draws up its own rules of procedure, but those of the Inter-American Conference for the Maintenance of Peace, held at Buenos Aires in 1936, are typical of those of the general Pan American Conference. It is therein specifically provided that, " except in cases expressly indicated " all " proposals, reports, and projects under consideration by the conference shall be considered approved when they have obtained the affirmative vote of an absolute majority of the delegations represented by one or more of their members at the meeting where the vote is taken." [34]   Each delegation is given a single vote.[35] A quorum of two-thirds is required for a vote on any of the subjects on the program of the Conference.[36]   An extraordinary majority of two-thirds is required to dispense with committee consideration of any project,[37] to suspend the rules of procedure,[38] and to modify the rules.[39] A majority vote suffices for all decisions in the committees but the minority has the privilege of presenting its view to the plenary session of the Conference.[40]

The significance of this departure from the rule of unanimous consent is greatly lessened by two factors. First, the conventions, agreements, and recommendations approved by majority vote in the conference are gathered

---

[33] *Ratification of Agreements and Conventions Concluded under the Auspices of the League of Nations* (League Doc. A. 6 (a). 1937. Annex I. V).

[34] Pan American Union, *Regulations of the Inter-American Conference for the Maintenance of Peace, Buenos Aires, 1936,* Art. 22.

[35] Art. 17.   [37] Art. 19.   [39] Art. 29.
[36] Art. 18.   [38] Art. 21.   [40] Art. 10.

together in a Final Act for signature, but participating states may withhold their signatures from any part thereof. Thus, at the Buenos Aires Conference of 1936, the United States delegation withheld signature on two of the eleven instruments embodied in the Final Act.[41]   Second, no obligation is imposed upon any state without its consent being expressed through ratification.   States failing to sign have not even the obligation to consider ratification. Indeed, in the case of some conventions, no obligation extends to any state until all have ratified.[42]   On the other hand, the usual practice is to allow the convention to become effective as between ratifying states.[43]   The practice varies, of course, with the subject matter of the conventions involved.

In the first seven International Conferences of American States a total of thirty-nine conventions and treaties were adopted [44] and twenty-eight conventions, treaties, and protocols have been offered by special conferences.   However, many of the conventions have been poorly ratified.   The sixty-seven treaties and conventions have received only five hundred and eighty ratifications and adhesions by the twenty-one states members of the Pan American Union.[45] Only one convention has been ratified by all.[46]   Forty have been ratified by less than one-half.

It does not appear that the failure of general ratifica-

---

[41] *Bulletin of the Pan American Union,* Aug., 1937, p. 646.

[42] For example, Article 14 of the Convention on the Pan American Union provides the Convention must be ratified by all 21 states before becoming effective.   Final Act, *Sixth International Conference of American States, Havana, 1928.*

[43] Cf. Art. 4 of the Convention on Private International Law, *ibid.*; Hudson, *International Legislation,* IV, 2279.

[44] No treaties or conventions were signed at the First Conference, Washington, 1889-90.

[45] Figures from Pan American Union, *Status of the Treaties and Conventions Signed at International Conferences of American States and at Other Pan American Conferences.*   Revised to July 1, 1938.

[46] The Sanitary Code drafted at Havana, 1924.

tion properly can be laid at the door of majority proposal. In the first place, although conventions may be proposed by majority vote in the Conference, every effort is made to secure unanimity or a close approximation of unanimity. The preparatory work is largely in the hands of the Governing Board of the Pan American Union, a body on which all members have representation through their diplomatic representative at Washington or, in the absence of such representation, by a special representative, and which by tradition and precedent adheres to the rule of unanimity.[47] Consequently, the agenda can not contain subjects that some members are unwilling for the Conference to consider. This stands in marked contrast to the preparation of the agenda for International Labor Conferences, a function which is performed by the Governing Body, a body on which many members of the organization are without representation and which acts in such cases by majority vote.[48] Moreover, in the International Conferences of American States when differences appear in the discussions in the plenary sessions and committees, resort frequently is had to sub-committees in an endeavor to find a formula which can be accepted unanimously. The very success of such endeavors may hinder occasionally general ratification since unanimity is sometimes achieved at the expense of a good convention.

In the second place, when member states are dissatisfied with the work the majority rule has permitted the Conference to accomplish, it is their privilege to withhold signature from any or all the instruments included in the Final Act. Yet the number of signatures withheld has not been great and there remain 588 unratified signatures. This suggests that the low ratification score results from factors other than the failure to achieve complete agree-

---

[47] See below, p. 233.
[48] Art. 9 a, Standing Orders of the Governing Body of the International Labor Office.

ment in the Conference. Among these factors may be the failure of the Conferences until recent years to provide for any "follow-up machinery," such as the International Labor Organization has, for securing ratifications,[49] and the attitude of indifference shown by some states toward the work of the Conferences.[50]

Representative bodies in three other unions, the International Telecommunications Union, the Metric Union, and the International Office of Public Health, have power to amend the terms of conventions by majority vote, the amendments entering into force for those states consenting to them. The International Telecommunications Convention, signed at Madrid, December 9, 1932,[51] provides for its own revision by conferences of plenipotentiaries of the contracting governments assembled by virtue of a decision by a previous Conference or upon request of at least twenty contracting governments directed to the Swiss Government.[52] The provisions of the Regulations annexed to the Convention are revised by Administrative Conferences, each Administrative Conference fixing the place and date of the next meeting.[53] Each Conference is free to adopt its own rules of procedure, taking as a basis the rules of the previous Conference and modifying them as it sees fit.[54] In practice, the Conferences have provided that all propositions are adopted by an absolute majority of votes. In case of an equal division, a proposition is considered rejected.[55] However, if the proposed measure appears to

[49] The Seventh Conference (1933) provided the Union might send its representatives into the states for the purpose of promoting the "examination, approval, ratification and deposit of ratifications of treaties and conventions." *Seventh Conference,* Final Act, p. 71; Wilcox, *The Ratification of International Conventions,* p. 209.

[50] The Argentine Republic, for instance, has signed fifty-four instruments and ratified four of them.

[51] *L. N. T. S.,* CLI, 5; Hudson, *International Legislation,* VI, 109.
[52] Art. 18.   [53] *Ibid.*   [54] Art. 20.
[55] Art. 22, Règlement intérieur de la Conférence de Madrid, in *Documents de la Conférence Radiotélégraphique Internationale,* II, p. XLVII.

any delegation to be of such a nature as to prevent its government from ratifying the new act, it may express a formal refusal to associate itself with the vote of the majority.[56] By decision of the Cairo Conference of 1938, voting power is now awarded on a basis of strict equality to " the countries listed in Article 21 of the Internal Regulations." In fact this " equality " means plural voting privileges for some because the enumerated " countries " include colonial areas and groups of colonial areas.[57]

Article 8 of the Madrid Convention provides for abrogation among the contracting countries of earlier radio and telegraph conventions and of the regulations affixed thereto.[58] The Convention and attached Regulations entered into force for the ratifying powers January 1, 1934.[59] Should future Radiotelegraphic Conferences provide for abrogation of earlier instruments upon the entering into force of the new among ratifying powers, ratification might well become a formality as in the Universal Postal Union. Indeed, the new Radio Regulations annexed to the Madrid Convention were put in force by several states on the date fixed without formal ratification or accession.[60]

Probably of greater significance for the purposes of this study are the procedures and powers of the International Committee of the International Office of Public Health. As established by the terms of the International Arrange-

---

This accords with the practice of earlier Telegraph Conferences. Cf. Art. 10, Règlement, *Documents de la Conférence Télégraphique Internationale de Paris* (1925), II, 24.

[56] Art. 23, Règlement.

[57] For consideration of this problem, see below, p. 281.

[58] The International Telegraphic Conventions of Paris (1865), *B. & F. State Papers*, LVI, 295; Vienna (1868), *ibid.*, LIX, 322; Rome (1872), *ibid.*, LXVI, 975; St. Petersburg (1875), *ibid.*, LXVI, 19; International Radiotelegraph Convention of Berlin (1906), *ibid.*, XCIX, 321; London (1912), *L. N. T. S.*, I, 135; Washington (1927), *ibid.*, XCII, 412.

[59] Arts. 6 and 40 of the Convention.

[60] Hudson, VI, 133.

ment and the *Statuts* annexed thereto,[61] signed December 9, 1907, at the Sanitary Conference held in Rome, the International Committee was given no powers beyond those of an advisory character nor was it definitely authorized to reach decisions by majority vote. Yet the body has evolved a procedure in which majority rule finds complete acceptance and its powers have been extended beyond an advisory nature.

The terms of the Arrangement and the annexed *Statuts* provided for the establishment of an International Office at Paris. The Office was charged with receiving information from the health authorities of the participating states upon health conditions in their states and upon fulfillment by their respective governments of the terms of the Sanitary Conventions. This information was to be brought to the attention of the member states.[62] The International Committee, composed of technical representatives, one being named by each state, was created to supervise the Office. The *Statuts,* however, do not grant these representatives equal voting power but instead give each delegate a number of votes inversely proportional to the number of the category selected by his government for participating in the cost of maintaining the Office.[63]

---

[61] *B. & F. State Papers,* C, 466. The original contracting states were Great Britain, Belgium, Brazil, Spain, the United States, France, Italy, Netherlands, Portugal, Russia, Switzerland, and Egypt. Of those present at the Conference of 1907, only Roumania failed to sign and ratify. She has since adhered in accordance with Article 6 of the Arrangement (1921). Other adhering powers: India, Peru, Tunis (1908); Australia, Bulgaria, Mexico, Persia, Sweden (1909); Algeria, Argentina, Canada (1910); Turkey (1911); Bolivia, Chile, Norway (1912); Denmark, Monaco, Uruguay (1913); French Indo-China (1914); Union of South Africa (1919); French West Africa, Madagascar, Morocco, Poland (1920); Czechoslovakia (1922); Japan, New Zealand (1924); Dutch Indies (1925); Luxemburg, Sudan, U. S. S. R. (1926); British Colonies, Belgian Congo (1927); Germany, Irish Free State (1928); French Equatorial Africa (1929); Kingdom of the Hedjaz (1932).

[62] Arts. 2, 4, 5 of *Statuts.*

[63] Art. 6.

For this purpose, six categories are provided. Of the original twelve members of the Union, eight were placed in the first class, three in the third, and one in the fourth. Adhering states may select their own class and it is always permissible for a state to change to a higher class.[64] The Committee is required to meet at least once a year in sessions of unlimited duration. In practice, it has been meeting twice a year in sessions generally lasting about ten days, the sessions being held in April or May and again in October. The Committee elects its own President for a period of three years and a Director and a Secretary-General. The Director, who is responsible for appointing and removing all other employees of the Office, is accountable to the Committee.[65] The budget is voted annually by the Committee but it may not exceed a fixed amount without consent of all signatory states.[66] Thus the *Statuts* provided for placing policy control, within the narrow limits set by the Arrangement, in the hands of the International Permanent Committee, and actual supervision of administration in the hands of the Director, the latter being accountable at all times to the Committee.

Neither the Arrangement of December 9, 1907, nor the *Statuts* annexed to it contain any clause stating how decisions are to be taken in the meetings of the Committee. Nor has the Committee itself seen fit to adopt any formal regulations of its own upon this subject. Consequently, the only rule bearing upon the matter at all is Article 6 of the *Statuts* providing that each representative has a number of votes in the Committee inversely proportional to the number of the class selected by his government. In actual practice, this rule is never applied. The *Statuts* assign

[64] Art. 11.
[65] Art. 8.
[66] The amount was originally fixed at 150,000 francs per annum but this has been increased. Cf. *Comité Permanent, Procès-verbaux de la session d'octobre-novembre,* 1919, p. 240.

varying numbers of votes to the members of the Committee but the Committee never bothers to count them up. Instead, the Committee, composed as it is of medical technicians, rules propositions are adopted when approved by a substantial majority of the individuals present. When the Committee is considering the desirability of expressing an opinion or of approving a report, the President asks if it has the approval of all members present. When no contrary opinion is expressed, which is frequently the case, the proposition is, of course, adopted. In case a few delegates oppose, this fact is mentioned in the *procès-verbaux*, but the resolution stands as a valid action of the Committee. When the proposition is opposed by a large minority group, it is not the practice to push it to adoption by counting votes. Rather, it is modified in such manner as to become acceptable to a larger number of delegates or the proposition is abandoned.[67] Consequently, it may be said that, in the absence of any rule to the contrary in the documents laid down by the Conference of 1907, the Committee has established for itself the right to take decisions by majority vote. In practice, this is interpreted as a majority vote of the individuals present, it being understood that propositions will not be pushed to adoption unless the majority favoring is large. However, should occasion demand, it would always be possible to resort to Article 6 of the *Statuts* which assigns members varying numbers of votes.

Thus the Permanent Committee of technicians, in the absence of restrictive rules to the contrary, devised for itself a procedure adequate for its needs, a procedure which did not permit a small minority to block adoption of reports approved by substantial majorities. It will be noted, of course, that when this procedure was developed the organization was limited in function to the collection of information relative to public health and to the bring-

[67] Statement of the Director to the writer, January 5, 1937.

ing of that information to the attention of the appropriate authorities in the signatory states. The Committee had no authority to supervise the execution of the provisions of the sanitary conventions. Neither had it the power to amend the conventions nor even to propose officially amendments for acceptance of the states. However, in the course of a few years the Committee came to command such respect that several attempts were made, one successfully, to increase markedly the powers of the body.

An extension of powers was attempted first in conjunction with a plan to bring the organization under the League of Nations in accordance with the provisions of Article 24 of the Covenant. The plan, which had the approval of the Permanent Committee of the International Office [68] and the Second Committee of the Assembly of the League,[69] was adopted by unanimous vote of the Assembly, December 10, 1920.[70] The plan envisaged the establishment of a General Committee and a Standing Committee. The former was to consist of the delegates serving on the Permanent Committee of the International Office of Public Health augmented by delegates appointed by members of the League not parties to the Arrangement of 1907. The Standing Committee was to consist of delegates named by the states having permanent Council seats, five members elected by the General Committee (having regard to their scientific attainments and to geographical representation),[71] the president of the General Committee, a representative of the League of Red Cross Societies, and one chosen by the Governing Body of the

[68] Office International d'Hygiène Publique, *Comité Permanent, Procès-verbaux de la session d'octobre-novembre,* 1920, pp. 119 ff.

[69] *Records of the First Assembly,* Second Committee, pp. 150 ff.

[70] *Ibid.,* Plenary, p. 338.

[71] This stipulation was inserted in the proposal by the Second Committee of the Assembly after the representative of Argentina had urged a plan of representation by continents. (*Records of the First Assembly,* Second Committee, p. 237.)

International Labor Organization. The Standing Committee was to be authorized to draw up draft health conventions or to propose revision of existing ones, such draft conventions or draft revisions being referred to all member states for ratification when approved by two-thirds vote of the General Committee. The plan, it will be noted, resembled closely that provided in the Constitution of the International Labor Organization for the proposal of labor conventions.

Thus the Second Committee of the Assembly had planned, and the Assembly had approved by unanimous vote, a new technic for the development of international sanitary law. The majority action of the existing organization was to be retained and at the same time its powers increased. But the success of the plan depended upon securing the consent of all states parties to the Rome Arrangement of 1907. When it became apparent the United States would not consent, the plan approved by the Assembly of the League of Nations had to be abandoned.[72]

Again, at the Sanitary Conference held in 1926, some attempt was made to confer upon the Permanent Committee power to amend the sanitary conventions subject to subsequent ratification by the parties to the conventions. The proposal was made in recognition of the important part the Office and Committee had played in the preparation of the changes in the conventions actually proposed in the Conference. However, some members of the Conference considered conferring upon the Permanent Committee the power to propose amendments by majority vote too much of an innovation in international usage and so the plan was dropped.[73]

[72] Cf. C. Vitta, "Le droit sanitaire international," *Recueil des Cours,* 1930, III, 592; Schücking and Wehberg, *Die Satzung des Völkerbundes* (2d ed.), pp. 749 ff.

[73] Vitta, p. 582.

Finally, by the terms of the International Sanitary Convention for Aerial Navigation, signed at the Hague, April 12, 1933, in force, August 1, 1935,[74] the Permanent Committee was authorized to propose amendments to an international convention. Any party to this convention desiring to introduce modifications therein may communicate proposals to the Government of the Netherlands. The latter will then inform the International Office of Public Health, which, if it thinks fit, will prepare a protocol amending the convention. The protocol prepared by the Office, which is under the control of the Permanent Committee, will then be sent by the Government of the Netherlands to all the parties to the convention and the governments will be asked if they accept the proposed modifications. Acceptance may result either from explicit approval or from failure to notify objections within one year after the circular is issued. When the number of express or tacit accessions represents at least two-thirds of the parties to the convention, the Government of the Netherlands will so notify the International Office and the contracting parties. Six months from the date of this notification the amendments will enter into force among the acquiescing states. The old convention continues to apply among the other states.[75]

The provision that initiative in the proposal of amendments must come from the government of a state party to the convention is, of course, in accordance with well established practice. But the retention of this seems inconsequential compared to the fact that the convention

---

[74] *L. N. T. S.,* CLXI, 65. The convention has been ratified for the following: Monaco, Egypt, Netherlands, Great Britain and Northern Ireland, Syria, Lebanon, Australia, Morocco, Tunis, Roumania, Germany, Sweden, Austria, Poland, United States, Italy and Belgium. Accessions are as follows: Bolivia, Brazil, Iraq, Sudan, British Colonies and Protectorates and Territories under Mandate, Chile, Turkey, Papua, Norfolk Island, New Guinea under Australian mandate.

[75] Art. 61.

entrusts the actual formulation of amendments to a body which by long usage acts by majority vote, and further provides these amendments become effective upon the explicit or tacit approval of a part only of the parties to the convention. Here, certainly, is recognition that the old method of unanimous consent to proposal and unanimous consent through ratification is not suitable for keeping sanitary and air law up to the needs of the international society. Indeed, the innovation in established practice was so great that Grenville T. Emmet, representing the United States at the 1933 conference, signed with the reservation that " no amendments to the convention will be binding on the Government of the United States or territory subject to its jurisdiction unless such amendments are accepted by the Government of the United States." [76]

The regulations attached to the Convention for the Unification and Improvement of the Metric System, signed at Paris, May 20, 1875,[77] may be amended upon proposal of the General Conference of the Metric Union but such amendments enter into force only for states voting for them and for such others as later indicate their consent. Amendment of the Convention proper appears to require unanimity in a conference of revision and ratification by all participating states.

From its first session, the General Conference of the Metric Union, a body formed from delegates of all contracting states,[78] has exercised by majority vote powers of considerable breadth. By terms of the Convention and

---

[76] *L. N. T. S., CLXI*, 103.

[77] G. F. von Martens, *Nouveau recueil général de traités,* 2d series, I, 663; *B. & F. State Papers,* LXVI, 562; *B. P. P.,* 1875, LXXXIII. As revised Oct. 6, 1921, *L. N. T. S.,* XVII, 46.

[78] The following states are members of the Metric Union: Germany, Argentina, Belgium, Bulgaria, Canada, Chile, Denmark, Spain, the United States, Finland, France, Great Britain, Hungary, Italy, Japan, Mexico, Norway, Peru, Portugal, Roumania, Jugoslavia, Siam, Sweden, Switzerland, Uruguay.

attached Regulations it is charged with " undertaking the necessary measures for the propagation and perfecting of the Metric System," with the sanctioning of new metrological determinations which have been made between sessions, and with the selection of members to serve on the International Committee of the Union.[79] Neither the Convention nor the attached Regulations contained an explicit statement concerning how decisions were to be reached in the General Conference. The nearest approach to this was the provision of Article 7 of the Regulations to the effect that each state should have the right to one vote. To a diplomatic conference, such a provision generally means one thing: decisions reached by unanimous consent. However, the General Conference, dealing with the matter at its first session, did not feel constrained to adopt such an interpretation. The Conference decided that, since there was a total of eighteen votes in the Conference,[80] decisions would require ten votes to be valid.[81] All subsequent Conferences have likewise followed the majority rule. That the Conference, given opportunity, should adopt this rule seems quite natural. Most of the delegates sent to it have been scientists of recognized standing rather than diplomatic officers. The inconveniences of the unanimity rule may be tolerated by the latter but others will see little reason for its maintenance. Moreover, many of the delegates sent to the meetings of the General Conference had previously served as members of the International Metric Commission, a body which took its de-

---

[79] Art. 7 of the Regulations. The International Committee, which supervises the Bureau and directs the metrological work, was originally composed of 14 members nationals of different states (Art. 8 of Regulations attached to Convention of 1875). In 1921, membership was increased to 18. (Art. 2, Convention of 1921.)

[80] Only sixteen states were represented in the Conference, but Austria and Hungary and Sweden and Norway were each awarded separate votes.

[81] L'Union Internationale des Poids et Mesures, *Comptes rendus des séances de la première Conférence Générale*, p. 19.

cisions by majority vote,[82] and some were continuing to serve on the new International Committee which was entitled, by terms of the Convention and Regulations, to decide by majority.[83] Familiar practices were carried over in so far as possible to the procedure of the General Conference. Hence, majority vote has been used for the election of the members of the International Committee by the General Conference,[84] in the determining of procedural questions such as the appointment of special commissions,[85] in the adoption of metric standards,[86] and even in the amendment of the Regulations attached to the Convention.[87] However, in the latter case, the President explained that those states whose delegates abstained or cast negative votes would not be bound until they had given their assent.[88] At the Fifth Conference, when absolute unanimity was obtained for amendments to Articles 6 and 20 of the Regulations, pertaining to the budget and individual state contributions, respectively, the President ruled the articles in their amended form might go into force immediately without waiting for ratification by the contracting states.[89] The practice of the Conferences, therefore, suggests that, while changes in the Regulations may be proposed by majority vote, the new obligations extend only to those states which consent. By virtue of the

[82] Report to the Board of Trade upon the Formation and Proceedings of the International Metric Commission at Paris, 1869-1872, *B. P. P.,* 1873, XXXVIII.

[83] Art. 12 of Regulations. But a unanimous vote of the Committee is required to adopt a budget exceeding 250,000 francs. Should the budget exceed 300,000 francs or should the Committee desire to make a change in the system of calculating the contributions as fixed in Article 20 of the Regulations, unanimity is necessary together with the consent of the General Conference. It is further provided that such a decision is valid only if no member state expresses a contrary view in reply to the notification given it. Art. 2, Convention of 1921.

[84] *Première Conférence,* p. 44; *Cinquième Conférence,* p. 28.

[85] *Cinquième Conférence,* p. 43.

[86] *Ibid.,* p. 50.   [88] *Ibid.,* p. 57.

[87] *Première Conférence,* p. 59.   [89] *Cinquième Conférence,* p. 26.

amendments to the Convention made in 1921, any change in the financial clauses or any extension of the scope of the work of the Bureau requires unanimity in the Conference.[90]

Thus far we have examined cases in which an international organ acting by some form of majority vote may propose draft conventions or draft amendments to existing conventions, the instruments so proposed becoming binding upon all ratifying parties. There remains at least one case in which an international organ is competent to propose by vote of an extraordinary majority amendments to a convention, the amendments so proposed entering into force only if ratified by all parties to the convention. Article 34 of the Convention on Air Navigation, signed at Paris, October 13, 1919,[91] provides:

> Any proposed modification of the articles of the present convention shall be examined by the International Commission for Air Navigation, whether it originates with one of the contracting states or with the commission itself. No such modification shall be proposed for adoption by the contracting states, unless it shall have been approved by at least two-thirds of the total possible votes.
>
> All such modifications of the articles of the convention (but not of the provisions of the annexes) must be formally adopted by the contracting states before they become effective.

This provision for proposal of amendments to the Convention by two-thirds vote was written into the Convention, it will be recalled, on motion of the United States delegation.[92] The intention of the American delegation and those who supported its proposal was to make modification of the fundamental law of the Air Regime less difficult than is alteration of most multilateral treaties.

---

[90] Arts. 1, 2, Convention of 1921.
[91] *L. N. T. S.,* XI, 173.
[92] *La Documentation Internationale,* VIII, 60, and above, p. 86.

To some extent this aim has been secured although there is considerable evidence to suggest that the amending procedure is yet too rigid for desirable development of international air law. On two occasions, the Commission has submitted amendments to the member states over the opposition of one or more states. One of these received unanimous ratification and consequently entered into force, while the other has thus far failed. The first and successful instance occurred at the extraordinary session of June, 1929, when an amendment was proposed to the fourth paragraph of Article 15 by vote of 27 for to 4 against. The dissenting states were the British Empire, the Netherlands, Sweden, and the United States.[93] It was approved at a session of the Commission at which only member states were represented, received ratification by all and entered into force May 12, 1933. At the seventeenth regular session an amendment was again proposed over opposition. This time the Commission adopted a draft text of a chapter relating to " aircraft destined to ensure communications of importance for the working of the League of Nations." Such aircraft were to be permitted " to enjoy all the rights accorded to state aircraft of the contracting states other than military, customs, or police aircraft." This amendment was opposed by one state, Japan.[94] It has not come into force.

Moreover, the knowledge that amendments will enter into force only when ratified by all member states frequently causes delegations to withhold the proposal of changes because of opposition from some quarter. The withdrawal by the British delegation of an amendment to Article 16 proposed by Canada is a case in point.[95]

On other occasions the Commission has decided to forego the proposal of amendments even though approved

---

[93] Minutes of the Extraordinary Session, 1929.
[94] *Official Bulletin,* XVII, 25.
[95] *Ibid.,* V, 25.

by all members of the Commission because it has not been
considered expedient to prepare a separate protocol for
each modification of detail. Hence, at the eighteenth session the Commission postponed proposal of amendments
to Article 26 [96] and to Article 19.[97] Again at the twenty-
second session the Commission postponed amendments to
Articles 9 and 16 which had the support of the entire
body.[98] Finally, at the twenty-third session the Commission decided to unite in a single protocol amendments to
fourteen different articles of the Convention, some of the
amendments so proposed having been approved for as
long as five years.[99]

However, perhaps the strongest evidence of the undue
difficulty caused by the amending process is found in the
experiences of the Commission in obtaining unanimous
ratification of the " perfecting amendments " proposed in
the early sessions and at the extraordinary session of 1929.
It will be recalled that these were undertaken with the
definite purpose of making acceptance of the Convention
more general. The success of the Air Regime was in large
measure dependent upon their prompt acceptance by the
member states. Yet the Commission had the greatest
difficulty bringing these amendments into force. Indeed,
in order to make effective the amendments proposed to
Articles 5 and 34 by the protocols of October 27, 1922,
and June 30, 1923, respectively, it was necessary to take
action which virtually amounted to the dismissal of Bolivia
from the Air Regime. On August 30, 1923, the Bolivian

[96] *Ibid.*, XVIII, 38.
[97] *Ibid.*, p. 41.
[98] *Ibid.*, XXII, 74, 121.
[99] *Ibid.*, XXIII, 95. In this connection it should be noted that the International Commission for Air Navigation is not alone in its need for an
adequate procedure for securing minor changes in its convention. Although the International Labor Organization has now developed a procedure for general revision of labor treaties (see above, p. 116) it possesses no procedure for making the small changes which frequently need
to be made.

Minister in Paris had sent the Secretary-General of the International Commission for Air Navigation the following message: " Unforseen circumstances compel the Bolivian Government to withdraw from the I. C. A. N." [100] As Article 43 of the Convention requires notification of the French Government for denunciation of the Convention, the Secretary-General quite properly interpreted the Bolivian message merely as notice that Bolivia would not be represented at the sessions of the Commission. By the sixth session of the Commission, Bolivia and the Serb-Croat-Slovene State alone were preventing the amendments to Articles 5 and 34 from coming into force. Moreover, Bolivia was sending no representative to the sessions and had ignored all communications addressed to her by the Secretary-General. Consequently, the Commission adopted a resolution instructing each delegation present to ask its government to bring diplomatic pressure upon Bolivia to secure response to the communications.[101] Inasmuch as this failed to produce the desired results, the Commission adopted the following extraordinary resolution at its seventh session:

> Whereas the Commission has again examined the Communication which the Bolivian Minister in Paris made to the Secretary-General . . . on the 30th of August 1923. . . .
>
> And whereas since that communication the Bolivian Government has ceased to take part in the work of the Commission and has not yet paid its contribution to the expenses of the Commission. . . .
>
> The Commission considers that the above mentioned communication of the 30th of August 1923 . . . must be considered as being a denunciation of the convention. . . .
>
> The Commission, in order to ascertain the exact intentions of the Bolivian Government, directs the Secretary-General:
>
> To bring this Resolution to the knowledge of the Bolivian Government forthwith, requesting it to state whether the Com-

[100] *Ibid.*, V, 13.   [101] *Ibid.*, VI, 23.

10

mission has interpreted its intentions rightly, adding however that *if no reply shall have been received to the contrary within four months from the date of such communication, the telegram of the 30th of August 1923 will be definitely considered as a denunciation within the terms of Article 43. . . .*[102]

The Bolivian Minister at Paris finally notified the French Government that it had been the intention of Bolivia to denounce the convention,[103] and so when the Serb-Croat-Slovene State finally deposited her ratification the amendments to Articles 5 and 34 came into force.[104]

Somewhat similar difficulty was encountered in obtaining ratification of the amendments proposed in June and December, 1929. A resolution of May, 1932, requested that diplomatic pressure be brought upon Chile, Persia, and Uruguay to hasten ratification.[105] Chile quickly responded with ratification and Uruguay ratified on May 17, 1933. Persia, after waiting until April 20, 1933, gave notice of denunciation of the convention. Since Article 43 provides that there must be notice of one year for denunciation, the amendments could not properly be considered in force until April 20, 1934. The Commission, however, has considered them effective from May 17, 1933, the date of Uruguay's ratification.[106]

In spite of the difficulties encountered by the Air Regime in altering its basic law in such fashion as to promote the fullest development of air communications, it seems very unlikely that change can be made in the near future in the requirement of unanimous ratification of amendments. The development of air communications and of civil aviation generally is tied up far too closely with preparations for war and defense for any state to permit basic changes in the terms of the Convention by which it is bound without its own consent. Such will not

[102] *Ibid.*, VII, 21.　Italics added.
[103] *Ibid.*, XII, 3.
[104] *Ibid.*, p. 17.
[105] *Ibid.*, XX, 35.
[106] *Ibid.*, XXII, 56.

be possible until the collective security so long sought has become a reality.

Conceivably, the obstruction caused by small states not greatly interested in the Air Regime might be obviated by changing the amending clause to one like that provided in the Covenant of the League of Nations. There, amendments enter into force when ratified by all the states composing the Council and by a majority of those composing the Assembly. States failing to ratify may prevent the altered text from being binding upon them by exercising their right of denunciation. Although this rule has permitted the adoption of two amendments, of comparatively slight importance, over the negative votes of certain small states, without in either case causing their withdrawal from the League of Nations,[107] it is believed such a plan would have distinct disadvantages for the Air Regime. From its inception until the amendment to Article 34 entered into force May 17, 1933, there has been a constant struggle to rid the Convention of derogations from the principle of state equality.[108] The battle having been won, the small states would never consent to their reinsertion.

Needless to say, it would be neither possible nor desirable to depart from the rule of unanimous ratification without making an exception for the larger powers or without awarding them greater voting strength in the body which brings forward amendments to the Convention. Although the experience of the League of Nations and international bodies generally indicates that the small states show little or no disposition to adopt new rules over the opposition of the great powers when possessing the power to do so, it seems unlikely that the larger powers would consent to a rule for the Air Regime which might

[107] Greece opposed an amendment to Article 6 of the Covenant (*Records of the Second Assembly,* Plenary, p. 885) and Cuba and Uruguay later opposed an amendment to the same article (*ibid.,* p. 886).

[108] See below, p. 267.

force them to denounce the treaty in order to prevent basic changes being made in the Convention. Nor would it be desirable to provoke denunciation by any of the great powers, for one of the chief handicaps of the regime has been the non-participation of two important European states—Germany and the Union of Soviet Socialist Republics.

Perhaps the most feasible method of eliminating some of the difficulties caused by the rule of unanimous ratification for amendments to the Convention lies in a gradual building up of the content of the Annexes. Changes in the Convention are considered matters of high policy; changes in the Annexes are dealt with on the administrative level. It is not suggested that the problem can be solved by a wholesale transplanting of Convention articles to the Annexes, although if the Convention were being drafted today quite possibly more of its provisions would be relegated to that category. It is suggested, however, that in view of the interpretation placed by the International Commission for Air Navigation on its own powers,[109] the Annexes may be expected to expand to embrace and regulate new situations. While the Convention remains virtually static the Annexes will be developed. Although the cumbersome process of amending Convention articles remains, the existence of a workable process for changing the Annexes may prevent the Convention amending process from forcing stagnation on the Air Regime.

[109] See above, p. 93.

CHAPTER V

Majority Vote in Bodies Having Power of Sanction

International practice presents but few examples of bodies of an international character which have been empowered to supervise or control by majority vote the fulfillment of international undertakings by the participating states. In general, application is controlled exclusively by the government of each contracting state. Each decides for itself the existence and the extent of its own obligations under the instrument in question.

Perhaps the best known example of an international organ possessing extensive supervisory powers is the Permanent Sugar Commission set up by the Brussels Convention of March 5, 1902,[1] in an effort to eliminate in the production of sugar the wasteful bounty systems.[2] This Commission, which functioned until 1920, was composed of one delegate from each contracting state.[3] The states bound themselves to suppress " direct and indirect bounties by which the production or exportation of sugar may profit," [4] not to impose duties upon non-bounty fed sugar beyond a maximum rate fixed in the Convention,[5] and to impose a countervailing duty upon the import of bounty-fed sugar.[6] The Commission was authorized by terms of the Convention to determine whether any contracting state

---

[1] *B. & F. State Papers*, XCV, 6; Sir Edward Hertslet's *Commercial Treaties*, XXIII, 579. The convention also may be found in Appendix C to Sayre, *Experiments in International Administration*.

[2] Cf. Sayre, pp. 117 ff.; N. Politis, " L'Organisation de l'Union Internationale des Sucres," *Revue de science et de législation financières*, 1904; Reinsch, *Public International Unions*, pp. 49 ff.

[3] Art. 7 of the Convention. The original parties to the convention were Great Britain, Germany, Austria-Hungary, Belgium, Spain, France, Italy, Netherlands and Sweden. Hungary and Austria were given separate representation. Four other states, including Russia, later adhered.

[4] Art. 1. [5] Art. 3. [6] Art. 4.

was granting any direct or indirect bounty on the production or exportation of sugar, to determine whether the non-exporting states (Spain, Italy and Sweden) continued in that special condition, to deliver opinions on contested questions, to determine the existence of bounties in non-signatory states and the amount of compensatory duty which should be charged, to prepare for consideration of member states requests for admission to the Union, and to authorize the levy of an increased surtax by any of the contracting states against another by whose sugar its markets were being flooded to the injury of national production.[7] All decisions of the Commission could be reached by majority vote, each contracting state having a single vote. Such decisions normally came into effect within a period of two months. However, each contracting state had the privilege of appealing within eight days after notification any decision taken in respect to the determination of non-exporting countries and in respect to the existence of bounties in non-contracting states, but the appeal was always back to the Commission itself. The new decision of the Commission, which could likewise be reached by majority vote, was final and entered into force within two months of its delivery.[8]

Thus the Commission was used primarily for the determination of facts, but upon the basis of such findings the contracting parties were obliged to alter their domestic regulations in accordance with their previous convention undertakings. In numerous instances the existence of bounties in states not parties to the Convention was discovered by the Commission, necessitating the application of countervailing duties by all contracting states.[9] The final collapse of the Union, which was foreshadowed by

---

[7] Cf. Art. 7, 8, and Final Protocol.

[8] Art. 7.

[9] Cf. *Commission Permanente sur le Régime des Sucres, Procès-verbaux,* 1903-1904, pp. 26, 110; 1904-1905, pp. 34, 66, 142.

the withdrawal of Great Britain and Italy in 1913, resulted
apparently from the divergence of interest between sugar
producing and sugar consuming countries.[10]

At the present time, three other international organs are
authorized to exercise by majority vote powers of a somewhat extraordinary character in respect to supervision of
fulfillment of international undertakings by national administrations. Two of these bodies, the Governing Body
of the International Labor Organization and the Permanent
Central Opium Board established by the convention
adopted at the Second Opium Conference, Geneva, 1925,[11]
have authority to apply " sanctions " for failure of participating states to fulfill their obligations under labor and
opium conventions, respectively. The third, the International Sugar Council, established by virtue of the International Agreement regarding the Regulation of Production and Marketing of Sugar, signed at London, May 6,
1937,[12] may recommend " sanctions " and has wide powers
in respect to the controlling of export quotas. By terms of
the Convention for Limiting the Manufacture and Regulating the Distribution of Narcotic Drugs, signed at Geneva,
July 9, 1931,[13] the Permanent Central Opium Board also
has powers for control of exports.

By the terms of Article 408 of Part XIII of the Treaty
of Versailles, each member of the International Labor
Organization agrees to make an annual report to the
International Labor Office on the measures taken to give
effect to the conventions to which it is a party, and in
Articles 409 to 420 " sanctions " or " measures of enforcement " are provided in accordance with two procedures, one growing out of " representations " and the
other from " complaints." " Representation " to the Inter-

[10] Cf. Sayre, pp. 129 ff.
[11] *L. N. T. S.*, LXXXI, 317.
[12] Cmd. 5461. H. M. Stationery Office, 1937.
[13] *L. N. T. S.*, CXXXIX, 301.

national Labor Office that a convention is not being
observed may be made by any industrial association of
employers or of workers. The Governing Body may
communicate this representation to the government against
which it is made and invite from it a statement. If no
statement is received within a reasonable time or if the
statement when received is not deemed by the Governing
Body to be satisfactory, the Governing Body has the
right to publish both the complaint and the statement, if
any, made in reply to it.[14] Thus representation can lead
to the sanction of publicity only.

The " complaint " procedure may be opened only by a
member state or by the Governing Body acting on its own
motion or on receipt of a complaint from a delegate to the
Conference. Although the Governing Body may, if it
thinks fit, communicate with the government named in the
" complaint " as set forth in the procedure under " representation," resort may be made to a Commission of Inquiry
consisting of three persons nominated by the Secretary-
General of the League of Nations from a panel composed
in advance on nomination of the member states. In nomination of the panel, each state agrees to name three
persons of industrial experience one of whom shall be a
representative of employers, one of workers, and the third
a person of independent standing. The qualifications of
each are examined by the Governing Body which may, by
two-thirds vote, refuse to accept any nomination. When
the Secretary-General appoints a Commission of Inquiry
one member must be elected from each section of the
panel and no one may be named who has been nominated
by a state directly involved in the complaint. The Commission of Inquiry is authorized " to prepare a report
embodying its findings on all questions of fact relevant
to determining the issue between the parties and contain-

[14] Arts. 409-410.

ing such recommendations as it may think proper." Further, " it shall also indicate . . . the measures, if any, of an economic character against a defaulting Government which it considers to be appropriate, and which it considers other Governments would be justified in adopting." The report is to be communicated by the Secretary-General to the governments concerned. Any government directly concerned may then carry the matter to the Permanent Court of International Justice whose decision affirming, varying, or reversing any of the findings or recommendations of the Commission of Inquiry shall be final. In the event of a member failing to carry out the recommendations of the Commission of Inquiry or the decision of the Court, any other member may take against the defaulting state the measures of an economic character suggested in the report or decision. " Sanctions " must be lifted when the defaulting state informs the Governing Body that it is complying with the report or decision and when this fact is ascertained either by a Commission of Inquiry named by the Secretary-General to verify the contention or by the Permanent Court.[15] All decisions of the Governing Body in respect to the instigation of the " representation " or " complaint " procedures are taken by simple majority vote except that, by the terms of Article 412, rejection by the Governing Body of an individual nominated by a government to serve on the panel from which commissions of inquiry are drawn requires a two-thirds vote.[16]

[15] Arts. 411-420.

[16] See Standing Orders of the Governing Body of the International Labor Organization. Majority vote in the Governing Body was not explicitly provided for in the Constitution of the International Labor Organization, but it was clearly implied. Article 393 gives the Governing Body authority to determine its own rules of procedure. In the matter of the vote necessary for reaching decisions, the Constitution places only the one limitation noted upon the freedom of the Governing Body. If a two-thirds decision was intended to suffice for a matter of such delicate character as the rejection of an individual named by a government to serve on the panel from which the personnel of Commissions of Inquiry are drawn, clearly a simple majority was intended to suffice in other cases.

Although many members of the Commission of the Peace Conference which drafted the Constitution of the Labor Organization considered the sanctions clauses of supreme importance,[17] resort to the articles has not been frequent. However, the " representation " procedure has been invoked on several occasions. In 1924 the Japanese Seaman's Union filed a representation against non-enforcement by the Japanese Government of the Convention of 1920 on the Placing of Seamen.[18] In 1930 the trade unions of Latvia called attention to the failure of the Latvian Government in respect to the same convention.[19] In neither case was the protest published inasmuch as the Governing Body found the explanation of Japan satisfactory, and in the case of Latvia, the existence of circumstances which made application of the convention exceedingly difficult.[20] However, in 1936, the representation of the Madras and Southern Mahratta Railway Employees Union concerning the alleged failure of the Government of India to secure effective observance of the Unemployment Convention of 1919 was published.[21] The complaint procedure has been utilized on only one occasion. At the Conference of 1934 demand was made by the Indian workers' delegate, Jamnadas Mehta, that a Commission of Inquiry be named to examine enforcement by the Government of India of the hours of work convention adopted at Washington in 1919. The Governing Body decided to publish the complaint.[22]

Even though the " sanctions " clauses have not been used extensively their presence in the Constitution of the

[17] See particularly the remarks of Vandervelde, Barnes, Fontaine and Baron Mayer des Planches, Minutes of Proceedings No. 25 (March 17, 1919), in Shotwell, *Origins*, II, 255 ff.

[18] *Official Bulletin*, IX, 262.

[19] *Ibid.*, XVI, 29.

[20] Cf. Wilson, *Labor in the League System*, pp. 225-227.

[21] *Official Bulletin*, XXI, 16.

[22] *Ibid.*, XX, 15.

International Labor Organization is significant as a departure from the usual nature of international commitments. States members of the International Labor Organization have consented to procedures which allow appeals to be brought by their own nationals, as well as by others, against any failure on their part to comply with their international obligations under the labor conventions which they have ratified. Decisions to publish or to resort to a commission of inquiry may be taken by majority vote of a body in which no state has more than a single vote.[23] Further, the recommendations of the Commission of Inquiry or of the Permanent Court, if appeal is taken, are binding, and failure to comply may permit other member states to take measures of an economic character against the defaulting state.

The sanctions powers conferred upon the Permanent Central Opium Board by the Geneva Convention of 1925 [24] are somewhat less far-reaching than those with which Part XIII of the Versailles Treaty arms the International Labor Organization. The Board is authorized by the Convention to receive from the contracting parties detailed statistics upon the production, manufacture, distribution and trade in narcotic drugs.[25] The Convention further provides that the Board shall watch the course of international trade. If the information at its disposal leads the Board to conclude that excessive quantities of any drug covered by the Convention are accumulating in any country or that there is a danger of a country becoming a center of illicit traffic, the Board may ask the country in question, through the Secretary-General of the League of Nations, for explanations. In the event that no explana-

[23] By the terms of Art. 411, any state not represented in the Governing Body is entitled to send a delegate to take part in the proceedings during " representation " or " complaint " directed against itself.

[24] *L. N. T. S.*, LXXXI, 317.

[25] Arts. 22 and 23 of the Convention.

tions are offered, or that those put forward are unsatisfactory, the Board may call the matter to the attention of the contracting states and to the Council of the League. In addition, it may recommend that no further exports of the substances covered by the Convention be made to the country at fault until the Board is satisfied that the situation is again as it should be. The country named by the Board or any exporting country which is not prepared to accept the recommendation may bring the matter before the Council of the League of Nations. A report dealing with the situation may be published by the Board, which, after communication to the Council, must be forwarded to all contracting countries.[26] The Board possesses no authority to invoke penalties but instead must rely upon the results of publicizing the situation and upon the recommendation of restrictive measures. These powers may be exercised by the Board acting upon its own initiative or upon that of any contracting state [27] and may extend to non-contracting as well as to contracting states.[28] All decisions of the Board relative to these matters may be taken by an absolute majority of the whole number of the Board,[29] but should the decision not be unanimous, the views of the minority must also be stated.[30]

The Convention on Limitation of 1931 [31] further adds to the powers of the Permanent Central Opium Board. Each contracting party is required to furnish annually to the Board estimates of its drug needs.[32] These are examined by a Supervisory Body composed of four members, one being appointed by the Advisory Committee on Traffic in Opium, one by the Permanent Central Board, one by the Health Committee of the League, and one by the International Office of Public Health. The Body has

[26] Art. 24.
[27] Art. 25.
[28] Art. 26.
[29] Art. 19.

[30] Art. 24.
[31] L. N. T. S., CXXXIX, 301.
[32] Art. 2.

power to fix its own rules of procedure. If any contracting state fails to supply the Board with an estimate the Supervisory Body may draw one up for it, and it is authorized also to supply estimates for non-contracting states and for the colonial territories of contracting states for which the contracting metropolitan states have not accepted the obligations of the Convention. Estimates submitted by the contracting states may be amended by the Supervisory Body only with the consent of the government concerned.[33] With these estimates which have been supplied by the governments and fixed by the Supervisory Body in its hands, the Permanent Central Opium Board is in possession of a powerful weapon of control. If any contracting country appears to be violating its obligations under the Convention, the Board, acting by majority vote, may request explanations and ultimately publish the statements in accordance with the procedure laid down in the Geneva Convention of 1925.[34] The Convention further adds to the powers of the Board by providing that contracting governments must notify the Board of any authorization for the export to non-contracting states of drugs covered by the Convention. If the request for export amounts to five kilogrammes the Board must be asked whether the export will cause the estimates for the importing country to be exceeded. If the Board decides that such would be the case, the contracting countries have obligated themselves not to permit the export.[35] Thus the Board has final authority in respect to exports amounting to five kilogrammes or more to non-contracting countries. For exports to contracting countries, its control rests upon the power to request explanations and to publicize its findings.

The Permanent Central Opium Board which exercises these powers of control by majority vote is not a body on

[33] Art. 5.   [34] Art. 14.   [35] *Ibid.*

which all contracting states find representation. Rather, it consists of eight persons " who by their technical competence, impartiality and disinterestedness will command general confidence," appointed by the Council of the League of Nations with the United States and Germany being invited to participate.[36] The members serve for five year terms and are eligible for reappointment. They may hold no office which places them in a position of direct dependence upon their governments.

Of all the conventions conferring upon international bodies power to exercise some control over national administration the recent International Agreement regarding the Regulation of Production and Marketing of Sugar,[37] negotiated in pursuance of the decision of the World Monetary and Economic Conference of 1933, is perhaps most interesting. The purpose of the contracting governments is " to assure consumers of an adequate supply of sugar in the world market at a reasonable price not to exceed the cost of production, including a reasonable profit of efficient producers." [38] Basic export quotas for the free market are set for thirteen exporting countries,[39] and the other five exporters are limited to set quotas.[40] The four importing countries assume various obligations in

[36] Art. 19 of Geneva Convention of 1925. When the first and second appointments were made in December, 1928 and October, 1933, Germany was a member of the Council. The United States participated but insisted that the Council was acting as an electoral body in conjunction with an American representative and not sitting as the Council. This helps to establish the fact that the Board is an international institution deriving its life from a treaty and not a subsidiary of the League. See S. H. Bailey, *The Anti-Drug Campaign,* p. 119 n.

[37] Signed at London, May 6, 1937, Cmd. 5461, H. M. Stationery Office, 1937.

[38] Art. 2.

[39] Art. 19. The countries are Belgium, Brazil, Cuba, Czechoslovakia, Dominican Republic, Germany, Haiti, Hungary, Netherlands, Portugal, Peru, and the U. S. S. R.

[40] Arts. 10, 12, 13, 19. The countries are South Africa, Australia, France, Philippines, and Jugoslavia.

respect to the limitation of their own production and exports and the maintenance of existing consumption levels.[41]

The Agreement is administered by an International Sugar Council composed of delegates of the participating governments and an Executive Committee, both sitting in London.[42] The first session of the provisional Council, acting before the Agreement was officially in force, was held July 5, 1937.[43] Although representation on the Council is equal, all states having three delegates,[44] voting power is distributed among exporting and importing countries somewhat in accordance with the importance of the countries as exporters or importers, respectively, and in such fashion that the ratio of exporting and importing votes shall always be 55 to 45.[45]

[41] Arts. 9, 11, 14, 16, 17. The countries are China, India, the United States, and the United Kingdom.

[42] Arts. 29, 30.

[43] *The Times* (London), July 6, 1937. Ratifications have now been deposited by 18 states. Cf. K. Wilk, " The International Sugar Régime," *American Political Science Review*, XXXIII, 860.

[44] Art. 31.

[45] The following table of votes was established by Article 37:

Exporting Countries:

Union of South Africa	2	Haiti	1
Australia	3	Hungary	1
Belgium	1	Netherlands	9
Brazil	2	Peru	3
Cuba	10	Philippines	1
Czechoslovakia	3	Poland	2
Dominican Republic	3	Portugal	1
France	3	U. S. S. R.	5
Germany	4	Jugoslavia	1
			55

Importing Countries:

China	5	United Kingdom	17
India	6	United States	17
			45

Should any signatory fail to ratify or should a participating power with-

The Council, which meets at least once a year, elects its own officers, determines their powers and fixes their terms of office; estimates, at least twenty days before the beginning of each quota year, the requirements of consumption of the free market for that year; appoints such permanent or temporary committees as it sees fit; approves the annual budget which may not, except with the express consent of all governments, exceed twelve thousand five hundred pounds per year, each state's contribution being proportionate to its number of votes; obtains and publishes such statistics and other data as it considers desirable; endeavors to secure the accession of such non-signatories as it considers desirable; and in general, exercises all the powers necessary to carry out the Agreement.[46] In addition, the Council may fix the quota and determine the vote in the Council of acceding states;[47] increase or decrease quotas, such changes being proportional to the basic quotas fixed;[48] re-distribute quotas which contracting governments have notified the Council are not to be used;[49] authorize the accumulation of sugar stocks in any country beyond the twenty-five percent of annual production " if it considers that such action is justified by special circumstances ";[50] recommend to the contracting governments the prohibition or restriction of sugar imports from countries having infringed the Agreement;[51] and authorize the suspension of the obligation under the Agreement for any importing country in which, because of the workings of the Agreement, an acute shortage of sugar develops, or for an exporting country where the Agreement has unreasonably diminished market possibilities.[52]

---

draw, the votes allotted to the delegation are to be re-distributed, *pro rata,* among other countries in the group. If a non-signatory accedes, the Council is to decide upon the number of votes it shall be allotted, the number being deducted, *pro rata,* from among the countries in the group.

[46] Art. 33.
[47] Arts. 19, 37.
[48] Arts. 20, 21.
[49] Arts. 24.
[50] Art. 26.
[51] Art. 44.
[52] Art. 51.

Except where otherwise provided in the Agreement, all decisions of the Council are taken by a simple majority of the votes of the contracting governments represented at the meeting.[53] At least one-third of the governments must be represented for a decision to be valid.[54] However, extraordinary majorities and even unanimity are required for some of the more important actions of the Council. A unanimous vote is required to fix the basic quota of a non-signatory government which accedes to the Agreement.[55] Proportionate reduction in quotas may be voted only with the consent of all members of the Council representing countries entitled to basic quotas or to participation in the reserve.[56] Quotas may be increased, however, by a three-fifths vote.[57] The recommendation of prohibition or restriction of imports from a country infringing the Agreement requires a three-fourths vote,[58] as does a decision to relieve a government from its obligations under the instrument.[59]

The Executive Committee is composed of nine members, three representing importing countries, three producers of cane sugar, and three producers of beet sugar. The Governments of the United Kingdom and of the United States are assured of representation as importers for the whole life of the Agreement, the remaining seat being filled annually by the country designated by the governments of the importing countries. Cuba and the Netherlands are assured of constant representation as cane sugar producers, the remaining seat rotating for one year periods among Australia, the Dominican Republic, Peru, the Union of South Africa, and Brazil. For the beet sugar producers Czechoslovakia, Germany, and the Soviet Union were given representation during three of the five years the

[53] Art. 38.
[54] Art. 36.
[55] Art. 19.
[56] Art. 21.
[57] Art. 20.
[58] Art. 44.
[59] Art. 51.

11

Agreement is to run, France and Poland during two years, Belgium one year, and Hungary and Jugoslavia have six months each.[60] Each member of the Committee has one vote except the delegates of the United States and the United Kingdom who have two votes each. All decisions are by majority vote, five members constituting a quorum.[61] The Committee is permitted to exercise any powers which the Council shall delegate to it except the powers of reducing quotas, allotting additional quotas, determining the conditions under which non-signatories accede, recommending " sanctions " against states infringing the Agreement, and relieving contracting states of their obligations under the instrument.[62] One of the chief functions of the Executive Committee appears to be that of suggesting to the Council an increase in quotas whenever a sudden and excessive rise of price appears probable. If the necessary three-fifths vote is obtained by telegraph, additional quotas may be released. Otherwise, the Chairman of the Executive Committee may summon a special meeting of the Council.[63]

Thus, the instrument confers all real power on the Council, a body on which all member states are assured of constant representation. Although it is significant that measures may be recommended against governments infringing the Agreement and that governments may be relieved of their obligations under the Agreement by some form of majority vote, it should likewise be noted that unanimity is required for the reduction of quotas in contrast to the extraordinary majority requisite for increase. The convention, it would seem, represents the maximum concession exporting countries are willing to make to assure the stability of the sugar market. The Council, acting without the consent of all, may decide the moment

[60] Art. 39.
[61] Art. 42.
[62] Art. 40.
[63] Art. 41.

has come to ease the strain by permitting an increase in accumulated sugar stocks in some or all participating states. It may even decide without consent of all to free a government from its obligations under the Agreement or to recommend measures against a violator. But decisions to extend further the basic obligation of the Agreement to reduce sugar production may be taken only with the consent of all concerned.

By way of summary, it may be said that none of the four international bodies which have been considered in this chapter, namely, the Permanent Sugar Commission of 1902-1920, the Permanent Central Opium Board, the Governing Body of the International Labor Organization, and the International Sugar Council, have been in possession of power to add to the international commitments of the member states without the consent of the parties. Three of the organs have or did have power to make determinations of fact by majority vote, such determinations controlling the action of governments within the terms of the undertakings. Thus a decision by the Permanent Sugar Commission to the effect that a certain state was granting a bounty obligated all participating states to impose a countervailing duty, the amount of which was fixed by the Commission. A finding by the Permanent Central Opium Board to the effect that additional exports of narcotic drugs to a non-contracting state will cause the estimates of legitimate need of the area concerned to be exceeded prevents contracting states from authorizing any export of five kilogrammes or more without violating their international undertakings. No government party to the Sugar Agreement of 1937 may increase its sugar exports over the basic units set in the Agreement without the International Sugar Council finding, by three-fifths vote, that the requirements of the market justify it.

Three of the organs considered have power to watch over the governments in the performance of their obligations under the agreements or conventions and to impose or to recommend by some form of majority vote remedial action against violators. In this respect, the powers of the Governing Body of the International Labor Organization are most advanced, for it may, acting under the " representation " procedure, focus public attention on the defaulting state; or acting under the " complaint " procedure, instigate investigation which may actually result in the application of sanctions of an economic character. The Permanent Central Opium Board may, on its own authority, decide by majority vote to publish its findings in respect to states violating the opium conventions and it may recommend to the contracting governments the restriction of drug exports to the states considered at fault. The International Sugar Council is restricted in its " sanctions " clause, which it applies by three-fourths vote, to the recommendation " that the other Contracting Governments shall prohibit or restrict the import of sugar from the country which has infringed the Agreement."

Finally, it should be noted, the arming of a body such as the International Sugar Council with power to decide by majority vote represents in international organization something quite different from the equipping of a body like the Permanent Central Opium Board with powers of a similar character. Departure from unanimity is, of course, more significant when representation is by states or governments as in the International Sugar Council. A majority decision there means that one or more governments have been defeated by the vote of a combination of others. In contrast, the Permanent Central Opium Board is in no sense representative of states or governments. The members can not even hold positions which place them under any direct control of their governments. Their findings are those of experts. They do not represent the expression of state or government policies. Consequently, questions of state prestige do not enter. The United

States has not been " out-voted " by other powers though a decision may be taken over the head of the one national of the United States on the Board. The remarkable thing in respect to boards or commissions so constituted is not that they are given power to act by majority vote but that they are given powers. The Governing Body of the International Labor Organization stands somewhere between these two positions. Its membership is made up in part of representatives of governments and in part of persons selected as individuals by the functional groups in the Conference. However, inasmuch as every state named in a " representation " or " complaint " is entitled to representation on the Governing Body during the hearing of the action, it would seem that governments could here be " out-voted," not by a body of other governments but by a body in which the representatives of governments and individuals are united.

The equipment of the Governing Body of the International Labor Organization with such extraordinary powers of sanction to be exercised without the consent of all must be attributed, it would appear, to a combination of several circumstances. In the first place, the Peace Conference itself worked to some extent in an atmosphere of idealism. International commitments were to be enforced by collective action. Second, there existed in the minds of many statesmen in 1919 very real fear of bolshevism. If radicalism on the part of labor was to be prevented, an effective organization for accomplishing some of the things sought by labor must be created. These two circumstances combined to induce the Conference to turn the drafting of the Labor Organization constitution to a Commission composed in large part of men with whom considerations of effectiveness would weigh more heavily than adherence to established international practices. The idealism of some and the fear of radicalism by others help to explain the acceptance of the work of the Commission by the Conference without major change being made.

The extraordinary powers, to be exercised by majority vote, which have been conferred by governments upon the other bodies herein considered, sprang much more directly from the experience of states with attempts at international cooperation in the fields involved. The stability of the world sugar market could not be secured by leaving each state free to produce, export, and consume as it saw fit. Nor could it be secured through mere agreement to restrict production and exports to certain amounts. Production conditions and consumption demands change with rapidity. The situation, the regulation of which was sought, is ever-changing. Effective regulation necessitates the creation of an international authority equipped to apply the basic terms of the agreement to the new situation with promptness. Hence, unanimity had to be discarded in large part for the more convenient rule of majority decision. Substantially the same may be said of international control in the field of narcotic drugs. Advance determination of the legitimate needs of contracting states is valuable. But such a determination is even more valuable as an instrument of control when there exists an international authority which may call attention to accumulations of supplies in excess of the estimates and which may by effective procedure determine when circumstances justify importation of amounts beyond the pre-stated needs.

CHAPTER VI

Decision in International Bodies Controlling
Territory

There are but few instances in which territory has been placed under the control of an international body.[1] One of the earliest modern cases is that of the Cape Spartel Lighthouse which commands the southern entrance to the Strait of Gibraltar on the Atlantic coast of Morocco. By the terms of the Convention of May 31, 1865,[2] the government of Morocco agreed to construct the lighthouse, its direction and administration to be vested in the representatives of the contracting powers.[3] The representatives of the contracting powers, the personnel being drawn from the diplomatic corps at Tangier, were also charged with establishing " the necessary regulations for the service and superintendence of this establishment," no modification to be made in these articles except by common agreement of the contracting states.[4] In accordance with this provision, *règlements* governing the procedure of the Commission were adopted at a meeting held July 11, 1865,[5] the *règlements* remaining in force to the present time. Although

[1] The arrangements for the government of Schleswig-Holstein and Lauenburg from 1864 to 1866 under the condominium of Austria and Prussia, for the Sudan under the condominium of Great Britain and Egypt, and for the New Hebrides under Great Britain and France do not fall within the scope of this study.

[2] *Treaties, Conventions, International Acts, Protocols and Agreements between the United States of America and Other Powers, 1776-1909,* comp. William M. Malloy, I, 1217. The parties to the convention were the United States, Austria, Belgium, France, Great Britain, Italy, Netherlands, Portugal, Spain, Sweden and Norway, and Morocco.

[3] Art. 1.   [4] Art. 4.

[5] *Phare de Cap Spartel, Conseil d'Administration,* pp. 34-35, cited by G. H. Stuart, " The International Lighthouse at Cape Spartel," *A. J. I. L.,* XXIV, 773.

these rules may be modified only with unanimous consent, they permit the Commission to reach its decisions in respect to the administration and supervision of the lighthouse by majority vote. Participating powers have equal voting privileges and, although it was suggested at one time that financial contributions be proportionate to the volume of trade, provision was made for equal sums to be paid by each power.[6]

Although the lighthouse is within the International Zone of Tangier established by the Treaty of December 18, 1923,[7] the Statute of Tangier has made no change in the control of the lighthouse. Indeed, it makes no mention of it. It would not appear that the Commission, deriving its authority from the Treaty of 1865, would have any obligation to recognize a jurisdiction derived from a subsequent international convention to which several of the powers maintaining representation on the Commission are not parties. Consequently, the Cape Spartel Lighthouse Commission continues to function as an independent international agency within the area of the International Administration established by the Tangier Statute of 1923.

By the terms of the Convention on the Organization of the Statute of the Tangier Zone, signed at Paris, December 18, 1923,[8] and revised July 25, 1928,[9] " the maintenance of public order and the general administration " of

[6] Ten countries now participate: Belgium, France, Great Britain, Italy, Netherlands, Norway, Portugal, Spain, Sweden and the United States. Austria-Hungary discontinued payments during the war as did Germany and Russia which had adhered March 4, 1878, and May 31, 1899, respectively. L. F. Schmeckebier, *International Organizations in which the United States Participates,* p. 28.

[7] *L. N. T. S.,* XXVIII, 541.

[8] *Ibid.*; Hudson, *International Legislation,* II, 1191. The parties were France, Great Britain and Spain.

[9] *L. N. T. S.,* LXXXVII, 211; Hudson, II, 1219. The revision was undertaken largely to facilitate the participation of Italy which joined the three original parties in revising the convention.

the region described as the Tangier Zone is entrusted to a Mendoub nominated by His Shereefian Majesty,[10] to a Committee of Control consisting of the *consuls de carrière* of the powers signatory to the Act of Algeciras,[11] to an international legislative Assembly presided over by the Mendoub and composed in part of persons selected by the consulates and in part by the Mendoub,[12] and to an administrator and three assistant administrators named by His Shereefian Majesty, originally on nomination of the Committee of Control but more recently on nomination of the Assembly. The four must be nationals of powers signatory to the Act of Algeciras and no two may be of the same nationality.[13]

General legislative authority for the Zone is conferred upon the Assembly representing the foreign and native communities. "In consideration of the number of nationals, volume of commerce, the property interests and the importance of local trade at Tangier of the several signatories of the Act of Algeciras," the Assembly is composed of four French and four Spanish members, three British and three Italian, and one American, Belgian, Dutch, and Portuguese each nominated by their respective consulates. In addition, the Assembly includes six Mussulman subjects of the Sultan of Morocco nominated by the Mendoub and three Jewish subjects of the Sultan selected by the Mendoub from a list of nine names submitted by the Jewish community.[14] This Assembly, which in fact is a municipal legislative body constituted in a somewhat unusual fashion, naturally reaches decisions by majority vote. However, its powers are severely restricted,

---

[10] Art. 29.   [11] Art. 30.   [12] Art. 34.

[13] Art. 35. The number of assistants was increased from two to three by the revision of 1928 so that Italy might have equality with Great Britain, France, and Spain.

[14] Art. 34. Italian representation was increased from two to three by the revision of 1928.

for many propositions require approval by the Committee of Control to become valid and any law or regulation voted by the Assembly may be vetoed by the Committee of Control within fifteen days after notification of its passage, the Committee being obliged in such cases to cite the provisions and principles of the Statute with which the proposition adopted is in conflict.[15]

Although the Mendoub retains certain powers of administration in respect to the native population,[16] responsibility for administration, in general, belongs to the administrator and his three assistants,[17] nationals of the four parties to the revision of 1928 and in fact nominated by their respective consulates at Tangier.

Above the Assembly and the administrator and assistants stands the Committee of Control consisting of the *consuls de carrière* of the powers signatory to Algeciras, subject, of course, to the modifications imposed by the Tangier Convention. By Article 9 Germany and Austria-Hungary were excluded from all share in the control of the area. Moreover, since the World War Russia has given up all her interests in Morocco, Sweden has no *consul de carrière* at Tangier, and the United States has not adhered to the Statute. Consequently, the Committee consists of but seven members, the consuls of Belgium, France, Great Britain, Holland, Italy, Spain, and Portugal.[18] Each member of the Committee has one vote. The presidency of the Committee rotates for one year terms. The Committee is required by the convention " to ensure the observance of the regime of economic equality and the provisions of the Statute." [19] To that end it may veto laws or regulations enacted by the Assembly and require the removal of administrative officers. In general, all decisions of the Committee of Control are reached by

[15] Art. 31. [16] Art. 29. [17] Art. 35.
[18] G. H. Stuart, *The International City of Tangier,* p. 167.
[19] Art. 30.

majority vote. In case of an equal division, a second discussion must be held within eight days, the President, on
this occasion, possessing a casting vote.[20] For certain
actions extraordinary majorities and even unanimity are
required. A three-fourths vote is required for approval
of any abrogation or modification by the Assembly of any
of the numerous regulations drawn up for the Zone by
commissions of British, Spanish, and French experts, governing such things as liquor shops, the practice of medi-
cine, the protection of historic monuments, and the working of quarries.[21] A similar vote is necessary to demand
of His Shereefian Majesty the removal of an administrator[22] or the head of the customs service.[23] Disputes
between the customs service and the Administration of
the Zone may be settled by the Committee by a majority
vote, but if the dispute relates to the creation or suppression of posts, a three-fourths majority is required.[24] A
unanimous vote of the Committee is required for approval
of the establishment of a local interurban postal, telegraph, and telephone service replacing those maintained
by the powers,[25] for approval of abrogation or modification of any of the legal codes applied by the Mixed Court
which has replaced the consular jurisdictions,[26] or to permit the establishment in the Zone of games of chance.[27]

The German territory of the Saar constituted for a time
another example of a region placed under control of an
international commission. By Article 49 of the Treaty of
Versailles, Germany " renounced in favor of the League
of Nations, in the capacity of trustee, the government of
the territory," the inhabitants of the area retaining their
German nationality. Although the government of the
territory was restored to Germany in 1935, following the

[20] Art. 31.
[21] Art. 32.
[22] Art. 35.
[23] Art. 38.

[24] *Ibid.*
[25] Art. 14.
[26] Art. 32.
[27] Art. 52.

plebiscite held in conformity with the provisions of the Treaty of Versailles, this example of international government is sufficiently recent and important to necessitate consideration here.

The Saar Statute, which appears as an Annex to Section IV of Part III of the Treaty of Versailles, was drafted by a committee composed of André Tardieu (France), Headlam Morley (Great Britain) and Charles H. Haskins (United States), and incorporated into the Treaty by the Council of Four without change in respect to the governmental structure provided.[28]   By the terms of this Statute the government of the territory was entrusted to a Governing Commission composed of five persons chosen by the Council of the League of Nations for one year terms but eligible to reappointment.   Of the five, one was required to be a citizen of France, one a native inhabitant of the Saar Basin, not a citizen of France, the remaining three to belong to three countries other than France or Germany.[29]   Within the territory the Governing Commission was granted " all the powers of government hitherto belonging to the German Empire, Prussia, or Bavaria, including the appointment and dismissal of officials, and the creation of such administrative and representative bodies as it may deem necessary." [30]   The laws and regulations in force in the territory on November 11, 1918, except war measures, were to continue to apply.   However, the Commission was authorized to amend these " after consultation with the elected representatives of the inhabitants in such manner as the Commission may determine." [31]   The imposition of new taxes, other than customs duties, likewise required previous consultation with the elected representatives of the inhabitants.[32]   However, the right to be consulted in no sense gave the local assem-

[28] Cf. M. T. Florinsky, *The Saar Struggle*, p. 5.
[29] Treaty of Versailles, Part III, Sec. IV, Annex, Ch. II, pars. 16, 17.
[30] *Ibid.*, par. 19.   [31] *Ibid.*, par. 23.   [32] *Ibid.*, par. 26.

blies nor the Advisory Council established in 1922 power to prevent an opposed ordinance from becoming operative. From the first the Commission correctly took the position that it had power to decide on and to put into effect legislation, provided that the elected representatives of the inhabitants were consulted. This view was upheld by the Council of the League of Nations.[33] The Commission was debarred by the Statute from making any change in the legal regime for the exploitation of the mines, without previous consultation with the French Government, unless such changes were necessitated " by some regulation respecting labor adopted by the League." [34]

The principle of majority decision found complete acceptance in the Statute. Not only could all decisions of the Commission be reached by simple majority vote [35] but provision was made that decisions of the Council of the League, in respect to all matters dealt with in the Annex, could be made by a like vote.[36]

The Memel Harbor Board may be cited as a final example of an international body which was charged with the administration of territory. By the Convention of May 8, 1924, concerning the Territory of Memel,[37] between Lithuania and the British Empire, France, Italy, and Japan, the area was declared to constitute, under the sovereignty of Lithuania, a unit enjoying legislative, judicial, administrative, and financial autonomy.[38] Lithuania further agreed to give effect to certain engagements in respect to the port of Memel contained in Annex II

[33] League of Nations, *Official Journal,* 1922, p. 382.

[34] Treaty of Versailles, Part III, Sec. IV, Annex, Ch. II, par. 23.

[35] *Ibid.,* par. 19.

[36] *Ibid.,* par. 40.

[37] *L. N. T. S.,* XXIX, 85; Hudson, II, 1265. Memel was ceded by Lithuania to Germany on March 22, 1939 (*New York Times,* March 23, 1939), thus making impossible the continued functioning of the Board.

[38] Art. 2.

to the Convention.[39]   By the provisions of this document
the port was placed under the control of a Harbor Board
consisting of three members appointed for three year
terms and eligible for reappointment.   One, representing
Lithuanian economic interests, was appointed by the
Lithuanian Government; the second, representing the
economic interests of the Memel Territory, was appointed
by the Directorate of the Territory; the third, who was not
to be a citizen of Germany, Lithuania, or Poland was
appointed by the Advisory and Technical Committee for
Communications and Transit of the League of Nations.
The last named was expected to devote particular attention to the protection of the international economic interests served by the port.[40]

The Harbor Board was entrusted with the administration, operation, upkeep, and development of the port.[41]
The budget it drew up required the approval of the
Lithuanian Government.   The annual report of the Board
on the fulfillment of its tasks under the Convention was
presented both to the Directorate of the Memel Territory
and to the Advisory and Technical Committee on Communications and Transit.[42]   All decisions of the Board
were taken by majority vote.[43]   The composition and
powers of the Harbor Board were subject to modification
on proposal of the Lithuanian Government approved by
majority vote of the Council of the League of Nations,
the Council majority including the votes of the four other
parties to the Convention of May 8, 1924.[44]

On the basis of the four cases of international control
of territory examined, certain conclusions may be sug-

[39] Art. 3.
[40] Art. 5, Annex II.   [42] Art. 7.
[41] Art. 6.   [43] Art. 8.
[44] Art. 14. Inasmuch as Japan had ceased to be a member of the League
prior to the termination of the Statute by the cession of Memel to Germany, Japanese consent would have had to be secured in some other way.

gested. In the first place, when an international authority is charged with actual administration of an area, that is, with the enactment of ordinances and the direction of administrative officers, convenience virtually dictates use of the simple majority rule just as convenience has necessitated such a rule in municipal bodies charged with like duties. Thus, such a rule is found in the *règlement* for the Cape Spartel Lighthouse Commission, as well as in the Saar and Memel Statutes, even though the *règlement* was drawn up by a diplomatic body to regulate the procedure of a commission representing states as such.[45]

In the second place, under certain circumstances majority rule may be better suited than unanimity for protecting the interests of participating states. In such situations, the majority principle is adopted readily enough. The drafters of the Statute for the Tangier Zone were aware that majority rule afforded greater protection than unanimity. It will be noted that the Committee of Control is not charged with direct powers of government. It neither enacts ordinances nor appoints administrative officers directly. Its chief powers lie in vetoing acts of the Assembly alleged to be in violation of the Statute and in requiring the removal of administrative officers who fail in their duties. Obviously, with such duties majority decision is more suitable as a protective device than is unanimity. For the most part, unanimous consent, or consent by an extraordinary majority of the Committee is requisite only for positive approval of some action altering the rights of the participating states in the area. Undoubtedly, the same consideration, i. e., that majority

---

[45] It will be noted that state representation was not completely excluded by the Saar and Memel Statutes. One member of the Saar Commission had to be of French nationality and another a resident of the Saar not French. Evidence indicates the French nationals always looked upon themselves as representatives of the French Government even though appointed by the Council of the League. On the Memel Harbor Board, one member was appointed by the Government of Lithuania.

rule affords greater protection to the powers than unanimity, was present when the provisions for majority rule were written into the Saar and Memel Statutes. The powers had no desire to arm either the German national on the Saar Commission nor the appointee of the Lithuanian Government on the Memel Harbor Board with an absolute veto by requiring unanimous consent in either body. This is further substantiated by the provision in the Saar Statute that all decisions of the Council of the League of Nations in respect to the Saar may be made by majority vote when decisions of that body normally require unanimous consent.[46]

[46] For other deviations from unanimity in the Council designed to facilitate enforcement of the clauses of the peace treaties against the defeated powers, see above, p. 22.

CHAPTER VII

DECISION IN INTERNATIONAL RIVER COMMISSIONS

During the last one hundred and forty years numerous international commissions have been established for regulation of the navigation and other uses of rivers of international concern. In each case, where such commissions have included representatives from more than two states, some deviation from unanimity has been made. In some cases, provision for majority decision has appeared in the terms of the convention establishing the organ. In others, it has been inserted after an interval. However, since the commissions vary widely both in the extent to which majority decision is accepted and in legal competence, some consideration of the powers and procedure of each body is necessary before any generalizations concerning the majority rule in the practice of the river commissions can be offered.

The Central Commission for the Navigation of the Rhine

Of the international river commissions, that established for the Rhine may lay claim to the longest history. As early as August 15, 1804, a convention was entered into between France and the Arch-chancellor of the German Empire, providing for the creation of an international authority for river control.[1] Passage tolls on vessels and cargoes, with a fixed maximum in each case, were to be collected at established points by joint administration. The two powers united in the appointment of a director-general and each appointed two inspectors. These united to form a governing board with a seat at Mayence. Although the chief functions of the director-general and

---

[1] Martens, *Recueil des principaux traités,* VIII, 261.

inspectors were supervision of such things as toll collection and maintenance of channels and tow paths, a board consisting of the director-general and two inspectors, one representing each power, enjoyed some rule-making authority. However, regulations adopted in this fashion, although applied immediately, had only provisional validity until approved by the governments of the powers concerned. Appeals from the decisions of toll officials were heard by a board constituted in the same fashion, this board likewise acting by majority vote. Final appeal might be taken to a central commission, assembling annually at Mayence, consisting of the local French prefect, a commissioner appointed by the Arch-chancellor, and a third appointed by the two.[2]

However, the origin of the present Central Commission for the Navigation of the Rhine may be traced quite directly to the agreement reached concerning the Rhine at the Congress of Vienna.[3] Navigation of the river, " along its whole course, from the point where it becomes navigable to the sea (*jusqu'à la mer*)" was made free for the commerce of all nations. Regulation of this free river was given to the riparian states, the regulation to be exercised through a Central Commission acting as a meeting of state representatives rather than as an independent administrative organ. The Commission, assembling at Mayence for two sessions each year, consisted of one representative of each state.[4]

The chief functions of the Commission, as given in Article 10, were " to establish a perfect control over the observance of the general regulations, and to constitute an

[2] Cf. J. P. Chamberlain, *Regime of International Rivers*, pp. 164 ff.; E. J. Clapp, *The Navigable Rhine*, pp. 11 ff.; G. Haelling, *Le Rhin*, pp. 56 ff.

[3] Regulations for the Free Navigation of the Rhine, Hertslet, *The Map of Europe by Treaty*, I, 75.

[4] Arts. 11 and 21. The riparian states were France, Netherlands, Baden, Bavaria, Hesse, Hesse-Nassau, and Prussia.

authority which may serve as a means of communication between the states of the Rhine upon all subjects relating to navigation." Somewhat more specifically, the Commission was charged with the appointment of a chief inspector and with supervision and control of that officer; the appointment of three deputy inspectors who together constituted a permanent administrative authority; the publication of an annual report on the state of navigation of the Rhine; and, finally, the drawing up of regulations for navigation of the Rhine which, when approved by the governments, would take the place of the existing articles.[5] The Commission was also charged with acting as a court of appeal in cases involving disputes relating to the collection of duties. Each state was charged with the establishment of a judicial authority for each office for the collection of duties located on its territory, the judicial authority to hear cases in the first instance. Appeal was then to lie either to a state tribunal of second instance or to the Central Commission.[6]

It may therefore be said that the original commission was charged by terms of the Convention with three types of functions more or less distinct from one another: the selection of the chief administrative officer and the control of all the administrative staff, rule making, and review of decisions by judicial bodies of first instance. The method of taking the decisions and the nature of the obligations imposed by them differed somewhat in each case. Although, in general, the rule of state equality was observed in the make-up of the Central Commission, it was discarded in the selection of the chief inspector and the three deputy inspectors. The former was elected by majority vote of the Commission, but the commissioners did not cast equal votes. For this purpose the Prussian commissioner possessed one-third of the total vote, the French

[5] Arts. 12, 16, 21, 32.   [6] Arts. 8, 9.

and Dutch commissioners one-sixth each, and the remaining third of the voting power was divided among the commissioners of the German states, other than Prussia, in proportion to the extent of their respective possessions on the banks of the Rhine. The three deputy inspectors were chosen by the states rather than by the Commission. The first was chosen by Prussia, the second, alternately by France and the Netherlands, and the third by the German states, other than Prussia, by whatever method they agreed upon. The Commission possessed power to dismiss any of the inspectors but to do so required a two-thirds vote. When voting on this question, voting power was distributed among the commissioners in the same way as when electing the chief inspector.[7]

In all other matters, the most important of which may be described as the drafting of regulations and the review of decisions by courts of first instance, decisions were taken by an absolute majority of votes and each commissioner possessed a vote of equal weight.[8] However, a very important difference existed between the nature of the obligations imposed by decisions in the two cases. Judgments rendered in review cases were final, no further appeal being allowed.[9] But in other cases, i. e., those in which the Commission was exercising rule-making authority, decisions were not binding on the states until consent was given by their commissioners.[10]

Little change of importance was made in the competence, composition and procedure of the Central Commission by the Treaty of Mayence, March 31, 1831,[11] the Treaty of Mannheim, October 17, 1868,[12] or even by the Treaty of Frankfort, May 10, 1871.[13] By the Treaty of

[7] Arts. 13, 14.
[8] Art. 17.
[9] Art. 9.
[10] Art. 17.
[11] *Rijndocumenten* I, 212.
[12] *Ibid.*, p. 80; Martens, *Nouveau recueil général*, XX, 355.
[13] Hertslet, *The Map of Europe*, III, 1954.

Mayence the Commission was charged with reporting to the states on the manner in which regulations for the conduct of navigation were being applied, suggesting new regulations to them, and recommending to the appropriate state authorities the undertaking or the hastening of work for the improvement of the river bed, tow paths, or any other projects useful to navigation.[14] The appellate jurisdiction of the Commission was to be exercised only in cases involving fifty francs or more.[15] The treaty specified in somewhat more detail the system of weighted voting to be used in the election or removal of the chief inspector,[16] and the number of deputy inspectors was increased from three to four.[17] Decisions continued to be by majority and were made obligatory for those states whose commissioners had voted for them.[18]

At the time of the Treaty of Mannheim, the number of parties represented on the Commission had been reduced by one by reason of the annexation of Nassau by Prussia following the War of 1866. Otherwise, the provisions in respect to the personnel of the Commission remained unchanged.[19] Some changes were made, however, in the powers to be exercised. The new convention charged the Commission with four functions. First, it was to examine all complaints made concerning the application of the

[14] Art. 93.

[15] Art. 86.

[16] Art. 95. Prussia was assigned 24 votes, France 12, Netherlands 12, Baden 11, Hesse 6, Bavaria 4, and Nassau 3.

[17] Art. 101.

[18] Art. 94 was as follows: " La Commission centrale prendra ses décisions à la pluralité absolue des voix, qui seront émises dans une parfaite égalité. Mais ses membres devant être regardés comme des agens des Etats riverains, chargés de se concerter sur leurs intérêts communs, ses décisions ne seront obligatoires pour les Etats riverains, que lorsqu'ils y auront consenti par leur commissaire.

" Elle pourra non plus émettre en son nom des lois et de nouvelles ordonnances, ni imposer à un Etat riverain quelconque de nouvelles obligations, qu'il prétendrait ne pas avoir contractées."

[19] Cf. Art. 43.

convention or any of the subsidiary rules made by common agreement of the riparian states. Second, it was to give consideration to all propositions submitted by the riparian governments concerning Rhine navigation, particularly to those envisaging completion or modification of the existing convention or any of the subsidiary regulations entered into by the governments. Third, it was to continue to render opinions in cases appealed from the locally established courts of first instance. Finally, it was charged with the preparation of an annual report on the state of Rhine navigation.[20] Decisions continued to be taken by majority vote but the Commission was weakened slightly inasmuch as its decisions were obligatory only when approved by the governments,[21] exception being made, of course, for decisions rendered by the Commission as an appeal tribunal. The reduction of the membership from an uneven to an even number resulted in the President of the Commission, elected annually by the members, being given a casting vote in appeal cases.[22] Almost the last vestige of state inequality disappeared from the Commission with the abolition of the office of chief inspector and, consequently, of the system of weighted voting used for his election and removal.[23]

In 1871, France ceased to be a riparian by reason of her forced cession of Alsace and Lorraine to the German Empire. Although this meant that by the terms of the Treaty of Versailles, February 26, 1871, confirmed by the

[20] Art. 45.

[21] Art. 46 was as follows: " Les résolutions de la Commission centrale seront prises à la pluralité absolue des voix, qui seront emises dans une parfaite égalité. Ces résolutions ne seront toutefois obligatoires qu'après avoir été approuvées par les Gouvernements."

[22] Art. 44.

[23] The member states continued to share unequally in the common expenses of the Commission. The expenses were divided into 72 parts, Baden paying 11, Bavaria 4, France 12, Hesse 6, Netherlands 12, and Prussia 27. Art. 9, *Protocale de Cloture*. Each state continued to pay its own commissioner. Art. 47.

Treaty of Frankfort, May 10, 1871, the entire upper river had passed into German hands, it did not cause any major change in respect to the Rhine Commission. The terms of the Constitution of the German Empire left to the states virtually complete control of internal navigation, subject, of course, to respect for existing treaty arrangements. Hence, the Central Commission was able to continue as before, the French representative being replaced by one named by the Reich Government to sit for Alsace-Lorraine.

In summary, one might say that during this period the Commission enjoyed substantially the status of a diplomatic agency for the riparian powers. It had no authority to adopt in its own name new laws or regulations for Rhine navigation. Although it might suggest new regulations or the modification of existing ones by majority vote, the rule that no new obligation could be imposed upon any state without its consent, tended to throw the Commission back on use of the unanimity rule. Only when sitting as an appeal tribunal deciding upon the rights of individuals did the Commission resemble an independent international agency. And even here, the arming of this body with final jurisdiction probably resulted less from a community interest in uniform interpretation of the fluvial law than from a desire on the part of each state to permit their nationals recourse to a tribunal in which their own state would be represented. This conclusion seems to be warranted by the fact that the Commission was not given exclusive final jurisdiction.

The Treaty of Versailles, June 28, 1919, brought important changes in the Rhine Commission. By terms of Article 354 of that treaty, the Convention of Mannheim of 1868 was to continue to govern navigation of the Rhine subject to such modification as the Versailles Treaty itself provided. By reason of her annexation of Alsace and Lorraine, France had again become a riparian. Moreover, she became a riparian with special privileges. Article

358, for instance, gave her the right to take water from the Rhine to feed navigation and irrigation canals (constructed or to be constructed) and also exclusive right to the power derived from works of regulation on the river between the two extreme points of the French frontier, subject to payment to Germany for half the power actually produced.[24]   To a lesser extent Belgium and Switzerland, the latter for the first time considered a riparian, were given special status.   By Article 361 Belgium was permitted to draw from the Rhine water for a deep-draught Rhine-Meuse navigable waterway, provided the construction be undertaken within twenty-five years. Switzerland, by Article 358, might, on her demand, exercise rights on the part of the river forming her frontier comparable to those granted France on her frontier, subject, however, to such request being approved by the Central Commission.   Germany was to facilitate these undertakings in various ways.   For example, she was to permit France to construct such works as were necessary on the German bank of the Rhine as well as on her own bank.[25]   Should Belgium undertake her deep-draught waterway, Germany was bound to construct, in accordance with the plans of the Belgian Government approved by the Central Commission, that part situated within German territory.   Failing execution by Germany, the Commission itself might undertake the work.[26]   However, the exercise of these rights was not to be permitted to interfere with the navigability of the Rhine nor to involve any increase in the tolls formerly levied.   To assure these results the Central Comission was elevated to the position of guardian, all schemes for development requiring its approval prior to their execution.[27]

But the Commission could not be raised to such a stra-

---

[24] For the special position of France see Articles 65 and 354-362 of the Versailles Treaty.

[25] Art. 358.   [26] Art. 361.   [27] Art. 359.

tegic position without at the same time making fundamental changes in its constitution.   In the French view,
merely to return to France the seat held prior to 1871
appeared futile.   The Rhine concessions made to her by
terms of the treaty would be defeated by a Commission
on which hostile representatives predominated.   A majority must be favorably inclined toward the interests of
France.   Nor must the representatives of a single state
have power to prevent the Commission from arriving at
decisions with legal validity.   Consequently, as examination of the drafting of the Rhine clauses at the Paris Conference will reveal, the French delegation showed determination from the first to establish a definitely pro-French
majority on the Central Commission and to provide for
effective majority decision.   The first aim resulted in
marked departure from the rule of state equality which
had, in a general way, been observed in the Rhine Commission, and the inclusion for the first time of non-riparian
states.   The second aim, somewhat less successfully executed, led to an attempt to make the Commission less a
diplomatic agency for recording the wills of member
states and more nearly an independent administrative
agency taking effective decisions by majority vote.

As early as December 2, 1918, the Foreign Affairs Commission of the French Chamber of Deputies had started
clamoring for French preponderance on the Rhine Commission.[28]   Consequently, it is by no means surprising that
the initiative should have been taken by the French Government in supplying draft plans for reconstitution of the
Central Commission to the Commission of the Peace Conference established for consideration of matters pertaining
to ports, waterways, and railroads.   At the session of
March 13, 1919, the French delegation submitted their
first plan for constitution of the new Central Commission.

[28] W. J. M. Van Eysinga, *La Commission Centrale pour la Navigation
du Rhin*, p. 109.

They suggested that it be composed of one representative each from the Netherlands, Belgium, and Switzerland; one from each of the German riparian states now constituted or which might in the future be constituted; representatives of France to a number equal to those of the Netherlands, Belgium, Switzerland, and the German states; and one representative each from the United States, Great Britain, and Italy. In addition, the seat of the Commission was to be moved from Mayence to Strasbourg and the presidency was to belong always to one of the French delegates.[29]

The plan, which undoubtedly called for more French representation than France expected to receive, did not evoke a hearty response from all delegations. Crespi (Italy) pointed out that actually the part of the Rhine on which France should have an influence was rather limited. Incontestably, the greatest part of the river lay in German territory. To give France such a preponderant influence in the Commission would appear impossible. It would be better to award France the same representation as Germany.[30] General Mance (Great Britain) expressed a similar view.[31] In defense of their plan the French delegates declared it was essential that Germany should not have a majority on the Commission. Because of their commercial relations with her, the neutral states could be expected to vote with the German delegates. It followed, therefore, that France must have representation equal to that of Germany and the neutrals in order that the balance might be held by the more or less disinterested non-riparian powers. They conceded, however, it was possible that Belgium might, in general, vote with France, making representation equal to Germany, Netherlands, and Switzerland suffice for France.[32]

On March 15, France submitted a second plan. This

[29] *La Documentation Internationale,* VI, 151.
[30] *Ibid.,* p. 155.　　　　[31] *Ibid.*　　　　[32] *Ibid.*

called for two representatives each for Netherlands and Switzerland; one for each of the German riparian states (four); representation for France equal to the total for Netherlands, Switzerland, and Germany; and two each for Great Britain, Italy, and Belgium, and for the United States if the latter would consent to be represented. The President was to be one of the French delegates and the seat of the Commission was to be at Strasbourg.[33] However, the American, British, and Italian delegates were unwilling to accept a plan which on its face appeared to carry such gross over-representation of France. Consequently, Crespi proposed a compromise plan which was accepted by the Commission and later by the Conference. Netherlands and Switzerland were to have two seats each; the German riparian states four; France four, with the right to appoint an additional representative as President; and Great Britain, Italy, and Belgium two each. Whatever be the number of members present, each delegation was to have power to record a number of votes equal to the number of representatives allotted to it.[34] Prior to the adoption of this plan, the United States delegation in the Commission had announced the decision of its government against accepting representation in the Central Commission.[35]

French preoccupation with the securing of a definite majority on the Central Commission suggests expectation on their part that decisions would be taken by majority vote. One of the American delegates, M. O. Hudson, pointed out to them that they were giving an exaggerated importance to majorities in the Central Commission so long as Article 46 of the Convention of Mannheim continued in force.[36] By terms of that article resolutions

[33] *Ibid.*, p. 181.
[34] *Ibid.*, p. 193. See also Article 355 of the Treaty of Versailles.
[35] *Ibid.*, p. 173.   [36] *Ibid.*, p. 174.

adopted by the Central Commission are obligatory only after having been approved by the governments. Although the chief French delegate, M. Claveille, attacked the article as one imposing an intolerable procedure,[37] the French were not successful in securing its termination. The chief obstacle to this proved to be the Netherlands, one of the parties to the Convention of Mannheim but not party to the Treaty of Versailles. The changes in the Convention of Mannheim sought through the terms of the Versailles Treaty could have legal validity only when consented to by the Netherlands. That the Dutch had no intention of surrendering their veto rights on acts of the Central Commission was quite apparent from the statements of their representatives before the Waterways Commission of the Peace Conference. Under the Convention of Mannheim, they declared, each riparian had one vote and decisions had been taken by unanimity. The system had worked very well and the Dutch saw no reason to alter it.[38]

The result of this difference was compromise. The protocol regarding the adhesion of the Netherlands to the modifications introduced by the Treaty of Versailles in the Convention of Mannheim, signed January 20, 1921, contained no provision relative to the matter.[39] It did, however, provide that the Netherlands should be represented by three commissioners rather than by the two assigned in Article 355. The Netherlands' desire to increase her representation may be explained by the quest for prestige quite as much as an appreciation that, in fact, majorities were going to be more important than they had been under the old order.

When the Commission actually assembled at Strasbourg, it became apparent that the Allies desired to interpret the Convention as amended by the Treaty of

[37] *Ibid.*, p. 174.   [38] *Ibid.*, p. 300.   [39] *L. N. T. S.*, XX, 113.

Versailles as permitting majority decision of a binding character. The Netherlands delegation desired to adhere strictly to the letter of Article 46 of Mannheim, and assign legal validity to the Commission's rulings only after the consent of member states had been obtained.[40] The result was the negotiation of an additional protocol, signed March 29, 1923, in which a compromise interpretation was accepted. The protocol was as follows:

> In view of the differences of opinion with regard to the interpretation to be given to the stipulations concerning the resolutions adopted by the Central Commission for the Navigation of the Rhine, and for the purpose of ensuring the practical working of that Commission pending the coming into force of the revised Act provided for under Article 354 of the Treaty of Versailles, the undersigned delegates of the Belgian, French, British, Italian, and Netherlands Governments have agreed that the said stipulations shall be applied in the following manner:
>
> The Resolutions of the Central Commission for the Navigation of the Rhine shall be adopted by a majority of votes.
>
> No state shall be obliged to take steps for the execution of any resolution which it may have refused to approve.
>
> The present conclusion shall be considered as an integral part of the Protocol signed at Paris on January 21, 1921.[41]

Although it would not appear that this protocol could be obligatory for either Germany or Switzerland, the Commission has, in fact, adhered to the arrangement. Consequently, the adoption of this protocol marked a definite step away from the unanimity rule which had been virtually requisite under the unrevised Convention of Mannheim. Undoubtedly, the chief motivating force was the desire of France, shared to a lesser extent by other Allied governments, to create an authority which could not be brought to a standstill by opposition from Germany, or Germany and her neutral supporters. It appears equally

[40] Cf. Van Eysinga, pp. 113-114.   [41] *L. N. T. S.*, XX, 117.

clear that had it not been for the opposition of the Netherlands, France and the supporting Allies would have gone
further and adopted majority rule for the Commission
without any restrictions being attached.

In the actual practice of the Commission, the protocol
of 1923 does not seem to have interfered materially with
effective majority decision. In the first place, many of the
matters dealt with did not require governmental action by
all states. Consequently, the governments of minority delegates had no opportunity to veto the majority decision.
For example, if the Commission by majority vote had
authorized diversion of water by one power, opposing
states, having no duties in respect to the execution, would
have had no opportunity to prevent the decision from
becoming effective. In the second place, a definite community of interest existed in the maintenance of uniform
police regulations for the Rhine. Refusal by some to execute regulations would have introduced confusion no
riparian state desired. Although the exercise of certain
other powers by majority vote of the Commission might
appear more likely to have provoked refusal to execute,
in reality, that does not appear to have occurred on any
occasion.[42] In fact, the Commission gave some indication
of becoming an entity quite independent of the governments. This independence was shown in various ways. On
many occasions the Commission acted upon propositions
submitted to it with such rapidity as to make prior consultation with the governments quite impossible. The
spirit of independence also manifested itself in the relations between the Central Commission and other international administrative agencies. This movement in the
direction of independence from the governments should
not be attributed entirely to the power to act by majority
vote. Among other factors one might mention the presence
of representatives of non-riparian states less intimately tied

[42] Cf. Van Eysinga, p. 125.

to Rhine affairs, the naming by the governments of commissioners who were at the same time serving on other riparian commissions with the consequent tendency to carry over their practices to the Rhine Commission, and the presence of a secretariat desirous that the Commission should take the initiative.[43]

The denunciation by Germany on November 14, 1936, of Part 12 of the Treaty of Versailles relating to the Rhine, Danube, Elbe, Oder, Moselle, and Niemen rivers and to the Kiel Canal, accompanied by the withdrawal of commissioners,[44] was but a logical continuation of the policy of the party in power in Germany since January 1933, to terminate by unilateral act all unequal treaty stipulations imposed upon Germany. The action appears entirely unrelated to the activities of the Central Commission itself. The legal effect of Germany's unilateral denunciation does not appear entirely clear. Two powers, France and Czechoslovakia, lodged express protests with the German Government but Italy declared that under present conditions she would no longer take part in the work of the Commission.[45] It would appear that the Commission could have continued to function without German and Italian participation so long as the other states continued to send representatives to Strasbourg. However, the scope of the Commission's activity would naturally have been greatly reduced inasmuch as Germany would not recognize the validity of decisions reached by it. Appeals from German courts of first instance to the Central Commission were abolished immediately following the denunciation of November 14, 1936.

---

[43] *Ibid.*, pp. 120-135.
[44] *Times* (London), Nov. 16, 1936, p. 11.
[45] *Ibid.*, Dec. 3, 1936.

The European Commission of the Danube

All persons familiar with international affairs are aware of the conditions giving rise to international regulation of the Danube River.[46]   The Danube, as a highway for transport of grain from central Europe, has great commercial and political importance. Yet as late as the middle of the nineteenth century its navigation was made precarious by negligence on the part of Russia. The inconveniences inflicted far greater losses on such states as Great Britain and Austria than upon the territorial power responsible for tolerating them. It is not surprising, therefore, that numerous representations should have been made to Russia concerning the matter nor that the representations should, in general, have gone unheeded.[47]   The Crimean War, however, offered opportunity to adjust the situation. Freedom of navigation on the Danube and the creation of some supervisory authority were named by Great Britain, Austria, and France among the conditions for the peace. Consequently, the Treaty of Paris of 1856 laid down the fundamental law in respect to the Danube, a law which remained in force until May 16, 1939, when it was superseded by the provisions of the Convention signed at Sinaia, August 18, 1938.[48]

Actually, the settlement at Paris resulted in the creation of two commissions: a Danube European Commission, including non-riparian states, and intended to have tem-

[46] For brief accounts see Chamberlain, pp. 13-113; E. Krehbiel, " The European Commission of the Danube: An Experiment in International Administration," *International Conciliation*, No. 131, pp. 544 ff.

[47] See the correspondence between Great Britain and Russia respecting obstructions to the navigation of the Soulina channel of the Danube, 1849-1853, in *B. & F. State Papers*, XLIV, 417 ff.

[48] The Treaty of Paris will be found in Martens, *Nouveau recueil général*, XV, 710; *B. & F. State Papers*, XLVI, 8; Hertslet, *The Map of Europe*, II, 1250. For the Arrangement and Final Protocol relative to the Exercise of the Powers of the European Commission of the Danube, signed at Sinaia, Aug. 18, 1938, Miscellaneous No. 1, H. M. Stationery Office, 1939.

porary existence only, and a Danube River Commission
made up of riparians, intended as a permanent agency.
The former, composed of one representative each from
Great Britain, Austria, France, Prussia, Russia, Sardinia,
and Turkey, was charged with undertaking such works as
were necessary below Isatcha, to clear from the mouths of
the Danube the sand and other impediments which obstructed navigation. In order to meet the expenses of
such work, the Commission was authorized to levy duties,
the rates to be determined by majority vote, on the condition that the flags of all nations be treated on a basis of
perfect equality.[49] On the Riparian Commission, Austria,
Bavaria, the Sublime Porte, and Wurttemberg were represented by one delegate each, and three other commissioners, whose nominations should be approved by the
Porte, represented the three Danubian Principalities. This
commission was to prepare navigation and police regulations for the river, remove impediments to navigation
from the channel, order and cause to be undertaken all
necessary works throughout the whole course of the river,
and, after the dissolution of the European Commission,
undertake its work in respect to the mouths of the
Danube.[50] Adoption of navigation and police regulations
required the consent of all commissioners and subsequent
ratification by the powers.[51] The European Commission
was expected to complete its work in two years. Dissolution was to be pronounced by the signatory powers assembled in conference.[52]

In reality, however, it was the European Commission,
designed in 1856 to have temporary existence, which became the permanent regulatory body for the Danube. This
appears to have resulted from the tendency of the Riparian
Commission to be unduly solicitous of the interests of the
riparian states, sometimes at the expense of the non-

[49] Art. 16.   [50] Art. 17.   [51] Art. 19.   [52] Art. 18.

13

riparians whose interests were great, as well as from the very successful operation of the European Commission itself. The powers, meeting in conference at Paris in 1858, refused to ratify the rules of navigation drawn up by the Riparian Commission, and when Austria proposed dissolution of the European Commission in accordance with Article 18 of the Treaty of Paris, the representatives of France, Great Britain, Prussia, Russia, and Sardinia opposed.[53] Shortly thereafter Austria suggested that the European Commission be charged with drawing up police and navigation rules for the Danube and that its life be extended until such time as the powers were willing to transfer its functions to the Riparian Commission. This proposition was adopted June 20, 1861.[54] However, the legality and obligatory character of the regulations established remained in doubt until approved by the powers in the Public Act of November 2, 1865, ratifications of which were exchanged June 1, 1866. In addition to giving the navigation and police regulations contained in the annex the force of law, the agreement provided they might " be modified, according to need, by the European Commission or by the authority which shall be substituted for it by virtue of Article 18 of the Treaty of Paris." [55]

The affairs of the Danube were again discussed by a conference at Paris in 1866. No agreement could be reached on a date for transfer of the work of the European Commission to the Riparian Commission. The result was an agreement, later approved by the governments, to extend for five more years the life of the European Commission.[56] In 1871, British protests against Russian attempts to absolve herself from the Black Sea stipula-

[53] *La Commission Européenne du Danube et son œuvre de 1856 à 1931,* p. 18.
[54] *Ibid.,* p. 20.
[55] *B. & F. State Papers,* LV, 119.
[56] *La Commission Européenne du Danube,* p. 23.

tions in the Treaty of Paris, following the Franco-Prussian War, brought about another conference of the powers signatory to that treaty, meeting on this occasion in London. Great Britain proposed prolonging the life of the European Commission for twenty-six years. However, the other powers considered this excessive, and a compromise agreement was reached to extend the Commission's existence for another twelve years to April 24, 1883.[57] No change was made in the composition or powers of the Commission.

The Treaty of Berlin, July 13, 1878, brought important changes. Roumania was to be accorded representation on the European Commission, thus increasing its membership to eight, and the jurisdiction of the Commission which had extended only to Isatcha was extended to Galatz to be exercised "in complete independence of the territorial authorities."[58]   One year before the expiration of the term assigned for the duration of the Commission the powers were to come to an understanding in respect to its prolongation or the modifications they considered necessary to introduce.[59]   The European Commission, assisted by delegates of the riparians, was also authorized to draw up regulations in respect to navigation, river police, and supervision to apply from the Iron Gates to Galatz, to be in harmony with those issued for the river below that point.[60]   For this purpose the European Commission met with representatives of Bulgaria and Serbia, from December, 1880, to June, 1882, and formulated regulations the execution of which was placed under the supervision of a mixed commission composed of the Austro-Hungarian delegate as president, and one delegate each from the riparian states of Bulgaria, Roumania, and Serbia, and a fifth from the European Commission selected by

[57] Art. 4, Treaty of London, in Hertslet, *The Map of Europe,* III, 1919.
[58] Art. 53, in Hertslet, IV, 2759.   [59] Art. 54.   [60] Art. 55.

rotation from among the other members for a six months term.[61]

On the initiative of Great Britain, a conference of the states signatory to the Treaty of Berlin met in London in 1883 to negotiate in respect to the Danube. The resulting treaty, signed March 10, 1883, extended the jurisdiction of the Commission from Galatz to Ibraila [62] and extended the life of the Commission for a period of twenty-one years, dating from April 24, 1883.[63] Moreover, the powers of the Commission were to continue in force by tacit prolongation for successive terms of three years unless one of the parties to the treaty should notify, one year before the expiration of one of those terms, its intention of proposing modifications in the constitution or powers of the Commission. Provision was also made to the effect that all treaties, conventions, acts, and arrangements relating to the Danube and its mouths were maintained in force in so far as they were not abrogated or modified by the stipulations of the Treaty of 1883.[64]

From 1883 until interrupted by the World War, the Commission exercised its powers in accordance with the

---

[61] *La Commission Européenne du Danube,* p. 30.

[62] Art. 1, in Hertslet, *The Map of Europe,* IV, 3104.

[63] Art. 2.

[64] Art. 8. Roumania was not a party to the Treaty of 1883 and repeatedly denied its validity. The result was a situation of uncertainty as regards the powers of the European Commission upon the sector of the river between Galatz and Braïla, a situation which eventually led the states concerned, namely, Roumania, the territorial power, and France, Great Britain and Italy, the other powers represented on the Commission, to submit the matter to the Council of the League of Nations. The latter referred the matter to the P. C. I. J. for an advisory opinion. The majority of the Court found that the *de facto* situation before the war included the exercise by the European Commission of the same powers between Galatz and Braïla as below Galatz. Roumania had accepted the situation by accepting the Definitive Statute of the Danube in 1921. It mattered very little whether the actual exercise by the European Commission of its powers in the disputed sector was based before the war on a legal right or on mere toleration. *Publications of the P. C. I. J.,* Series B, No. 14 (1927).

Treaty of 1883. At the close of the war, provision was made in the Treaty of Versailles for resumption by the European Commission of the Danube of the powers it had possessed prior to the outbreak of the war. However, as a provisional measure, and for reasons which are quite apparent, membership was to consist only of representatives of Great Britain, France, Italy, and Roumania.[65] From the point where the competence of the European Commission ceased, the Danube system was placed under the administration of an International Commission.[66] Provision was also made for a conference of states nominated by the Allied and Associated Powers, attended by delegates of the defeated powers, to meet within one year for the purpose of drawing up provisions for a Danubian regime.[67] This conference, which took place at Paris in August, 1920, was attended by delegates from Belgium, France, Great Britain, Italy, Roumania, the Serb-Croat-Slovene State, and Czechoslovakia as well as by representatives from Germany, Austria, Bulgaria, and Hungary. The United States was invited to send a representative but the government found itself unable to do so.[68] For the most part, however, the attention of this conference was directed to the fluvial Danube to be placed under the newly constituted International Commission rather than to the maritime Danube which remained under the European Commission. Freedom of navigation was reaffirmed and the European Commission was declared to retain the powers and extent of jurisdiction it possessed before the war.[69] However, two slight changes should be noted.

---

[65] Art. 346.   [66] Art. 347.

[67] Art. 349 of Versailles. Corresponding articles appear in the Treaties of Saint-Germain (Art. 304), Neuilly (Art. 232), and Trianon (Art. 288).

[68] *Conférence Internationale pour l'Etablissement du Statut Définitif du Danube*, I, 6.

[69] Arts. 1, 5, 6, Definitive Statute of the Danube, in Great Britain, *Treaty Series,* 1922, No. 16; *A. J. I. L.,* Supplement, XVII, 13.

First, any European state which in the future " is able to prove its possession of sufficient maritime commercial and European interests at the mouths of the Danube " may, at its request, be accorded representation on the commission by a unanimous decision of the governments already represented.[70] Second, the powers of the European Commission can be terminated only by an international agreement concluded by all the states represented on the Commission.[71] The draft convention submitted to the conference by the French delegation, and used as a basis for discussion, had carried an article providing that the powers of the European Commission could be modified or terminated by means of an international agreement in which all states signatory to the present convention participated.[72] However, the German delegate objected to modification of the powers of the Commission by such a procedure, holding that, since the powers were given by the Treaty of Versailles, they could be modified only by the consent of the parties thereto. The result was amendment of the article on first reading to exclude any statement concerning modification and to provide for termination of the Commission by agreement of all the states represented on the Commission rather than by consent of the signatories to the present convention.[73]

The composition of the European Commission and the

[70] Art. 4. In the conference, the Greek delegation suggested that the Commission be made up of one delegate each from France, Great Britain, Greece, Italy, and Roumania and that its composition be modified by consent of four-fifths of the states represented on the Commission. (*Conférence Internationale pour l'Etablissement du Statut Définitif du Danube,* I, 48.) On March 1, 1939, Germany acquired membership through a Protocal signed at Bucharest by all states members of the Commission. (*Bulletin of International News,* March 11, 1939, p, 227.)

[71] Art. 7. The powers of the Commission were terminated by the agreement signed at Sinaia in August, 1938, in force, May 16, 1939. *Bulletin of International News,* June 3, 1939, p. 584.

[72] *Conférence Internationale pour l'Etablissement du Statut Définitif du Danube,* I, 9.

[73] *Ibid.,* I, 135 ff. and II, 544 ff.

scope of its powers were established by the international agreements reviewed above. It remained for the Commission itself, subject to the conditions imposed by the treaties, to determine its own rules of internal organization and procedure. At its first session, November 4, 1856, the Commission established itself at Galatz and made provision for creation of a Central Bureau composed of a Secretary-General and administrative staff, and for an Engineering Corps composed of a Chief Engineer and subordinate technicians. The Commission adopted a *Règlement* to govern its own procedure but this was the subject of frequent change between 1856 and 1878.[74]

However, after the Treaty of Berlin had increased the membership of the Commission and greatly increased its jurisdiction as well as virtually assuring the prolongation of its life, the Commission formulated a permanent *Règlement* governing its own operations. These rules, adopted in 1879, subject to amendments made at the first session of the Commission after the World War, May 24, 1920, remained in force until May 16, 1939, when they were modified by the terms of the Arrangement signed at Sinaia in 1938.[75]

Each year the Commission held two regular sessions at Galatz, one in the spring and one in the autumn.[76] At least three delegates were required to be present. Special sessions could be called on the request of three delegates, but such special sessions could be held away from the seat of the Commission only when the Commission so decided by unanimous vote.[77] The presidency rotated among the titular delegates in accordance with the alphabetical order

[74] *Commission Européenne du Danube*, pp. 65 ff.
[75] The rules appear in *Commission Européenne du Danube*, pp. 466 ff.
[76] Art. 4.
[77] Art. 7.

of the names of the states.[78]　Only titular delegates were permitted to sit in the extraordinary sessions.[79]

The rules of procedure provided for majority decision for two types of questions.　First, a majority vote sufficed in matters of form (*questions de forme*) such as those pertaining to the internal organization of the Commission, the relations of the Commission to its employees, and the execution of measures previously decided by the Commission.　Second, by virtue of the provisions of Article 16 of the Treaty of Paris (1856), a majority vote was sufficient for modification of the navigation tolls.　However, on questions of substances (*questions de fond*) unanimity was required.　Moreover, any titular delegate who was absent when a decision was taken, and not represented by his deputy, had the privilege of recording his vote in writing.　Decisions requiring unanimity became final only after two months had been allowed for the recording of negative votes by absent delegates.　For decisions requiring a majority only, but actually voted by less than a majority of the total membership of the Commission, a like period was allowed for the recording of the votes of absent delegates.[80]　A resumé of all propositions to be

[78] Art. 1. Since the War, each power represented on the Commission has named a titular delegate and a deputy. It is not at all unusual for several of the titular delegates to represent their countries on several international river commissions. Hence the provision for deputy delegates. For France, Italy, and Great Britain the deputy delegates are generally their consuls resident in Galatz. Lists of delegates and deputies from 1856 to 1930, may be found in *Commission Européenne du Danube,* pp. 75 ff.

[79] Art. 7.

[80] Art. 12 reads as follows: " Les décisions sont prises à la majorité des voix:

" (a) Quand il s'agit de questions de forme, notamment du service intérieur de la Commission, des rapports de la Commission avec ses employés, des détails des mesures arrêtées par le Plenum;

" (b) Lorsqu'il s'agit de modifier le Tarif des droits de navigation établi en vertu de l'article 16 du Traité de Paris du 30 mars 1856. ' Sur les questions de fond, pour lesquelles l'unanimité est requise, les déci-

discussed at a session of the Commission was sent to all delegates by the Executive Committee at least one month before the session convened.   Propositions presented in the course of the session could not, as a rule, be voted at the same meeting.   Propositions involving an increase in the tolls could be voted only at the regular session following that at which they were submitted.[81]

In the intervals between sessions of the Commission, the task of assuring the execution of its decisions and dealing with current administrative affairs fell on the shoulders of an Executive Committee.   This Committee was composed of the titular delegates, or their deputies, present at the seat of the Commission.   In practice, this meant that the work generally was carried forward by the consuls resident in Galatz who served as deputy delegates. Two constituted a quorum.   When only a single delegate was present he was invested with power to deal with current matters as well as those matters which would not permit delay.   Absent delegates were kept informed of the decisions taken.[82]   The decisions of the Executive Committee could be taken by majority vote in all cases in which a similar vote would suffice in a plenary session of the Commission.   In all other cases, unanimity was requisite.[83] On all questions of importance, the Executive Committee was obliged to consult the absent titular delegates.   Their replies were awaited for one month.   If replies were not received in that interval, the Executive Committee could act, but it had to give full account at the next plenary session of the measures taken.[84]   For the Commission to

---

sions prises à l'unanimité des Délégués présents deviennent définitives deux mois après leur communication aux Délégués absents, à moins d'un vote contraire formel émis par un ou plusieurs de ces Délégués, avant l'expiration dudit délai de deux mois.

" ' Les Délégués absents doivent aussi être consultés de la même manière quand il s'agit de décisions pour lesquelles la majorité suffit et qui n'auraient obtenu pendant la session que la majorité relative.' "

[81] Art. 5.   [82] Art. 13.   [83] Art. 19.   [84] Art. 20.

sit as a tribunal to hear appeals from the decisions of the
inspector of navigation or the captain of the port at Soulina in matters of policing, at least three titular delegates
or their deputies were required to be present.[85]

The powers of the European Commission, it must be
conceded, were quite remarkable. The body possessed distinct juridical personality. It had complete control over
navigation of the Danube to Braïla.[86] It laid and collected tolls on vessels using the river and those sums were
paid into its own treasury, giving the Commission a measure of financial independence. It established navigation
rules of an obligatory character. Lighterage, towage, and
pilotage facilities were under its supervision through its
control of the licensing of these services. It had complete control of the engineering work, the marking of the
channel, and the maintenance of lighthouses on the Isle
of Serpents and at the mouths of the river. It established
and operated hospitals for seamen at the port of Soulina.
All these functions were performed by employees appointed and subject to removal by the European Commission. Breaches of the navigation or toll regulations were
punished by fine or withdrawal of licenses, penalties being
inflicted in the first instance by administrative officers,
with appeal lying to the Commission itself. The Commission possessed no police force of its own but relied instead
upon use of the guard ships which the states members of

[85] Art. 15.

[86] The advisory opinion issued by the Permanent Court of International
Justice, Dec. 8, 1927, greatly strengthened the jurisdiction of the Commission. Not only did the majority of the Court hold that the powers of
the Commission were substantially the same between Galatz and Braïla as
below Galatz, a point long contested by Roumania, but they also rejected
all possibility of providing a territorial demarcation for the powers of
the Commission. They found the European Commission to exist for the
purpose of assuring freedom of navigation and equal treatment of all
flags. Hence a functional criterion for demarcation of the Commission's
powers was suggested as more suitable than a territorial definition. *Publications of the P. C. I. J.*, Series B. No. 14 (1927).

the Commission were authorized to keep at the mouths of the Danube. Each acted to enforce regulations against ships flying its own flag, that of Roumania, the territorial power, acting against the ships of those states not represented on the Commission. Criminal and civil jurisdiction remained, of course, in the hands of the Roumanian government.[87]

It must be recognized, however, that the states possessing representation on the Commission carefully guarded their own control over the exercise of these extensive powers. In the first place, the commissioners were in no sense independent of their governments. They were appointed and paid by their respective governments and, of course, were subject to removal at any time. In general, they were drawn from the diplomatic and consular services and were expected to act on the instructions given. As noted above, the rules of procedure were so formulated as to provide ample opportunity for instructions to be obtained. In the second place, the *liberum veto* was retained by each member state for use when occasion demanded. True, the tolls were fixed by the Commission by majority vote but in accordance with principles stipulated in the treaties. Likewise questions of form were settled by majority, only those involving matters of substance (*questions de fond*) being reserved for unanimous consent. But the Commission was never able to reach an agreement on the formulation of a precise definition of the line of division between the two classes of decisions.[88] Consequently, the rule remained in the somewhat vague form in which it was given in the *Règlement*. In the absence of clear precedents to the contrary, member states were in an excellent position to insist that *questions de*

[87] Cf. Chamberlain, pp. 95-96.
[88] See the statement of M. Albert Legrand, representative of France on the European Commission in 1919. *Conférence Internationale pour l'Etablissement du Statut Définitif du Danube*, I, 376.

fond be construed in a rather inclusive way when occasion demanded. Such important matters as amendment of the rules of navigation and decision in respect to the undertaking of engineering projects clearly fell within the *questions de fond* classification. Likewise, it may be suggested that the very liberal quorum provisions constituted an important deviation from unanimity. These rules did, in fact, materially facilitate the functioning of the body. It was able to proceed with its work without necessity of awaiting the presence of all delegates. But one should not overlook the carefully framed provisions of the *Règlement* designed to assure each government of being kept informed so that it might, if it deemed it desirable, veto propositions adopted provisionally in the absence of its own delegate. In this respect, the unanimity rule of the European Commission was more drastic in its operation than that of many other international organs wherein unanimity is deemed to have been achieved if all present and voting support the proposition in question.[89]

In reality, the greatest deviation from unanimity was found in the composition of the European Commission, a departure not wholly successful. From its creation in 1856, the Commission was an organ of the great powers of Europe supplemented by the territorial power, Turkey, and, after 1878, by Roumania as well. By provision of the Treaty of Versailles membership was provisionally reduced to include only representatives of France, Great Britain, Italy, and Roumania. The Statute of 1921 added that membership might be increased by unanimous decision of the represented governments to include " any European state which, in future, is able to prove its possession of sufficient commercial and European interests at the mouths of the Danube." Thus three great powers and

---

[89] For example, note how the rule is interpreted by the Council and Assembly of the League of Nations. Riches, *The Unanimity Rule and the League of Nations*, pp. 42 ff.

the territorial power most directly concerned had for themselves the function of regulation of Danube navigation below Braïla as well as the determination of when others were to participate in this regulation.

On May 16, 1939, the international control of the lower Danube, which had lasted since 1856, came to an end. The flag of the European Commission was lowered at Soulina and that of Roumania hoisted in its place.[90]   By terms of the agreement signed at Sinaia, August 18, 1938,[91] the European Commission of the Danube ceased to exercise the powers conferred upon it by earlier acts so that future arrangements may be compatible with the sovereign rights of Roumania.   Authority over the port of Soulina and the technical work at the mouths of the Danube passed to the Roumanian Government as did control over the corps of river pilots.[92]   Infringements of navigation regulations are now exclusively within the jurisdiction of the territorial power.[93]   The European Commission continues to exist, with membership widened to include Germany,[94] but its authority is restricted to drawing up navigation and police regulations, tariff schedules and plans for river improvement, all upon proposal of the Roumanian Government.   Decisions of the Commission in these matters are taken by majority vote, " but the vote of the Roumanian delegate must form part of the majority." [95]

[90] *Bulletin of International News,* June 3, 1939, p. 584.
[91] Miscellaneous No. 1, H. M. Stationery Office, 1939.
[92] Arts. 2, 3, 4.
[93] Art. 18.
[94] *Bulletin of International News,* March 11, 1939, p. 227.
[95] Arts. 6, 10.

CHAPTER VIII

DECISION IN INTERNATIONAL RIVER COMMISSIONS
(Continued)

The International Commission of the Danube

The activities of the International Commission of the Danube, created in accordance with Articles 347 of the Treaty of Versailles, 302 of the Treaty of Saint-Germain, 230 of the Treaty of Neuilly, and 286 of the Treaty of Trianon, pertained to the fluvial Danube from the point where the competence of the European Commission ceased (Braïla) to Ulm. In accordance with these articles it was composed of two representatives of German riparian states (Wurttemberg and Bavaria), one representative of each other riparian state (Austria, Czechoslovakia, Hungary, Jugoslavia, Bulgaria, and Roumania), and one representative of each non-riparian state represented on the European Commission of the Danube (France, Italy, and Great Britain). In accordance with treaty provisions, the Commission was to undertake provisionally the administration of the river in accordance with specified principles until such time as a definitive statute could be drafted by representatives of the states nominated by the Allied and Associated Powers.[1] In the Treaties of Saint-Germain, Neuilly, and Trianon it was also specified that decisions of this commission would be taken by majority vote.[2]

The Conference called by the Allied and Associated Powers for the purpose of drafting the Definitive Statute of the Danube assembled in Paris in August, 1920. Representatives of Belgium, France, Great Britain, Greece, Italy,

---

[1] Art. 348 of Versailles; Art. 303 of Saint-Germain; Art. 231 of Neuilly; Art. 287 of Trianon.

[2] Arts. 303, 231, 287, respectively.

Roumania, the Serb-Croat-Slovene State, and Czechoslovakia were present as well as delegates from Germany, Austria, Hungary, and Bulgaria. The United States was asked to send a representative but failed to do so.[3] The conference resulted in the production of a Statute which was signed July 23, 1921, and, ratifications having been deposited, entered into force June 30, 1922.[4]

The powers accorded by the Statute to the International Commission were definitely less far-reaching than those enjoyed by the European Commission. As noted above, the European Commission exercised what amounted, in essence, to state control over navigation within its domain. The International Commission, on the contrary, confined itself in large part to the role of supervisory authority.[5] On the portion of the Danube river system placed under its authority, the Commission was charged with seeing that no obstacle be placed in the way of unrestricted navigation; that there be access to and use of the ports and their equipment; that there be equality of treatment for the subjects, goods, and flags of all nations; and, in general, that the international character of the river system suffer no prejudice.[6] Each riparian state was authorized to draw up an annual program of work for the maintenance of the waterway which was submitted to the Commission for its certification of conformity with navigation requirements. On the basis of these plans a general program of important works of improvement was prepared by the International Commission.[7] Execution, however, was not by the Commission but by the riparian states themselves. However, when the latter were unable to

[3] *Conférence Internationale pour l'Etablissement du Statut Définitif du Danube,* I, 6.

[4] Great Britain, *Treaty Series,* 1922, No. 16, Cmd. 1754.

[5] Cf. G. Sherman, "The International Organization of the Danube under the Peace Treaties," *A. J. I. L.,* XVII, 438.

[6] Art. 10.

[7] Art. 11.

undertake the work, the Commission was authorized to do it.[8] Works undertaken by riparians for flood protection, irrigation, or the production of hydro-electric power could be forbidden by the Commission only when found detrimental to navigation. Final decision had to be given within four months after the riparian state had notified its desire to construct.[9]   States could impose navigation tolls to defray the initial cost or maintenance costs of works to improve navigation on authorization given by the Commission. When works were undertaken by the Commission itself, it also could lay tolls to meet the costs.[10]   Dues levied were required to be moderate in amount and based solely on tonnage of ships, never on goods transported. The system of assessment was subject to modification by unanimous vote of the Commission.[11] In event of a state being able to prove that the expenditures involved in the maintenance of a navigable channel substantially exceeded what would be required in the interests of its own traffic, the Commission could apportion the costs among the benefiting states.[12] Where the river formed the boundary of two or more states and when those states could not themselves agree on a program for maintenance of navigability or on sharing the costs, the Commission itself could determine the conditions under which the works were to be carried out.[13]   The International Commission could draw up navigation and police regulations. However, these regulations could only be brought into force by appropriate legislative or administrative act of the individual states. Policing was entrusted to the riparians themselves.[14] The Commission had no authority to punish offenders by fines or by the revoking of licenses as had the European Commission. Rather,

[8] Art. 12.
[9] Art. 14.
[10] Art. 16.
[11] Art. 18.

[12] Art. 15.
[13] Art. 18.
[14] Arts. 24, 25, 26.

offenders were dealt with in the courts of the riparian states, the Commission being informed of the measures taken.[15] The Commission itself was competent to decide all questions relative to the interpretation and application of the Statute. But any state which believed a decision of the Commission to be *ultra vires* or otherwise in violation of the terms of the Statute could submit the matter to the League of Nations. States territorially interested could appeal to the League against decisions of the Commission on other grounds. The Commission possessed a corresponding right to refer to the League any dispute arising from failure on the part of a state to comply with a decision of the Commission taken in virtue of its powers under the Statute.[16]

Although the Commission had important powers for guiding riparians through the planning of navigation works and the drafting of navigation regulations, in large part, its powers were of a negative rather than of a positive character. It stood as an agency ready to intervene whenever freedom of navigation or equality of treatment was threatened, whether the danger resulted from the neglect of a riparian, a direct act of interference, or inability of riparians to reach agreement for common action. Only in the event of failure by the riparians did the Commission assume powers of a positive character. Even in such a situation, it will be noted, its powers were limited. When the riparian failure involved neglect of works of maintenance, the Commission itself could act. However, when it involved instead, failure to enact legislation to assure equality of treatment to the goods and vessels of all nations, as guaranteed by the Statute, the Commission had no authority to substitute its own regulations. The best it could do was to appeal to the defaulting state and, that failing, appeal to the agency provided by the League of

[15] Art. 30.   [16] Art. 38.

14

Nations, for an opinion holding the riparian state internationally delinquent. Revision of the Statute, and consequently of the powers of the International Commission, could be undertaken on request of two-thirds of the signatory states. The request addressed to the French Government was required to specify the stipulations which appeared to require revision. In such circumstances the French Government agreed to summon, within six months, a conference of all signatory states.[17] Unanimity was, of course, required for adopting a revised text.

With three exceptions, decisions by the International Commission were taken by a two-thirds majority vote, at least two-thirds of the total membership being present.[18] Unanimity, however, was requisite for extending the jurisdiction of the Commission to cover waterways other than those named in Article 2 of the Statute.[19] A similar vote

[17] Art. 42.

[18] Art. 35 of the Statute is as follows: " The International Commission determines its own method of procedure by regulations drawn up in plenary session. When establishing the annual budget, the commission will decide upon the measures to be adopted to meet the general expenses of its administration. The commission fixes the number of its ordinary and extraordinary sessions and the place where they shall be held, and constitutes a permanent executive committee, composed of the commissioners or their deputies present at the seat of the commission, and responsible for carrying out the decisions taken during the plenary session and for proper conduct of the service.

" The presidency of the commission is held for a period of six months by each delegation in turn in the alphabetical order of the states represented.

" The commission may only validly deliberate when two-thirds of its members are present.

" Decisions are taken by a majority vote of two-thirds of the members present."

[19] Art. 9. Article 2 provides: " The international river system referred to in the preceding article consists of:

" The Morava and the Thaya where in their courses, they form the frontier between Austria and Czechoslovakia;

" The Drave from Barcs;

" The Tisza from the mouth of the Szamos;

" The Maros from Arod;

" Any lateral canals or waterways which may be constructed, whether

was required for altering the basis for assessment of the river tolls from that fixed in the Statute.[20] Either action would, in fact, have amounted to an amendment of the Statute. Consequently, it is not surprising that the powers should have insisted upon unanimity in such cases. The third deviation from the normal two-thirds rule was found in connection with the appointment of the administrative staff of the Commission. The chief of the permanent secretariat had to be chosen from among the nationals of a non-riparian state represented on the Commission (France, Italy, Great Britain). The chief of the technical department could be appointed by the statutory majority of the Commission if he was a national of a non-riparian state, whether represented on the Commission or not. But to appoint a national of a riparian state, unanimity was re-required. The chief of the navigation service had to be selected from the nationals of a European state not represented on the Commission. No restrictions were placed on the selection of the head of the accounting and tax-controlling department.[21]

As noted above, the Treaties of Saint-Germain, Neuilly, and Trianon all specified that decisions of the International Commission should be taken by majority vote. Undoubtedly the Allied powers included these majority stipulations in the terms of the treaties because the ex-enemy powers were being accorded representation. Maintenance of the customary unanimity rule would permit their deadlocking the Commission. It may, therefore, be of interest to discover how the two-thirds rule, with the exceptions indicated, came to be written into the Statute in place of the simple majority rule.[22] Following customary

---

to duplicate or improve naturally navigable portions of the river system, or to connect two naturally navigable portions of one of these waterways."

[20] Art. 18.   [21] Art. 27.

[22] To be sure, the treaties say "majority vote" which might be interpreted to mean a qualified rather than simple majority. However, Article

international practice, the French delegation, as host to
the conference, submitted a project for a convention which
was accepted as a basis for discussion. This project, as
one might expect, provided for decision by majority vote,
in case of equal division the President having a casting
vote.[23]   However, rival projects were submitted by the
delegations of Greece, the Serb-Croat-Slovene State, and
Roumania, and the Hungarian delegation submitted a
rather extended criticism of the French plan.   In the
projects of Greece [24] and Roumania,[25] no statements appear concerning the vote necessary for decisions in the
International Commission, implying acceptance of majority vote as specified in the treaty provisions.   In their
comments, the Hungarian delegation suggested the insertion of a requirement of a two-thirds majority vote for
decisions of peculiar importance or delicacy such as a
decision to divide maintenance costs among several states
rather than place the entire burden upon the particular
riparian state in whose territorial jurisdiction the maintenance work fell.[26]   The Serb-Croat-Slovene project, however, made a direct attack upon majority decision, an
attack which was carried into the debates of the conference by their representative, and which resulted in the
adoption of the more cumbersome two-thirds rule for the
Commission.   In the original project submitted by this
delegation it was not intended to eliminate majority decisions as such, but rather to make them completely im-
potent by adding the provision that a vote concerning a

---

362 of the Treaty of Trianon seems to substantiate the case for holding
a simple majority was meant. It reads as follows: "The High Contracting Parties agree that, in the absence of a subsequent agreement to the
contrary, the Chairman of any Commission established by the present
Treaty shall in the event of an equality of votes be entitled to a second
vote."

[23] *Conférence Internationale pour l'Etablissement du Statut Définitif
du Danube,* I, 8.

[24] *Ibid.,* I, 48.   [25] *Ibid.,* I, 66.   [26] *Ibid.,* I, 63.

question touching the "vital interests" of a state would be obligatory for it only in case its delegate had been present and had voted for it.[27] As each state would, of course, have been competent to determine for itself what matters touched its "vital interests," this would have amounted to introducing in the Statute a rule substantially identical with that carried in Article 46 of the Convention of Mannheim for the Rhine Commission.

When the conference reached consideration of the French article calling for decision by the Commission by a simple majority vote, the delegate of the Serb-Croat-Slovene State asked that it be amended to provide unanimity in questions involving "vital interests." [28] No other delegation supported this proposition although the delegation of Czechoslovakia declared in favor of a qualified majority in exceptional cases.[29] The Roumanian delegation urged that the Statute fix a quorum requirement of two-thirds or three-fourths but that decisions be taken by a simple majority, since it would seem that unanimity almost never could be obtained on all the diverse questions on which the International Commission would be expected to pronounce.[30] The President, M. Legrand (France), stated that to introduce the unanimity rule in a deliberative body such as the International Commission would condemn it to impotence. However, in order that agreement might be reached in the conference, he suggested amendment of the article to require the presence of two-thirds of the members of the Commission for valid deliberation and decision by two-thirds vote of those present. This suggestion was accepted by the conference.[31]

The requirement of unanimity when the head of the technical department (chief engineer) was selected from among the nationals of a riparian state was inserted on

[27] *Ibid.*, I, 55.
[28] *Ibid.*, I, 378.
[29] *Ibid.*, I, 377.
[30] *Ibid.*, I, 377.
[31] *Ibid.*, I, 378.

motion by the delegate of Roumania.[32] The provision authorizing the Commission to extend its jurisdiction to waterways other than those enumerated in Article 2 of the Statute was included on motion of Great Britain, actively supported by Belgium. It was their position that it would be regrettable to require a special conference and a new convention whenever it might seem wise to extend the jurisdiction of the Commission to waterways which had previously not been considered sufficiently navigable or sufficiently important to merit international control.[33] But the Roumanian delegate was again responsible for adding the unanimity requirement. It was his view that turning over such a power to an international river commission would constitute an invasion of state sovereignty. The British proposition would be acceptable only if accompanied by a requirement of unanimity for adoption of such a decision.[34] However, when the conference considered the power of the Commission to alter the basis for fixing tolls, positions were reversed. The unanimity requirement was here inserted on demand of the non-riparian great powers rather than by the small riparians. It was the British view, supported by Italy, that the basis fixed by the convention for establishing tolls should be modified only by agreement of the signatories or by unanimous vote of the Commission. The delegates of Austria, Roumania, and Greece suggested a qualified majority of the Commission while Czechoslovakia favored unanimity of the riparians.[35] The conference finally accepted the clause: " This system of assessment based on ship's tonnage may be revised by unanimous decision of the Commission at the expiration of a period of five years." [36]

The Commission first met, for organization purposes, in June, 1920. Two other sessions were held in Sep-

[32] *Ibid.*, II, 946.
[33] *Ibid.*, II, 506.
[34] *Ibid.*, II, 507.
[35] *Ibid.*, II, 694-695.
[36] *Ibid.*, II, 1186.

tember and December of the same year. From that time until November 14, 1936, when its work was interrupted by Germany's repudiation of the river clauses of the Versailles Treaty, the Commission had been holding two regular sessions of about two weeks duration each year, usually in June and November. In performing the functions given it by terms of the Statute, the Commission had not been without success. Among other things, it drew up a uniform set of navigation and police regulations, successfully administered the service at the Iron Gates and fixed the dues to be imposed upon ships utilizing it, examined the programs of maintenance work submitted annually by the states, and, in some cases, had even taken the initiative in inducing the states to take prompt action in keeping the river in satisfactory condition.[37] However, many of the important questions submitted to the Commission had not been decided by that body but rather decision had been postponed. Undoubtedly, this resulted, in part, from the fact that decision to act meant an increase in the budget of the Commission, an increase which could be met only by contributions from states already experiencing budget difficulties or by the imposition of navigation dues which the Commission was loath to impose. At the same time, it should be recognized that postponements were not infrequent on questions of principle or even administrative detail in no way involving immediate financial obligation.[38] This suggests that the two-thirds rule, written into the Statute to satisfy a single power so that unanimity might be achieved in the drafting conference of 1920, proved something of an obstacle to the successful functioning of a body representing the views of ten different powers.

[37] Cf. League of Nations, *Report on Danube Navigation submitted to the Advisory and Technical Committee for Communications and Transit* (League Doc. C. 444(a). M. 164(a). 1925. VIII), pp. 51 ff.

[38] Cf. *ibid,* Annex IX, for a summary of the decisions taken and matters postponed by the Commission during its first six years of activity.

The Permanent Technical Hydraulic System Commission of the Danube

The Treaty of Trianon, June 4, 1920, provided in Article 293 for the creation of a Permanent Technical Hydraulic System Commission of the Danube to be composed of one representative of each state territorially concerned, with a chairman appointed by the Council of the League of Nations. The Commission was established with headquarters at Rome. Regulations pertaining to the functioning of the body were drawn up and approved May 27, 1923, in a convention entered into by Austria, Hungary, Roumania, Jugoslavia, and Czechoslovakia. They entered into force September 30, 1924.[39]

The Commission was charged in particular with supervision of the execution of all interstate compacts or agreements pertaining to canalization, drainage, irrigation and such other matters made under authority of Article 292 of the Treaty of Trianon. It could perform such other functions as were entrusted to it by unanimous agreement of the interested states.[40]

In general, decisions were taken in this body by majority vote, four members constituting a quorum. However, a state whose delegate had voted with the minority had no obligation to take measures for the execution within its territory of a majority decision unless it later gave its express consent. In case of an equal division of votes, the Council-appointed President of the Commission had no casting vote.[41] In the performance of a few functions, such as the preparation of a list from which the President could provide himself with assistants, decisions were valid only when taken by unanimous vote.[42]

[39] Hudson, *International Legislation*, II, 1022.
[40] Art. 3, Regulations.
[41] Art. 11, *ibid*.
[42] Art. 9, *ibid*.

The International Commission of the Elbe

By Article 340 of the Treaty of Versailles provision was made for placing the Elbe under the administration of an international commission composed of four representatives of the German riparian states bordering on the river, two representatives of Czechoslovakia, and one each from Great Britain, France, Italy, and Belgium. Whatever the number of delegates present, each delegation was to have the right to record a number of votes equal to the number of representatives allotted to it. Clearly, the intention was to provide enough representation for the non-riparian Allied powers to assure the newly constituted state of Czechoslovakia an outlet to the sea through German territory by way of the Elbe. In accordance with treaty stipulations, the powers concerned appointed plenipotentiaries who met at Dresden for the purpose of drawing up a Statute of Navigation for the Elbe. The convention was signed February 22, 1922, and entered into force July 18, 1924.[43]

By terms of the Statute, the Elbe system, which was placed under the authority of the Commission, comprised the Elbe from its confluence with the Vltava (Moldau) as far as the open sea, and the Vltava from Prague to its confluence with the Elbe. The system was subject to extension by decision of the riparian state or states territorially concerned, with the unanimous approval of the Elbe Commission.[44]

The powers of the Commission were, in large part, restricted to a supervisory character. In no sense did the convention authorize it to exercise what might be called state control over the Elbe or Elbe navigation. By Article 2 of the Statute the Commission was charged:

[43] *L. N. T. S.,* XXVI, 219. Also in Great Britain, *Treaty Series,* 1923, No. 3, and *A. J. I. L.,* XVII, Supplement, 227.
[44] Art. 1.

(a) To supervise the conservation of the freedom of navigation, the maintenance in good order of the navigable channel and the improvement of the channel;

(b) To pronounce upon complaints arising out of the application of the present convention and likewise of the regulations which it contemplates;

(c) To decide whether the tariffs applied are in accordance with the conditions laid down by the present convention;

(d) To pronounce upon the claims preferred in appeal before it:

(e) And, in general, to exercise the powers arising out of the provisions of the present convention.

The Commission will secure that all inquiries and inspections which it judges useful are carried out by the persons appointed by it for that purpose. It must provide for the participation of the authorities of the riparian states in all inspections and journeys carried out by itself or by persons appointed by it.

Among the powers of the Commission which arose from terms of the Statute were a number pertaining to the maintenance of transit privileges. The riparian states were required to draw up lists of places for the approval of the Commission where masters or owners shipping goods under seal might, under riparian supervision, break seals in order to tranship the cargo or lighter the boat.[45] The Commission was to be notified of all public ports where masters, owners, and raftsmen were allowed to discharge or unload cargo or to take shelter.[46]

The Commission had some powers in respect to navigation licenses. Each riparian had exclusive authority to grant permits to its own residents, but those not habitually resident in either received permits either from one of the riparians or from the Commission itself.[47] Permits might be withdrawn only by the granting authority but the Commission was authorized to demand revocation by giving

[45] Art. 21.   [46] Art. 24.   [47] Art. 29.

proof of incompetence involving danger to navigation.[48] The Commission was empowered to establish a form for " identity papers " to be held by all members of crews sailing the Elbe.[49] It approved drafts of regulations for river police submitted by the riparians and could " fix the definitive text of these regulations." However, they were put in force only by the appropriate legislative or administrative act of the riparian state.[50]

Each riparian carried out at its own expense the works for the maintenance of the channel and towing paths within its jurisdiction. In that section constituting a frontier between Germany and Czechoslovakia, the two states were instructed to reach a common accord concerning the work to be done and the apportioning of the expense. Failing such an agreement, the Commission was authorized to decide what was to be undertaken and how the costs were to be met.[51] Riparians furnished the Commission with the description of all works they proposed to undertake (other than current maintenance work on channel and tow paths), particularly that in respect to flood control, irrigation, and hydraulic power. The Commission could prohibit the execution of such works only in so far as they might entail consequences prejudicial to navigation.[52] In exceptional circumstances, the Commission was authorized to decide that large improvement works for navigation purposes justified the imposition of dues fixed at moderate rates. A decision to this effect was valid only if it expressed the opinion of at least seven of the ten delegates.[53] On the basis of the proposals of a riparian state, the Commission could adopt a program of improvement works, the execution of which was a matter of primary interest. Riparian states were bound to execute such work programs if the programs involved no direct

[48] Art. 32.
[49] Art. 33.
[50] Art. 37.

[51] Arts. 39, 40.
[52] Art. 41.
[53] Art. 42.

financial obligation on their part.   However, under no
circumstances could works be undertaken if the state on
whose territory they were to be executed opposed them
on the score of " vital interests." [54]

Each riparian was required to make provision for
tribunals to hear cases arising out of breaches of the river
police regulations and other matters affecting navigation.[55]
Appeal from judgments pronounced by such tribunals
might be brought either before an appellate court of the
country in which the judgment was pronounced or before
the Commission.[56]   The appellate jurisdiction of the Com-

[54] Art. 43.

[55] Art. 44.

[56] Art. 46. On January 27, 1923, the states signatory to the Elbe Convention entered into a Supplementary Convention in respect to the jurisdiction of the tribunals referred to in the Convention. The Supplementary Convention was signed at Prague and entered into force July 18, 1924. (*L. N. T. S.,* XXVI, 253.) Articles 1, 2, and 4 are as follows:

Article 1. " The tribunals provided for in Article 44 of the Statute of Navigation of the Elbe of Feb. 22, 1922, have jurisdiction, in so far as navigation above Hamburg and Harburg is concerned:

(i)   To investigate and pronounce judgment on breaches of police regulations in respect of navigation;

(ii) To decide disputes relative to:
  (a) Damages caused by masters, owners, and raftsmen during a voyage or in coming alongside;
  (b) The amount of salvage dues and other indemnities arising from shipwreck;
  (c) The engagements and obligations existing between proprietors, masters, owners, raftsmen, pilots, hands, and passengers;
  (d) The payment of dues levied under Article 42 of the Statute of Navigation above mentioned.

Article 2. " The competent tribunal according to Article 1 is:

In the case of paragraph (i) the tribunal within whose jurisdiction the offense was created.

In the case of paragraph (ii) (a) and (b), the tribunal within whose jurisdiction the damage was caused or assistance given.

In the case of paragraph (ii) (c), the tribunal within whose jurisdiction the contract is to be performed.

In the case of paragraph (ii) (d), the tribunal within whose jurisdiction the dues are payable."

Article 4. " The appeal to the Commission for which provision was made in Article 46 of the Statute of Navigation lies in the cases, and

mission, it will be noted, resembled closely that given the Rhine Commission in the Convention of 1815. It does not appear to have been designed to secure uniformity in the interpretation of the river law, for if that had been the case, the appellate jurisdiction would have been lodged exclusively in the Commission. Rather, it seems to have been established as a means of guarding the nationals of a state from possible prejudice in the courts of another state.

All questions arising among the parties relative to the interpretation and application of the Statute were to be settled by the Commission. In event of a dispute arising out of decisions of the Commission on the ground of incompetence or violation of the Statute, each contracting state was recognized as having the right to refer the matter to the League of Nations. On all other grounds, the appeal to the League for settlement of the dispute was reserved to the states territorially interested.[57]

Finally, the Commission was empowered to seek uniformity in the law and regulations applicable to commerce and navigation on the Elbe, as well as uniformity in the general conditions governing labor employed in navigation of the waterway, by drawing up draft conventions for submission to the interested states.[58]

As the above summary shows, the powers of the Commission were generally of a supervisory or standard-setting character. It had authority to protest against actions in violation of the Statute and power to refuse authorization of actions by riparian states which the Commission be-

---

under the conditions, laid down for appeals by the general legislation of the country in which the judgment of the court of first instance was delivered. In the case, however, of a dispute arising between employers and employees, nationals of the above state, and tried by a tribunal of that country, an appeal to the Commission will only lie when all parties agree to submit to the jurisdiction of the Commission."

[57] Art. 52.
[58] Art. 48.

lieved would be prejudicial to the ends sought by the convention. Likewise it possessed ample authority for guiding the riparians in such things as the preparation of navigation regulations and the performance of river works. The Commission's few powers of a positive character, such as that of issuing and revoking navigation permits to residents of non-riparian states, were designed, like its appellate jurisdiction, as devices for correcting possible prejudicial action by the riparian states rather than for substituting the jurisdiction of the Commission for that of the territorial states.

Subject to a few exceptions, which will be noted presently, all decisions by the Commission were taken by a simple majority vote. When the Commission was sitting in its judicial capacity as a court of review three members representing three different states constituted a quorum. On all occasions deliberations were valid when four delegates were present representing a total of six votes. This meant that decisions could be taken in the absence of a German delegate only when all the five other member states were represented. Only when the Commission was sitting as a court of review did the president[59] possess a casting vote when votes were equally divided. Ordinarily, whatever the number of its delegates present, each delegation possessed a number of votes equal to that of the representatives to which it was entitled. However, when sitting as a court, each delegate possessed but a single vote.[60]

[59] By the terms of Article 4 of the Statute the presidency rotated among the *members* of the Commission rather than among the *delegations*. Thus a German served four-tenths rather than one-sixth of the time. Article 4 of the Final Protocol provided, however, that two delegates of the same nationality might not immediately succeed one another nor might a delegate be president more than once in ten years.

[60] Article 6 of the Statute is as follows:

" The deliberations of the Commission will only be valid if four delegations, representing at least six votes, are present or represented.

" The decision of the Commission will be taken by a majority of votes,

For the performance of one function a vote by an extraordinary majority of the Commission was required. It was the intention of those drafting the Statute that in ordinary circumstances no tolls should be levied on navigation on the Elbe. However, in the event of large improvement works being required, the Commission could permit their costs to be wholly or partly covered by the imposition of tolls upon the classes of ships, boats, and rafts benefiting by the improvement works. But no dues could be fixed or authorized without the express approval of the Commission, the vote being valid only if it expressed the opinion of at least seven delegates.[61] Clearly, the extraordinary majority was required in this instance because it was not intended that the Commission should take this action so long as any possible substitute plan for meeting costs was available.

In two other cases, the Commission could act only by unanimous consent. First, the extent of the international system of the Elbe, over which the Commission had authority, could be extended to include waters not included in the terms as defined by the Statute only by decision of the riparian state or states territorially concerned, subject to unanimous approval by the Commission.[62] The inclusion of this requirement for unanimity in a Statute whose terms provide for simple majority decision in most instances does not appear incongruous, for the taking of

---

save in the cases mentioned in the present Convention where a special majority is required.

" The President has no casting vote when the votes are equally divided.

" Whatever the number of its members present, each delegation shall have a number of votes equal to that of the representatives to which it is entitled."

Article 9 of the Convention Supplementary to the Statute provides:

" The Commission can not decide an appeal unless at least three delegates, belonging to three different delegations are present.

" Judgment is given by majority vote, each delegate having one vote only. In case of an equality of votes the President has a casting vote."

[61] Art. 42.   [62] Art. 1.

such an action would amount, in fact, to an important amendment of the convention forming the basic agreement among the states in respect to the Elbe system and its regulation.

The other matter for which unanimity was required was the selection of the Secretary-General and the Assistant Secretary-General. The former was charged with the custody of the archives, the dispatch of the current business of the Commission, and the submission to the Commission of an annual report on the shipping situation and on the navigable state of the Elbe. The Assistant Secretary-General took part in the preparation of all business and, in the absence of the Secretary-General, acted in his capacity. The two could not be of the same nationality.[63] Unanimity was here insisted upon because it was generally appreciated that the effectiveness of the Statute depended in large part upon its actual administration by the Secretary-General. That being the case neither riparian was prepared to dispense with its veto on the selection of the person to serve. The circumstance of there being but two riparians explains the rather unusual provision for an Assistant Secretary-General to be selected in the same fashion as the Secretary-General and sharing in his work. These conclusions are supported by the terms of an agreement entered into by Germany and Czechoslovakia at the time the Elbe Statute was drafted. It follows:

With regard to filling the posts of Secretary-General and Assistant Secretary, provided for in the Elbe Statute, the German and the Czechoslovak Governments are agreed on the following points.

(1) The Secretary-General and Assistant Secretary shall be selected from nationals of the two riparian States.

(2) The Secretary-General and Assistant Secretary shall be appointed alternately by the two States, and shall hold office for

[63] Art. 7.

ten years. On the coming into force of the Statute, Germany shall appoint a Secretary-General.

(3) Both Governments, therefore, undertake to instruct their delegates to vote for the candidates respectively nominated as Secretary-General and Assistant Secretary, unless they have valid objections to raise against the person selected.

(4) In accordance with the Statute, the election of both officials shall be by a unanimous vote. Should it prove necessary, in the absence of unanimous vote, to employ substitutes to carry out the work pending the final appointment of these officials, the two Governments undertake reciprocally to apply the foregoing agreement (*mutatis mutandis*) with regard to these persons.[64]

German denunciation of the river clauses of the Versailles Treaty, November 14, 1936, coupled with the Italian policy of withdrawing commissioners, made impossible the continued functioning of the Elbe Commission after that date. It will be recalled that Article 6 of the Statute of the Elbe required the presence of at least four delegations with at least six votes for valid deliberation. The destruction of Czechoslovakia as an international person in March, 1939, and the incorporation of Bohemia and Moravia in the greater Germany, naturally eliminated all reason for continued existence of the Elbe Commission.

The International Commission of the Oder

By Article 331 of the Treaty of Versailles certain rivers, including the Oder, were declared international from a point specified in each case. The Oder was declared international from its confluence with the Oppa. The article also provided for the internationalization of " all navigable parts of these river systems which naturally provide more than one State with access to the sea, with or without transhipment from one vessel to another; together with lateral canals and channels constructed either

[64] *L. N. T. S.,* XXVI, 249.

to duplicate or to improve naturally navigable sections of the specified river systems, or to connect two naturally navigable sections of the same river." Article 341 placed the Oder under the administration of an International Commission to be composed of three representatives of Prussia and one representative each from Poland, Czecho-slovakia, Great Britain, France, Denmark, and Sweden. Article 343 provided that this commission should meet within three months from the date of the coming into force of the treaty and prepare a project for the revision of the existing agreements and regulations for the river. Finally, Article 344 provided that the project should designate the headquarters of the Commission and prescribe the manner in which its president was to be nominated; specify the extent of the Commission's powers, particularly in regard to the execution of works of maintenance, control, and improvement on the river system, the financial regime, the fixing and collecting of charges, and regulations for navigation; and define the sections of the river and its tributaries to which the international regime should apply.

In 1920 the Commission organized, established temporary headquarters in Paris, named a Secretary-General, and commenced the work of drafting a statute of navigation. However, difficulties arose in connection with defining the extent of the international regime. The Polish delegate maintained that the Warthe and the Netze should be internationalized only up to the Polish frontier while the Prussian delegate, supported by the representatives of the other powers, held that if the principle of internationalization of tributaries were to be adopted, it must be integrally maintained and the navigable portion of the tributaries situated in Polish territory should not be excluded from the international river system.[65]

[65] *Publications of the P. C. I. J.*, Series E., No. 6, p. 214.

No agreement had been reached by January, 1924, and, in consequence, the governments agreed the matter should be submitted to the Advisory and Technical Committee for Communications and Transit of the League of Nations. In November, 1924, this body adopted by majority vote a suggestion for conciliation but it was rejected by Poland, and Germany reserved opinion.[66]

The Oder Commission, with the approval of the governments represented thereon, then decided upon reference to the Permanent Court of International Justice, and, on November 29, 1928, the Court was asked to decide the following questions:

Does the jurisdiction of the International Commission of the Oder extend, under the provisions of the Treaty of Versailles, to the sections of the tributaries of the Oder, Warthe (Warta) and Netze (Notec), which are situated in Polish territory, and, if so, what is the principle laid down which must be adopted for the purpose of determining the upstream limits of the Commission's jurisdiction? [67]

The Court's judgment, adopted by 9 votes to 3, was given on September 10, 1929. In the opinion of the Court, the matter in dispute turned on the meaning to be given the words of Article 331 of the Versailles Treaty: " all navigable parts of these river systems which naturally provide more than one State with access to the sea." In the view of the Court, these words proved that internationalization was subject to two conditions: navigability and access to the sea for more than one state. But the navigability of the tributaries in question was not disputed in this case. Hence, it remained for the court to decide only on the application of the second condition. In the opinion of the Court, this condition refers to tributaries as such, so that if a tributary in its naturally navigable course

[66] *Ibid.*, p. 215.   [67] *Ibid.*

traverses or separates different states, it falls as a whole within the definition in Article 331. Accordingly, the tributaries do not cease to be international above the last frontier crossing its navigable course.[68]

With the question of the extent of jurisdiction cleared away by the judgment of the Permanent Court, the Commission was able to turn once more to the preparation of a statute of navigation. Such a statute has been prepared but up to the present time has not entered into force. In view of the German action of November 14, 1936, there now appears no prospect of obtaining the consent necessary for the draft statute to become operative.

Other International Waterway Commissions

The riparian commissions described above are without exception the product of multilateral treaties. In all these cases either the riparians number more than two or nonriparian states have been conceded to have an interest in the supervision of the river waters. In addition to these commissions, representing in every case four or more powers, there are a number which have been established by bilateral arrangement providing representation only for the two powers concerned. In some instances these bodies adhere strictly to the rule of unanimity. In other cases, they are permitted to reach all or a part of their decisions by majority vote. It will be appreciated that, where the latter is the case, this is something quite different from majority decision by a commission representing several powers. As equality of representation is maintained without exceptions for all commissions established by bilateral arrangement, majority vote never permits the taking of a decision over the adverse vote of *all* representatives of any one power.

[68] *Ibid.*, p. 220.

International Boundary Commission, United States and Mexico. The treaty between the United States and Mexico, December 30, 1853, provided that where the Rio Grande and Colorado Rivers marked the frontier between the two countries, the actual boundary line should be the middle channel of the stream.[69] But as the Rio Grande frequently changes its course, this meant a changing boundary. To prevent territory from being shifted back and forth between the two powers, provision was made in the Treaty of November 12, 1884, to the effect that in event of changes brought about by erosion, the middle point in the channel should continue to be the boundary. However, where changes were made by avulsion, the boundary was to follow the middle of the original river bed as defined by the Boundary Commission of 1852.[70] Thus, in theory, the boundary was stabilized except as it might move slightly by the slow process of erosion. But considerable uncertainty remained as to the exact location of the boundary, as no agency was provided to determine whether changes had in fact resulted from erosion or avulsion. Moreover, by terms of the same treaty, the two powers had forbidden the construction of jetties, piers, or other works tending to deflect the normal flow of the river.[71] Yet no authority was established for determining whether works being undertaken might have such effect.

On March 1, 1889, practical effect was given to the Treaty of 1884, by a convention providing for an International Boundary Commission to be composed of one commissioner appointed by each power, each assisted by a consulting engineer.[72] This commission was empowered to keep the boundary line up to date by determining after each change in the bed of the Rio Grande or Colorado whether it was the result of erosion or avulsion.[73] The

[69] Art. 1 in Malloy, *Treaties, U. S., 1776-1909*, I, 1121.
[70] Arts. 1, 2, in *ibid.*, I, 1159.   [72] Art. 2, in Malloy, I, 1167.
[71] Art. 3.   [73] Arts. 1, 4.

Commission was also empowered on complaint of local authorities of either country to determine whether works undertaken were in fact in contravention of the provisions of the Treaty of 1884.[74] Decisions reached by agreement of the commissioners are considered binding upon the governments unless notice of disapproval is given within one month. In event of failure to agree each commissioner shall so report to his government, the two governments agreeing to seek a solution by amicable methods.[75]

Although this convention was to remain in force only for five years,[76] it was renewed from time to time, the Convention of November 21, 1900, finally giving it indefinite duration.[77] By treaty of March 20, 1905, the work of the Commission was simplified by provision that the boundary should follow the existing channel of the stream, all " bancos " on the right bank belonging to Mexico and all on the left bank to the United States. However, in the event of a " banco " appearing with an area of more than 250 hectares or a population of more than 200 persons, the old bed of the river was to be considered the boundary.[78]

The International Joint Commission, the United States and Canada. In order to provide a method for settlement of controversies arising out of the use of waters along the boundary of the United States and Canada, Great Britain and the United States entered into a treaty concerning the matter on January 11, 1909.[79] The treaty lays down rules governing the use of the boundary waters and makes provision for an International Joint Commission to apply them. This Commission is composed of six persons, three appointed by the United States and three by Canada.[80]

---

[74] Art. 5.
[75] Art. 8.
[76] Art. 9.
[77] Malloy, I, 1192.

[78] Arts. 1, 2, 3, in *ibid.*, 1199.
[79] *B. & F. State Papers,* CII, 137.
[80] Art. 7.

By the terms of the Convention, the Commission is given three distinct functions. In the first place, it has "jurisdiction over and shall pass upon all cases involving the use or obstruction or diversion of the waters, with respect to which under Articles 3 and 4 of the Treaty, the approval of the Commission is required." Thus it has compulsory jurisdiction in all cases in which use, obstruction, or diversion of the boundary waters is sought either by one of the governments or by private persons. In such cases it may render decisions which are final. In reaching such decisions the Commission must be guided by the order of precedence prescribed by the treaty for the use of boundary waters wherein use for domestic and sanitary purposes is given first place, navigation second, and power and irrigation third. Decision in all such cases may be taken by majority vote of the Commission.[81] The Commission itself has provided in its rules of procedure, which Article 12 of the Convention authorized it to establish, that although a majority of the Commission may conduct hearings, "less than the whole number of the Commission shall not proceed to finally consider and determine any matter proceeding, or question which the Treaty creating the Commission, either in terms or by implication, requires or makes it the duty of the Commission to decide." [82] In case of equal division, the commissioners on each side make reports to their own governments. The two governments shall then endeavor to agree upon an adjustment of the matter, and if agreement is reached, it will be reduced to writing and communicated to the Commission for such further proceedings as may be necessary to carry out the agreement.[83] Although the Commission

[81] Art. 8.
[82] Rule 22. The Rules of Procedure of the International Joint Commission are printed as Annex B in C. J. Chacko, *The International Joint Commission.*
[83] Art. 8.

has dealt with more than a score of cases involving the use of boundary waters, in no instance does it appear to have been equally divided in respect to the rendering of a decision. In the first nineteen cases coming before the Commission in its judicial capacity, decision was reached by unanimous vote in all cases but one.[84]

In the second place, the Commission is authorized to act in the capacity of a commission of inquiry and conciliation. On the request of either the United States or Canada, the Commission is authorized to conduct an investigation and make a report upon any matter " involving the rights, obligations, or interests of either in relation to the other or to the inhabitants of the other, along the common frontier between the United States and the Dominion of Canada." Such reports " shall not be regarded as decisions of the questions or matters so submitted either on the facts or the law, and shall in no way have the character of an arbitral award." Unanimity is not requisite for the adoption of such a report, but should a report be arrived at by majority vote, the minority may also make a report. In case of equal division, separate reports are to be prepared.[85]

Finally, if the two governments desire, they may use the Commission as an arbitral tribunal with power to render a decision upon any question which the two governments shall submit to it. A decision may be rendered by majority vote and is binding. In case the Commission is equally divided or is otherwise unable to render a decision, the commissioners shall make a joint report to both governments or separate reports to their respective governments. The questions or matters involved will then be re-

[84] In the first decision rendered by the Commission, the Kettle Falls Case, the Commission divided 4 to 2. Chacko, p. 363.

[85] Art. 9. For a survey of the first six cases submitted to inquiry see Chacko, Ch. VI. In five of the cases reports were adopted by unanimous agreement.

ferred for decision to an umpire chosen in accordance with the procedure prescribed in Article 45 of the Hague Convention for the Pacific Settlement of International Disputes of October 18, 1907.[86] The Commission has never been called upon by the governments to act in the capacity of an arbitral tribunal.

Roya River Commission. December 17, 1914, France and Italy entered into a treaty for regulation of the use of the waters of the Roya River.[87] Provision was made for a Permanent Commission to be composed of an engineer appointed by France and one appointed by Italy. The Commission was authorized, after the commissioners had received instructions from their respective governments, to deal with applications for the construction of works involving utilization of the river water. Decision naturally depended upon the assent of both commissioners. If they were unable to work out a plan acceptable to both, the two governments agreed to consider what measures should be taken.

Mixed Technical Commission for the River Eneo. In a treaty made July 20, 1925, by Italy and Jugoslavia provision was made for the creation of a Mixed Technical Commission to supervise the necessary works in the River Eneo in order that the use of the waters for power purposes be not affected adversely.[88] The Commission was to be composed of six members, three appointed by each power.[89] The body was authorized " to decide all questions relative to the works and operations " and to " take steps to ensure that the use of the waters . . . for the production of power shall not be adversely affected by such works and operations." [90] Decisions of the Commission were valid only if adopted by the majority of *each* delegation.[91] In

[86] Art. 10.
[87] *B. & F. State Papers,* CVIII, 487.
[88] *L. N. T. S.,* LXXXIII, 87.

[89] Art. 2, Annex I.
[90] Art. 3.
[91] Art. 4.

the event of the failure of the Commission to reach a valid decision, the powers agreed to refer the question involved to arbitration, each party appointing one of its nationals, and the two naming a third from the nationals of a friendly power.[92]

German-Polish Mixed Committees for Frontier Waters. On January 27, 1926, Germany and Poland entered into a treaty providing that in Poland the slarosts and in Germany the district administrators (*Landräte*) should be responsible for the preservation and maintenance of the frontier.[93] Should these authorities be unable to arrive at agreements in respect to the performance of the duties incumbent upon them, Mixed Committees were to be established, consisting of three Polish and three German members, designated by the central authorities of the two contracting powers. Decisions of these Committees were in all cases to be taken by two-thirds vote except where otherwise specified in the terms of the treaty.[94] Unanimity, however, was requisite for decisions pertaining to the regulation of the obligation to maintain bridges and ferries, for any decision involving the establishment of new bridges or ferries, and for the allocation of the costs.[95] Two-thirds vote would appear to have sufficed for authorization of the construction of dams, watermills or other works which might affect the flow of the streams and the level of the waters.[96] Questions in respect to which the Mixed Commissions were unable to reach decisions were to be settled through the diplomatic channel.[97]

Spanish-Portuguese Commission for the Douro River. On August 11, 1927, Spain and Portugal entered into a treaty in respect to the regulation of the frontier section of

[92] Art. 4.
[93] Art. 5, *L. N. T. S.,* LXIV, 159.
[94] Art. 6.
[95] Arts. 24, 25.
[96] Cf. Art. 29.
[97] Art. 6.

the River Douro.[98] Provision was made for an International Commission to be composed of six members, three appointed by each government.[99] By terms of the convention, the Commission was given advisory and supervisory power and, within a restricted field, power to take decisions of a final character. Before the governments make any decision relative to the approval of hydro-electric works or to the authorization or transfer of concessions, the Commission must be heard.[100] The supervisory duties involve the policing of the international section of the waters, in accordance with the laws in force in each country, and the inspection of all works for the purpose of seeing that the terms of concession are fully observed.[101] The Commission is empowered to decide disputes arising out of servitudes, concessions, and such matters.[102]

Decisions of the International Commission are taken by majority vote. In case of equal division, a new vote is taken at the next regular meeting of the Commission.[103] There is, however, one very important qualification of majority decision. *Decisions* taken by the Commission in virtue of its powers granted in Article 18 are final only when adopted unanimously. If taken by majority vote they enter into force only with the express approval of the two governments or after an interval of thirty days has elapsed in which the governments may file objections.[104]

In the event of the Commission being unable to reach a decision, the matter is brought before the two governments to be settled by direct negotiations. Should direct negotiations fail to result in an agreement, the two powers agree to refer the matter to an arbitral tribunal composed of the Commission itself presided over by an umpire. If the dispute refers to a legal question, the umpire shall be

[98] *L. N. T. S.*, LXXXII, 131.
[99] Art. 14.
[100] Art. 17.
[101] Art. 19.
[102] Art. 18.
[103] Art. 21.
[104] Art. 16.

a legal expert appointed by the Permanent Court of International Justice. If the question at issue is of a technical nature, the umpire shall be an engineer appointed by the Zurich-Polytechnical Institute. Should the two governments not agree upon whether the dispute is of a legal or technical character, that question shall be decided by the Permanent Court.[105]

Summary

Examination of the procedure of international commissions which have been set up to regulate the use of rivers of international concern reveals that in every case in which more than two powers are represented some departure has been made from the rule of unanimous consent. However, wherever the commission may reach all or substantially all decisions by majority vote the competence of the body has been carefully guarded by the terms of the convention establishing the organ. Thus, decisions by the Central Commission of the Rhine and by the Permanent Technical Hydraulic System Commission of the Danube were reached by simple majority vote, but no state was obliged to take steps for the execution of any resolution which its representatives had refused to approve. For the most part, decisions by the International Commission of the Danube were reached by two-thirds vote and those by the Elbe Commission were reached by a simple majority, but the powers of both bodies were in large part, of a supervisory character. They authorized rather than required actions by the riparian states. The powers of the European Commission of the Danube were until 1939 much more extensive but it must be recalled always that in this body the undefined *questions de fond* required unanimous consent. Where waterways are controlled by but two states, each appointing a single commissioner, unanimity naturally is requisite for any decision. Where the states each

[105] Art. 21.

appoint several commissioners, convenience generally has dictated that decisions be reached by majority, but inasmuch as equality of representation is always maintained, it is never possible for a decision to be reached over the negative votes of all the commissioners of one power. Wherever a commission is endowed with powers of a judicial character majority action finds complete acceptance.

CHAPTER IX

DECISION IN ADMINISTRATIVE AND TECHNICAL COMMISSIONS

Public international unions show great variation in organization. As indicated earlier, the structure may consist of a bureau or central office supervised by either the government in whose territory it is located or by an international council, a committee or commission, and a periodic conference or congress. In several unions the only organ is the central office. Others possess in addition a commission or a periodic conference. Where the commission is provided in addition to a periodic conference, the power of the former generally is restricted to administrative supervision and the adoption of administrative regulations, new commitments resulting from the deliberations of the periodic conferences or from special diplomatic conferences. Where the commission, except for the central office, is the sole organ of the union its competence is sometimes more extensive. As we have noted, the conferences or congresses in some cases use the rule of unanimous consent while in other cases majority decision has been accepted. Although the commissions tend more generally to reach decisions by majority, here, too, some variation is found in their practices. As the following survey will show, the practice in this respect is related closely to the nature of the powers possessed and to the character of the personnel.

In several unions the body responsible for supervision of the central office is composed of persons selected as individuals rather than as representatives of states. Thus the Directing Committee of the International Hydrographic Bureau is composed of three individuals, technically qualified to direct the work of the Bureau, elected

228

by the Conference. When selecting members of this Committee the Conference uses a system of voting weighted in accordance with naval and mercantile tonnage under the flag of each member state.[1] The members of the Committee must be of different nationalities.[2] The Executive Committee of the International Relief Union is composed of seven persons elected by the General Council of the Union. Ordinarily a two-thirds vote is required for such election but the General Council may, if it sees fit, provide for election by a simple majority.[3] Both the Governing Body and the Managing Committee of the Nansen International Office for Refugees were composed of persons serving in their private capacity rather than as representatives of states. The former consisted of a President named by the Assembly of the League of Nations, four members from the Inter-Governmental Advisory Commission for Refugees named by that body, a member appointed by the Secretary-General of the League of Nations, a member appointed by the Director of the International Labor Office, three members of the Advisory Committee of the Private Organization for Refugees, and two selected from the principal relief organizations by two-thirds vote of the other members of the Governing Body. The Managing Committee consisted of the President of the Governing Body and two other members appointed by that body.[4] The International Committee of the Metric Union consists of eighteen members, nationals of different states, elected by the General Conference of the Union.[5] Although the members are required to be

[1] Arts. 35, 59 and Appendix E, *Statutes of the International Hydrographic Bureau,* Monaco, 1932. See below, p. 253.
[2] Art. 22, *ibid.*
[3] Arts. 4, 5, Statute of Relief Union, *L. N. T. S.,* CXXXV, 247.
[4] Arts. 5, 8, Statute of the Nansen International Office for Refugees, in League of Nations, *O. J.,* 1931, p. 309; Hudson, *International Legislation,* V, 872.
[5] Art. 2, Convention of 1921 modifying the Convention of May 20,

of different nationalities, they are selected primarily upon the basis of their scientific attainments. Finally, it will be recalled that the Governing Body of the International Labor Organization is made up in part of persons selected to represent governments and in part of persons selected as individuals by the employer and worker sections of the Conference.[6]

It so happens that each of the bodies just mentioned has been charged with duties of some importance in addition to the supervision of the bureaus or permanent offices of the unions. The Directing Committee of the Hydrographic Bureau may exercise, with certain exceptions, the powers of the Conference during the five year intervals between meetings of the latter body.[7] The Executive Committee of the Relief Union has very extensive powers in respect to the collection, employment, and investment of funds of the Union and, in case of disaster, may make decisions in respect to the organization of relief.[8] The Managing Committee of the Nansen Office was authorized to exercise all powers delegated to it by the Governing Body, the supreme authority of the Office.[9] The International Committee of the Metric Union is charged with the direction of all metrological works which the contracting parties decide to carry out in common.[10] The Governing Body of the International Labor Organization has important powers in respect to the preparation of the agenda of the Labor Conferences and in securing the compliance of member states with their obligations under the conventions.[11]

1875, for assuring the International Uniformity and Perfection of the Metric System, *L. N. T. S.,* XVII, 46.

[6] See above, p. 98.

[7] Art. 61 of the Statute of the Hydrographic Bureau.

[8] Cf. Arts. 7, 8, 9 of the Statute of the Relief Union.

[9] Art. 7, of Statute of Nansen Office.

[10] Regulations attached to the Convention of 1875, *B. & F. State Papers,* LXVI, 562; *B. P. P.,* 1875, LXXXIII.

[11] Arts. 400 and 408-420 of the Treaty of Versailles.

Although each of these bodies may be said to be charged with functions somewhat more far-reaching than those exercised by many commissions associated with public international unions, substantially all decisions of the bodies in question may be reached by simple majority vote.[12] This suggests that once powers have been delegated to bodies made up of persons over whom member states have no direct control, reason no longer exists for maintenance of the unanimity rule. The rule no longer possesses practical utility for the states, nor is it of any significance in relation to questions of prestige. Hence, the convenient rule of majority decision finds ready acceptance.

However, the personnel of permanent international commissions charged with supervision of central offices or bureaus is more frequently recruited on the state representative basis. In some cases there is a perfect equality of participating states or administrations both in number of representatives allowed and in voting power. This is true in respect to each of the following bodies: the Executive Committee of the International Institute of Refrigeration,[13] the Administrative Council of the International Exhibitions Union,[14] the International Committee of the International Office for Epizootics,[15] the Baltic Geodetic

[12] Cf. Art. 26 of the Statute of the Hydrographic Bureau; Art. 3 of the Statute of the Relief Union; Arts. 8 and 16 of the Rules of Procedure of the Nansen Office (*O. J.,* 1931, p. 746); Art. 13 of the Regulations attached to the Metric Convention of 1875; and the Standing Orders of the Governing Body of the International Labor Organization. A few exceptions to the simple majority rule should be noted: To adopt a budget for the Metric Union in excess of 250,000 francs, but not exceeding 300,000 francs per annum, a unanimous vote of the International Committee is required (Art. 2, Convention of 1921). A two-thirds vote of the Governing Body of the International Labor Organization is required to reject the nomination of an individual to the panel from which Commissions of Inquiry are drawn (Art. 412 of the Treaty of Versailles).

[13] Art. 5, Convention for the Foundation of an International Institute of Refrigeration, *L. N. T. S.,* VIII, 65.

[14] Art. 12, Convention concerning International Exhibitions, *L. N. T. S.,* CXI, 343; Hudson, IV, 2553.

[15] Art. 6, Agreement for the Creation of an International Office for Epizootics, *L. N. T. S.,* LVII, 135.

16

Commission,[16] the International Committee of the International Bureau of Intelligence on Locusts,[17] the Governing Board of the Pan American Union,[18] and the International Commission for Air Navigation.[19]   On certain other commissions representation is by states or administrations but voting power varies in accordance with financial contribution or some other formula.[20]   In this group are found the Permanent Committee of the International Office of Chemistry,[21] the Committee of the International Association for the Protection of Children,[22] the Permanent Committee of the International Institute of Agriculture,[23] and the Committee of the International Wine Office.[24]   If formal convention provisions only were considered, the International Committee of the International Office of Public Health also would fall within this class as Article 6 of the Statute attached to the Arrangement of December 9, 1907, provides that each representative shall have a number of votes inversely proportional to the number of the class selected by his government for contributing to the financial maintenance of the Office.[25]

[16] Art. 2, Baltic Geodetic Convention, *L. N. T. S.,* LXXIX, 167; Hudson, III, 1823.

[17] Art. 2, Agreement creating the International Bureau, and Art. 6, Organic Statute, *L. N. T. S.,* CIX, 121; Hudson, III, 1888.

[18] Art. 5, Statute of the Pan American Union, Resolution adopted at the *Fifth International Conference of American States,* Santiago, Chile, 1923.

[19] Art. 34 of Air Navigation Convention as amended, *Official Bulletin,* XXII, 56.

[20] For consideration of the various devices used in assigning votes see below, pp. 248 ff.

[21] Arts. 1, 3, Rules of the International Office of Chemistry, *L. N. T. S.,* CXXVII, 27.

[22] Art. 9, Statute of the International Association for the Protection of Children, in Hudson, II, 878.

[23] Arts 7, 10, Convention for the Creation of an International Institute of Agriculture, *B. & F. State Papers,* C, 595; Malloy, II, 2140.

[24] Office International du Vin, *Textes de l'Arrangement International et des Règlements,* Art. 5.

[25] *B. & F. State Papers,* C, 466.

In practice, however, each delegate casts but a single vote.[26]

Although majority decision finds wide acceptance in these bodies in which representation is by states, acceptance of the principle is somewhat less complete than in the organizations composed of individuals serving in such capacity. One of the bodies, the Governing Board of the Pan American Union, has always adhered strictly to the rule of unanimous consent in all its deliberations. Nor does there appear to be prospect of adoption of a more flexible procedure for this board inasmuch as the Convention on the Pan American Union, signed at the Sixth Conference of American States, Havana, 1928, but not sufficiently ratified to enter into force, makes provision in Article 6 to the effect that " whenever a state believes its vital interests are involved in a question or that an obligation may thereby be imposed upon it, such state may require that the resolution of the Board be adopted by unanimous vote." [27] Two others, the International Committee of the International Office for Epizootics and the International Committee of the International Bureau of Intelligence on Locusts, while adhering nominally to majority rule, are thrown back upon unanimity for some decisions by reason of convention stipulations requiring unanimous approval of the member states to render certain Committee decisions valid. Thus Article 5 of the Annex to the Epizootics Agreement requires approval of all the participating governments before a decision of the Committee to alter the list of animal diseases to which the arrangement applies becomes effective, while the Agreement creating the Bureau of Intelligence on Locusts provides in Article 12 of the Organic Statute attached to it that decisions modifying the regulations in respect to

---

[26] See above, p. 125.
[27] The convention, which will not enter into force until ratified by all twenty-one republics, had received fourteen ratifications up to July, 1938.

the organization of the Bureau are valid only with the consent of the governments.

Finally, provision for decision by extraordinary majorities appears somewhat more frequently in the commissions organized on a state representation basis that in commissions on which the personnel is selected as individuals. A two-thirds vote of the Administrative Council of the International Exhibitions Union is required to adopt internal regulations, to increase the budget, to reject a request for an international exhibition made by a contracting country, to authorize an exhibit when several countries are competing for it, or to authorize the holding of a general exhibit for longer than six months.[28] A three-fourths majority vote is required in the Permanent Committee of the International Office of Chemistry to allow an exception to the scale of contributions which is established on a population basis.[29] A two-thirds majority in the Committee of the Association for the Protection of Children is requisite for alteration of the internal regulations.[30] As previously noted, a three-fourths majority including at least two-thirds of the total possible vote is necessary for the most important decisions taken by the International Commission for Air Navigation.[31]

The citation of these cases in which unanimity or extraordinary majorities are requisite for valid decisions in international commissions charged, among other duties, with supervision of bureaus or central offices, should not cause one to lose sight of general practice in bodies of this character, namely, decision by simple majority vote. A number of factors appear to have contributed to this rather general acceptance of such a procedural rule. In

[28] Art. 12, Convention Concerning International Exhibitions.

[29] Art. 10, Rules of the International Office of Chemistry.

[30] Art. 22, Statutes of the International Association for Protection of Children.

[31] Art. 34 of Air Navigation Convention as amended May 17, 1933. See above, p. 79.

the first place, many of the functions dealt with are completely out of the realm of high policy. The matters dealt with by many of the unions are of concern to groups within states but are of little or no concern to states as political units. For example, the mere fact that the International Wine Office and the International Institute of Refrigeration, unlike hundreds of private international associations, owe their existence to conventions entered into by states does not indicate a *state* concern with the subject matter dealt with by these bodies beyond that in the works of the Red Cross or International Chamber of Commerce, both of which are private international associations.

Second, many of the conventions or arrangements carry stipulations to the effect that the organizations " may not in any way interfere with the administration of contracting states " [32] or that " all questions concerning the economic interests, the legislation, and the administration of a particular nation shall be excluded from consideration." [33] In general, the terms of the conventions or other basic instruments of the unions may be said to require the governmental bodies to confine their activities strictly within the scope of the agreements set forth in those documents.

Third, even though representation is by states, the personnel of the international commissions and boards herein considered is, with few exceptions, technical rather than diplomatic. This, itself, generally indicates that agreement has been achieved upon all matters of high policy

[32] Cf. Art. 2, Organic Statute of the International Bureau of Intelligence on Locusts.

[33] Cf. Art. 9, Convention of International Institute of Agriculture. For somewhat similar limitations in the scope of activity of unions see Arrangement, Office International du Vin, 1928, Protocole de Signature; Art. 6 of the draft Convention of the Pan American Union; Art. 3 of the International Convention for the Foundation of an International Institute of Refrigeration.

directly involved in the activity of the union, for states seldom consent to the appointment of technicians in positions of power until state interests have been secured. Furthermore, representation by technicians is very likely to result, in the absence of restrictive rules to the contrary, in the adoption of convenient and simple rules of procedure.

However, where representation is diplomatic, as in the Governing Board of the Pan American Union, the dictates of convenience will win but rarely over precedent which decrees that the representatives of states should not be placed in a position in which they can be out-voted by others. And where bodies possess powers of a technical character, but of such a nature that their application may impose new and important commitments upon participating states, such as those of the International Commission for Air Navigation or the International Committee of the Office of Epizootics, decision by extraordinary majorities or even by unanimity is likely to be retained.

In the three technical organizations of the League of Nations the principle of majority decision finds complete acceptance. The Economic and Financial Organization, which exists to advise the Council and the Assembly, has five constituent bodies: the Economic Committee, the Consultative Economic Committee, the Committee of Experts on Economic Statistics, the Financial Committee, and the Fiscal Committee. The members of the committees are appointed, in general, by the Council of the League of Nations, a few persons obtaining membership by reason of selection by other organizations such as the International Institute of Agriculture. The persons named are selected in their individual capacities as experts rather than as representatives of states. However, provision is made that the fifteen members of the Economic Committee must be of different nationalities [34] and a similar rule

[34] *O. J.*, 1927, p. 1454.

holds in respect to the ten members of the Fiscal Committee.[35] The committees are independent so far as their internal proceedings are concerned and, consequently, when unanimous agreement can not be obtained by process of discussion, majority vote has been held sufficient for decision. Numerous special conferences have been called by the Council of the League of Nations to consider draft conventions or less formal propositions prepared by committees of the Economic and Financial Organization. In these conferences procedural questions have been decided by majority vote but unanimity has been required " where possible " for formal adoption of resolutions. Where unanimity can not be obtained, the names of those in favor may be given, but the resolution does not stand as an act of the conference.[36]

The Communications and Transit Organization has two permanent organs: a General Conference and a Committee for Communications and Transit. The former is composed of representatives of all states members of the League and representatives of such non-League states as may have been admitted to participation in the Organization by resolution of the Assembly as well as representatives from such other states as may have been invited by the Council to participate in the particular Conference. Although majority vote suffices for ordinary decisions in the Conference, a two-thirds vote is requisite for adoption of the final text of conventions and recommendations.[37] The Committee for Communications and Transit is composed of persons appointed by members of the League and by non-League states members of the Organization. The total number of members to appoint persons to serve

[35] *Ibid.*, 1929, p. 1012; *ibid.*, 1934, p. 143.

[36] Cf. Art. 11, *Rules of Procedure adopted at the Economic Conference of 1927* (League Doc. C. 356. M. 129. 1927. II).

[37] Art. 22, *Statute of the Organization for Communications and Transit* (League Doc. C. 95. M. 48. 1938. VIII).

on the Committee is fixed every three years by the Assembly acting by majority vote. The Assembly also designates the member states whose nationals shall be called upon to form the Committee. Members of the League permanently represented on the Council are as of right entitled to one member each on the Committee. In selecting the states to designate the other members of the Committee, the Assembly is obliged to take into consideration representation of geographical areas, rotation of Council seats, and other such matters. Some rotation of state representation is secured by providing that not more than one-half of the states elected to appoint members can be re-elected and that no state can be elected more than twice consecutively.[38] The Committee performs the preparatory work for the Conferences and endeavors to make effective the work of past Conferences through measures designed to facilitate ratification of or accession to conventions. It carries out such other duties as are imposed upon it by virtue of resolutions adopted by the Assembly or Council of the League or by the Conference of the Organization.[39] In addition, important functions are imposed upon it by the terms of many international treaties and agreements. All decisions of the Committee may be taken by a simple majority vote.[40] Although representation in both the Conference and the Committee is by states it is, of course, technical in character.

The Health Organization of the League consists of two bodies in addition to a section of the Secretariat: the General Advisory Health Council (actually the Permanent Committee of the International Office of Public Health) and the Standing Health Committee. The latter consists of twenty members composed as follows: the President of the Permanent Committee of the International Office of Public Health, nine members of the Permanent Commit-

---

[38] Art. 4, *ibid.*   [39] Art. 7, *ibid.*   [40] Art. 12, *ibid.*

tee selected by that body for three year terms in such fashion as to assure representation of all states permanently represented on the Council, and ten members appointed for like terms by the Council of the League after consultation with the Standing Health Committee. Thus the personnel is technical and only in part representative of states. The Committee directs the health work of the League and is responsible for the technical direction of the Health Section of the Secretariat. Resolutions adopted by the Committee do not become effective until approved by the League Council and the Council does not act upon them until they have been approved by the Health Council. However, virtually all resolutions proposed by the Standing Health Committee receive approval of the Health Council inasmuch as the personnel of the two bodies is overlapping and inasmuch as the Health Council (Permanent Committee of International Office of Public Health) holds majority decision to suffice.[41] Decisions by the Committee are likewise taken by majority vote.[42]

In the bodies advisory to the League Council and Assembly and in which members are selected as individuals rather than as representatives of states, the principle of majority decision finds complete acceptance. Thus the Advisory Committee of Experts on Slavery, established by virtue of resolutions adopted by the Assembly and the Council,[43] may take all decisions by majority vote of the members present, a majority of the committee constituting a quorum.[44] The committee consists of seven members of different nationalities chosen by the Council, for undefined terms, for their special knowledge of slavery questions. The committee studies and gives advice concern-

[41] See above, p. 125.
[42] Art. 7, *Rules of Procedure, Health Committee* (League Document C. 10. M. 7. 1924. III).
[43] *O. J.*, 1933, p. 1628 (League Doc. A 34. 1932. VI).
[44] Art. 5, Rules of Procedure of the Advisory Committee of Experts on Slavery, *O. J.*, 1934, p. 222.

ing measures for securing the full compliance of states with the provisions of the 1926 Slavery Convention,[45] but Article 5 of the convention, dealing with forced labor, is recognized as beyond the committee's jurisdiction.[46]

The Permanent Mandates Commission, established by authority of Article 22 of the Covenant, consists of eleven members [47] selected for their personal merit and competence by the Council of the League. The members must be of different nationalities, a majority nationals of non-mandatory powers, and they may hold no offices which place them in position of direct dependence on their governments. Although in form the powers of the Commission are purely advisory, it has in fact become the agent of the Council through which international supervision of the mandate system is exercised. Nevertheless, all decisions of the body may be reached by majority vote, six members constituting a quorum.[48] However, if the Commission after hearing a report from a mandatory power is not in complete agreement on the report to be made to the Council, the minority, as well as the majority, may present observations.[49]

The Permanent Central Opium Board, as previously noted,[50] established in accordance with the provision of the International Convention adopted by the Second Opium Conference, February 19, 1925,[51] is composed of eight persons " who, by their technical competence, impartiality and disinterestedness, will command general

[45] League Doc. C. 210. M. 83. 1927. VI.
[46] O. J., 1933, p. 1628.
[47] Originally nine, but a resolution of the Council, Dec. 11, 1924, made M. Rappard, formerly head of the Mandates section of the Secretariat, an extraordinary member (O. J., 1924, p. 143), and on September 8, 1927, the Council increased the regular membership to ten to make possible the appointment of a German national (O. J., 1927, p. 1120).
[48] Art. 3, Rules of Procedure of Permanent Mandates Commission. The rules are printed as Annex III in Quincy Wright, *Mandates under the League of Nations*.
[49] Art. 8.   [50] Above, p. 145.   [51] L. N. T. S., LXXXI, 317.

confidence," appointed by the Council of the League assisted by representatives of the United States and Germany.[52]   The Board has power to watch the course of international trade in narcotic drugs, to ask through the Secretary-General of the League for explanations from countries in which accumulations appear dangerous, to call the attention of contracting governments and the Council to the matter, and even to recommend a cessation of further exports to countries in which the situation appears unsatisfactory.[53]   Reports of the Board are directed, however, to the Council of the League, and are communicated by that body to the contracting states.   Decisions are taken by an absolute majority of the whole number of the Board.[54]

The International Committee on Intellectual Cooperation, established by virtue of resolutions adopted by the Assembly and the Council,[55] is composed at the present time of seventeen members of different nationalities appointed by the Council for five year terms.[56]   Decisions of the Committee are reached by majority vote.[57]

In the advisory organizations in which state representation has found acceptance as a basis for membership, majority decision is less completely accepted.   It is provided for decisions in both the Advisory Committee on the Traffic in Opium and Other Dangerous Drugs and in the Advisory Commission for the Protection of Children and Young People.   The former, established in fulfillment of Article 23 of the Covenant " to assist and advise the Council " in combating the drug traffic, is composed of twenty-five members appointed by and representing governments.   The governments to appoint members are

---

[52] Art. 19 of the Convention.
[53] Art. 24.
[54] Art. 19.
[55] O. J., 1922, p. 535.
[56] Ibid., 1934, p. 114.
[57] Report of the International Committee on Intellectual Cooperation submitted to the Council, O. J., 1932, p. 1745.

named by the Council in such fashion as to include producers and consumers and manufacturing and non-manufacturing areas. The governments are urged to appoint members technically qualified to serve.[58] Decisions are taken by majority vote of those present, a majority constituting a quorum.[59]

The Advisory Commission for the Protection and Welfare of Children and Young People, established by resolution of the Council and Assembly adopted in accordance with the recommendation of the International Conference on Traffic in Women and Children, 1921, sits as two bodies: The Traffic in Women and Children Committee and the Child Welfare Committee. The personnel of the two committees is the same. The Council designates fifteen governments, including the governments of those states having permanent Council seats, to name one national each to serve for a five year term.[60] Decisions of the Committees are taken by majority vote, the chairman having a casting vote only on questions of procedure.[61]

In the Permanent Advisory Commission for Military, Naval, and Air Questions, however, unanimity is requisite for decision. This body, established in accordance with the provisions of Article 9 of the Covenant to advise the Council on the execution of the provisions of Articles 1 and 8, is composed of one military, one naval, and one air representative from each state represented on the Council, each state having one vote.[62] Other states members of the League shall, unless the Council decides otherwise, be invited to send a similar number of representatives to sit

[58] *O. J.*, 1934, pp. 112-113.

[59] Art. 7, Rules of Procedure of Opium Committee. League of Nations, *Opium Committee,* 123 (1).

[60] *O. J.*, 1933, pp. 806, 866, 1608.

[61] Rules of Procedure adopted April, 1933 (League Doc. C. 247. M. 129. 1933. IV).

[62] Arts. 1, 5, Revised Rules of Procedure of the Permanent Advisory Commission for Military, Naval and Air Questions, *O. J.*, 1924, p. 983.

in the Commission temporarily whenever a question directly affecting them is under consideration.[63]   Decisions of a procedural character may be taken by majority vote but the substantive recommendations of the Commission require unanimity.[64]   Although a provision is made for amendment of the rules of procedure by majority vote of the Commission, approval of the Council is requisite, thus making impossible abolition of the unanimity rule in the Commission without the consent of all.[65]   Some opportunity to circumvent the formal rule exists by reason of a provision permitting majority and minority reports to the Council in the event unanimity can not be reached, but no formal recommendations may be made.[66]

In the special organizations established by the League and by its subsidiary commissions such as the International Institute of Intellectual Cooperation (Paris), the International Museums Office, and the International Educational Cinematographic Institute (Rome), provision is always made for majority decision in the governing bodies.[67]

In summary, it may be said that both in the technical organizations of the League and in the bodies advisory to the League the principle of majority rule finds complete acceptance where the personnel is selected in their individual capacities rather than as representatives of states or governments. The stipulation frequently encountered, that individuals named for their technical competence must be nationals of different states, may be regarded as precautionary rather than as a device to secure state representation in fact.   Nor does the custom of including always

[63] Art. 2.   [64] Art. 18.   [65] Art. 24.   [66] Art. 18.

[67] Cf. Organic Statute of International Institute of Intellectual Cooperation, *O. J.*, 1925, p. 286; Statutes of the International Museum Office; Organic Statute of International Educational Cinematographic Institute, *O. J.*, 1931, p. 268. The International Educational Cinematographic Institute ceased its activities on January 31, 1938. League of Nations, *Monthly Summary*, Jan., 1938, p. 28.

in the personnel of certain bodies nationals of certain great powers and other states indicate that the members so named are in fact state representatives. It is much more a concession to the demands of state prestige than a yielding to state control. Hence, even where certain seats have become ear-marked for nationals of certain states, the power to decide still rests with a body free from direct governmental control. States affected by decisions of the body may be said to have yielded control at the time the body was established, and, consequently, no reason for insisting upon unanimity exists. No movement for establishment of the rule of unanimous consent shows itself even in those bodies, such as the Mandates Commission, in which the reports adopted relate frequently to matters which must be considered high policy.

When representation is by states, more hesitancy is shown in discarding unanimous consent even when the powers exercised by the organ in question are of a purely advisory character. This is particularly true where the advice to be tendered relates directly to a highly controversial matter of policy such as armaments. Few governments, in the present state of world affairs, will be willing to sacrifice their *liberum veto* when the sacrifice may well mean embarrassment for them through formal proposal of a proposition to which they can not consent.

CHAPTER X

From Equality to Qualitative Representation

Closely associated to the problem of the vote necessary for decisions in international bodies are the problems of representation and voting strength. Although it would appear that the doctrine of state equality could be interpreted quite properly as assuring merely the equal protection of the law or equality before the law, it has frequently been used as basis for a claim to equality of capacity for rights or political equality. Where such has been the case, the doctrine naturally has had a retarding effect upon international organization, for political equality involves recognition of the right of every interested state to participate upon a basis of equality both in representation and in voting strength. Moreover, although the rule of unanimity can not be said to be a consequence of the doctrine of state equality, its maintenance has been supported frequently as the best assurance of the maintenance of that equality.

But even though the political equality of states has been ardently championed by the statesmen of the small powers and has received considerable lip-service from those of the great powers, in the practice of states it frequently has been over-ridden or evaded. In the nineteenth century political conferences, political equality was but rarely maintained.[1] The record of the twentieth century is no different in this respect. On several occasions the greater political power of the large states has been recognized by according them greater representation than the

[1] Cf. E. D. Dickinson, *The Equality of States in International Law*, p. 281.

smaller states, or by all or part of the small states being excluded entirely from participation.[2]   However, the principle of equal representation received repeated recognition in the non-political conferences of the nineteenth century.[3]

In the permanent international organs which have been established no uniformity of practice exists in respect to the maintenance of political equality.   In a considerable number of them strict equality has been maintained both in representation and in voting strength.   This is the case, for example, in the Union for the Protection of Literary and Artistic Works, the Union for the Protection of Industrial Property, the Postal Union of the Americas and Spain, the Pan American Union, the International Bureau of Intelligence on Locusts, the Baltic Geodetic Commission, the Central Office for International Transport by Rail, the International Relief Union, the International Office for Epizootics, the International Exhibitions Union, and in the amended constitution of the International Commission for Air Navigation.   Equality is provided also for the inactive Spanish-American Commission for Air Navigation.[4]   It was likewise provided for in the Permanent Bureau of Analytical Chemistry,[5] but this convention has never entered into force.   However, equality in financial maintenance is provided for only one of these organizations, the International Bureau for Intelligence on Locusts,[6] and here comparatively little difference exists

[2] In the Commissions named by the Preliminary Peace Conference at Paris in 1919 the large powers, in general, had two representatives each and the small powers, designated to serve, one each.   Many decisions were reached without any participation by the smaller powers.

[3] Dickinson, p. 282.

[4] Art. 34, Spanish-American Convention on Aerial Navigation in Hudson, III, 2019.

[5] *Art. 2, Règlement,* Convention and Regulation for a Permanent Bureau of Analytical Chemistry, *B. & F. State Papers,* CXIV, 585.

[6] Art 1, *L. N. T. S.,* CIX, 121.

among the participating states in material resources. As previously noted, equality of representation and voting power is in all cases provided for river and boundary water commissions made up of representatives of but two states.[7] It was maintained likewise in the Permanent Technical Hydraulic System Commission of the Danube on which five states were represented.[8]

In several other permanent organs equality is maintained for those states that participate, but all having direct interest in the subject dealt with are not afforded an opportunity to participate. Representation on the Cape Spartel Lighthouse Commission is restricted to those powers parties to the Convention of 1865[9] and representation on the Committee of Control of the Tangier Zone is reserved for states signatory to the Act of Algeciras.[10] A much more serious deviation from equality was found, however, in the constitution of the European Commission of the Danube. Here representation was confined to Roumania, Great Britain, Italy, and France[11] although any European state " able to prove its possession of sufficient maritime, commercial and European interests at the mouths of the Danube " might have been accorded at its request representation on the Commission by a unanimous decision of the governments already represented.[12]

[7] Above, p. 218.
[8] Art. 1, Regulations of the Permanent Technical Committee in Hudson, II, 1023.
[9] Art. 1, in Malloy, *Treaties,* I, 1217.
[10] Art. 30, *L. N. T. S.,* LXXXVII, 211. By Article 9 of the Tangier Convention, Germany and Austria-Hungary, signatories of the Algeciras Act, were excluded from participation in the control.
[11] Art. 346, Treaty of Versailles.
[12] Art. 4, Definitive Statute of the Danube, in Great Britain, *Treaty Series,* 1922, No. 16; *A. J. I. L.,* XVII, Supplement, 13. On March 1,

In a number of other organizations a surface equality is maintained, but in fact an inequality exists because of the practice of admitting to full participation colonies, protectorates, or other possessions of participating states, thus giving certain members several times the representation and voting strength accorded other members. This is the practice of the Universal Postal Union, the International Telecommunications Union, the Metric Union, the International Institute of Agriculture, the International Office of Public Health, the International Wine Office, and the International Office of Chemistry. As a general rule, the extent to which a state's representation and voting strength may be supplemented through the device of colonial representation is controlled closely by the conference of the organization or by convention provisions. The Universal Postal Union may be cited by way of illustration. Article 2 of the Convention provides that membership in the Union may be effected by any country through giving notice to the Swiss Government through the diplomatic channel. Naturally, only sovereign states or areas possessing at least some degree of international responsibility are in a position to take this step for themselves. Special provision is made in Article 8 for non-sovereign areas possessing postal administrations which are, if not autonomous, to some extent distinct from that of the mother country or protecting state. Such areas may, by vote of the Congress, be accorded full membership in the Union including the right to vote and the duty to share in the expenses. Territories with this status are listed separately in the

---

1939, Germany acquired membership through a Protocol signed at Bucharest by all states members of the Commission. *Bulletin of Internaional News,* March 11, 1939, p. 227.

Convention.[13] Other colonies, protectorates or mandated territories may be accorded, on the declaration of the contracting party exercising authority over them, the benefits of the Convention but without the privilege of voting or the duty of contributing financially.[14] Finally, the Convention lists certain countries as belonging to the Union, but no separate representation or voting power has been accorded them.[15] By contrast, however, states members of the Metric Union are in a position to increase their voting strength in the Conference without obtaining consent. An amendment to the Convention adopted in 1921 permits " self-governing " possessions to accede either as dependencies or as contracting states in accordance with the

[13] Art. 8 of the Convention as amended at the Cairo Congress of 1934 is as follows: " The following are considered as forming a single country or Administration of the Union, as the case may be, within the meaning of the Convention or of the Agreements so far as concerns, in particular, their right to vote at a Congress or Conference, and in the interval between meetings, as well as their contribution to the expenses of the International Bureau of the Universal Postal Union.

1. The whole of the island possessions of the United States of America, except the Philippine Islands, and comprising Hawaii, Porto-Rico, Guam, and the Virgin Islands of the United States of America.

2. The Philippine Islands.

3. The Colony of the Belgian Congo.

4. The whole of the Spanish Colonies.

5. Algeria.

6. The French Colonies and Protectorates in Indo-China.

7. The whole of the French Colonies.

8. The whole of the Italian Colonies.

9. Chosen (Korea).

10. The whole of the other Japanese Dependencies.

11. Curacao and Surinam.

12. The Dutch East Indies.

13. The Portuguese Colonies in West Africa.

14. The Portuguese Colonies in East Africa, Asia, and Oceania."

[14] Art. 9.

[15] Art. 10: " The following are considered as belonging to the Universal Postal Union:

(a) Post Offices established by Union countries in territories not included in the Union;

(b) The Principality of Liechtenstein, as subordinate to the Postal Administration of Switzerland;

decision of the mother state.[16]   If the latter is elected, representation in the Conference and voting privileges follow.

In some international unions plural voting is provided for in accordance with the scale of financial contribution. Such provision is made for the International Institute of Agriculture, the International Wine Office, the International Office of Chemistry, and the International Office of Public Health. A similar provision may be found in the Agreement for the Creation of a Central Patent Bureau, signed at Paris, November 15, 1920,[17] but never sufficiently ratified to enter into force. In the Permanent Committee of the International Office of Public Health, and in both the Permanent Committee and the General Assembly of the Institute of Agriculture, equality of representation is provided, but members may cast a number of votes inversely proportional to the number of the class selected by their governments for participation in the financial maintenance of the union.[18] In the Institute of Agriculture five classes are provided and in the Office of Public Health, six. In regard to the International Wine Office, each state may

---

(c) The Faroe Islands and Greenland, as forming part of Denmark;

(d) The Spanish possessions in the North Coast of Africa, as forming part of Spain;

(e) The Valley of Andorra, as served by the Postal Administrations of Spain and France;

(f) The Principality of Monaco, as subordinated to the Postal Administration of France;

(g) Walfisch Bay, as forming part of the Union of South Africa; Basutoland, as subordinate to the Postal Administration of the Union of South Africa."

[16] Art. 2, Convention of 1921, *L. N. T. S.,* XVII, 46.

[17] Art. 17, in Hudson, I, 508.

[18] Arts. 6 and 11, Statuts Organiques de l'Office International d'Hygiène, *B. & F. State Papers,* C, 446. Also Art. 10, Convention for the Creation of the International Institute of Agriculture, *B. & F. State Papers,* C, 595. As previously noted, members of the Committee of the Office of Public Health do not in practice avail themselves of their right of plural voting. Above, p. 125.

send as many delegates to the meeting of the Committee as it sees fit, but each delegation is restricted to a number of votes equivalent to the number of units it chooses to contribute toward maintenance of the organization. Any state may contribute as many as five units, but under no circumstances may a group made up of " a power, its colonies, possessions, dominions, protectorates, or territories under mandate " cast more than a total of five votes.[19]   In the International Office of Chemistry each state or colony is accorded one representative in the Permanent Committee but votes are inversely proportional to the category of membership.   This, in turn, is determined in accordance with a scale of contribution based on population.[20]   Exceptions may be allowed by a three-quarters majority vote of the Committee.[21]   In the General Assembly of the proposed Central Patent Bureau votes were to be distributed in accordance with the ranking of the country for financial contribution, this to be determined at the first meeting of the delegates of the adhering countries, " account being taken both of the industrial importance and the population of each country." [22]   It will be noted that in the International Institute of Agriculture, in the International Wine Office, in the International Office of Public Health, and in the International Office of Chemistry the influence

[19] Art. 5, Arrangement.   Office International du Vin, *Textes de l'Arrangement International et des Règlements,* 1928.

[20] Art. 11, Rules of the International Office of Chemistry, *L. N. T. S.,* CXXVII, 27.   The table follows:

Category	Population in Millions	Votes	Units of Contribution
1	over 30	6	25
2	20–30	5	20
3	15–20	4	15
4	10–15	3	10
5	5–10	2	5
6	under 5	1	3

[21] *Ibid.*

[22] Arts. 17, 18, Agreement for the Creation of a Central Patent Bureau, in Hudson, I, 508.

of certain states may be enhanced both by the plural voting provisions and by colonial representation.

The distribution of representation and voting strength in accordance with financial contribution is justified on the principle that privilege ought to be apportioned in the same way as responsibility. It may also be asserted that, in those cases in which states are left free to select their own category of membership and where budgets are small enough to impose little financial burden, it represents a distribution in accordance with the interest of the states in the activities of the body in question. In a number of other international agencies, different means are used to the same end.

In some organizations unequal voting strength and representation are assigned arbitrarily by convention provision. For example, on the Central Commission for Navigation of the Rhine, France has five representatives, Germany four, Netherlands three, and Switzerland, Italy, Great Britain, and Belgium two each.[23] Whatever the number of delegates present each delegation may cast a number of votes equal to the number of representatives allotted to it. On the International Commission of the Elbe, the German riparian states have had four representatives, Czechoslovakia two, with one each from Great Britain, France, Italy, and Belgium.[24] Although in both these cases the fiction of votes in accordance with interest was maintained, the powers appear to have been more concerned in assuring Allied control of the commissions than in any exact determination of river interests.[25]

In certain other international agreements, the powers have adhered much more closely to the principle of votes

---

[23] Art. 355 of Treaty of Versailles and Protocol regarding adhesion of Netherlands, January 20, 1921, *L. N. T. S.,* XX, 113.

[24] Art. 340 of Versailles Treaty.

[25] See above, p. 175.

in accordance with interest.   The Agreement regarding the Regulation and Marketing of Sugar, May 6, 1937, provides for equal representation of the participating powers on the Council of the Sugar Regime but votes are distributed in accordance with what is considered to be the importance of the delegations as representatives of sugar exporting or sugar importing countries.[26]   The proportion between exporters and importers at 55 to 45, as fixed in the Agreement, is to be maintained.   The failure of a signatory state to ratify, the accession of a non-signatory, or the withdrawal of any state is to result in a re-distribution of votes, *pro rata*, among the exporting or importing countries in the class affected.   In the Conference of the International Hydrographic Bureau each member state is free to send two or more delegates, each delegation possessing for most questions a single vote.[27]   But in the election of the Directing Committee and the Secretary-General a system of plural voting is used, each delegation being assigned two votes and a number of supplementary

---

[26] Miscellaneous No. 3, 1937, Cmd. 5461. The table provided in Art. 37 is as follows:

Exporting Countries:

Union of South Africa	2	Haiti	1
Australia	3	Hungary	1
Belgium	1	Jugoslavia	1
Brazil	2	Netherlands	9
Cuba	10	Peru	3
Czechoslovakia	3	Philippines	1
Dominican Republic	3	Poland	2
France	3	Portugal	1
Germany	4	U. S. S. R.	5
		Total	55

Importing Countries:

China	5	United Kingdom	17
India	6	United States	17
		Total	45

[27] Arts. 53, 57, Statute of the International Hydrographic Bureau.

votes in accordance with its tonnage. The same system is used for the distribution of the financial obligations.[28]

In yet other organizations seats and votes are distributed in accordance with a formula embodied in the fundamental agreement. For example, in the Committee of the Committee of the International Association for the Protection of Children each member state has a minimum of two seats. This may be increased to a maximum of five in accordance with a formula giving additional seats to states having a certain number of associations participating in the work of the organization.[29]

[28] The table from Appendix E of the Statute as amended by the Third International Hydrographic Conference, Monaco, 1932, is as follows:

| States Members | Shares and Votes | | | Contributions |
	Fixed	Supplementary	Total	(gold francs)
Argentina	2	3	5	10,000
Brazil	2	3	5	10,000
British Empire (United Kingdom and Australia)..	2	15	17	34,000
Chile	2	1	3	6,000
China	2	3	5	10,000
Denmark	2	4	6	12,000
Egypt	2	..	2	4,000
France	2	7	9	18,000
Germany	2	7	9	18,000
Greece	2	5	7	14,000
Italy	2	7	9	18,000
Japan	2	7	9	18,000
Monaco	2	..	2	....
Netherlands	2	6	8	16,000
Norway	2	7	9	18,000
Peru	2	1	3	6,000
Poland	2	1	3	6,000
Portugal	2	2	4	8,000
Siam	2	..	2	4,000
Spain	2	4	6	12,000
Sweden	2	5	7	14,000
U. S. A...........	2	13	15	30,000
Total..........	44	101	145	286,000

Note: Monaco furnishes the headquarters for the Bureau and so pays no share in the expenses.

[29] Art. 9, Statutes of the International Association for the Protection of Children, in Hudson, II, 876.

Although equality is provided for in the Assembly of the League, the provisions of the Covenant in the matter of the composition of the Council constitute a significant departure from the principle of state equality. Likewise, in most of the technical organizations and advisory commissions of the League and in the special organizations associated with the League, in which states find representation as states, a somewhat similar departure from equality is made. The Statute of the Communications and Transit Organization provides for equality of representation for all states admitted to membership in the General Conference. But the Committee for Communications and Transit is composed of delegates appointed by a part only of the member states, including always the members of the League permanently represented on the Council.[30] Equality of representation is maintained on the General Advisory Health Council but the Standing Health Committee is composed of but twenty members selected in such way that each state permanently represented on the Council has a place.[31] The Advisory Commission for the Protection and Welfare of Children and Young People consists of fifteen members representing states, including always representatives of those states permanently represented on the Council.[32] Membership on the Permanent Advisory Commission for Military, Naval and Air Questions is restricted to representatives of the states members of the Council, with other states having the privilege of naming members when a special question directly affecting them is under consideration, unless the Council of the League decides otherwise.[33]

An exception to the general practice of affording special position to those states represented on the Council is

[30] Art. 4, *Statute of the Organization for Communications and Transit* (League Doc. C. 95. M. 48. 1938. VIII).

[31] *O. J.*, 1923, p. 1050.

[32] *Ibid.*, 1933, pp. 806, 866, 1608.

[33] *Ibid.*, 1924, p. 983.

found in the composition of the Advisory Committee on the Traffic in Opium and Other Dangerous Drugs. This body is composed of twenty-five members appointed by and representing states. The states to appoint members are named by the Council in such way as to include producing and consuming states, manufacturing and non-manufacturing states, and representatives of all geographical areas.[34] This formula is, of course, so broad as to leave the Council virtually free in the designation of states.

A much more significant use of a formula for classifying states for participation in international organization appears in the Constitution of the International Labor Organization. Equality of representation and voting power is maintained in the General Conference, each Member appointing two government delegates and two others representing respectively the employers and the workers.[35] The Governing Body, however, consists of thirty-two persons, sixteen of whom are government representatives, eight employer and eight worker. Eight of the sixteen government members are named by the states of chief industrial importance, the remaining eight being selected by the other government delegates in the Conference. By terms of the Constitution, any question as to which are the members of chief industrial importance is decided by the Council of the League of Nations.[36] In 1922, the Council determined the eight states to be Germany, Belgium, Canada, France, Italy, Great Britain, India, and

[34] *Ibid.*, 1934, p. 113.

[35] However, in the adoption of amendments to the Constitution of the Organization, the states which the delegates represent are not equal. An amendment proposed by two-thirds vote of the Conference enters into force when ratified by the states whose representatives compose the Council of the League and by three-fourths of the members. (Art. 422, Treaty of Versailles.) A similar limitation on equality in the League Assembly is made in Article 26 of the Covenant.

[36] Art. 393 of Treaty of Versailles as amended June 4, 1934.

Japan.[37] However, as previously noted,[38] in January, 1935, soon after the United States and Soviet Russia became members, the Governing Body ruled in the midst of an elective term that those two powers had displaced Belgium and Canada as states of chief industrial importance. Canada was again included after the withdrawal of Germany became effective, October 21, 1935. Consequently, by these two actions precedent was established both for changing the list by application of the formula and for making such changes whenever circumstances dictate. Permanent representation on the Governing Body is dependent, therefore, not upon rank as a great power or possession of a permanent Council seat. Rather, it is dependent upon continuous fulfillment of conditions set forth in a formula closely associated with the functions the organization is attempting to perform in the international society.

This survey reveals a considerable tendency in the structure of permanent international organization away from the strict equality of states. Equality of representation and voting power in permanent international bodies is more nearly the exception than the rule. However a substantial group of agencies continues to adhere to the principle. This appears justifiable in some cases. In the first place, if the organization is composed of and is of interest to states of substantially the same population and with substantially the same industrial development, the rule of equality will naturally be the most satisfactory basis on which to operate. This will not occur frequently but it is, perhaps, the case in respect to the International Bureau of Intelligence on Locusts and in respect to the Permanent Technical Hydraulic System Commission for the Danube. Second, when the organization is intended solely to promote cooperation among states in scientific or humani-

[37] *O. J.*, 1922, pp. 1160, 1184-1200.
[38] Above, p. 101.

tarian activities, departure from equality may not be worth the bother it would necessitate. In some such cases, the extent of representation is of little importance so long as all states whose cooperation is desired accept some representation. The Baltic Geodetic Commission would seem to be a case in point. Third, in a very few cases maintenance of equality may be justified as a device essential for preventing an international body from passing under the domination of a single great power or small group of great powers. The validity of this justification would seem to depend upon evidence of intent in each case in which it was advanced. It at least helps to explain, if not to justify, maintenance of strict equality in the International Conferences of American States and in the Governing Body of the Pan American Union. Finally, when the organization is committed to use of the rule of unanimous consent, as in the Union for the Protection of Literary and Artistic Works and in the Industrial Property Union, there is little reason for deviating from equality in representation and voting power. In such cases, the awarding of additional representation and votes to the larger powers, although it affords them some advantage in committee work, is chiefly of prestige value. So long as the *liberum veto* exists, the counting of votes is unimportant. Each state is equipped with the means of protecting its equality. It will be noted, however, that this works in a vicious circle for, so long as strict equality is insisted upon, the large powers hesitate to permit deviation from unanimity.

All too frequently, however, political equality is insisted upon where none of these conditions are present. States participating in international bodies rarely approach equality in population and development and in interest in the activity of the organizations. Frequently, real international cooperation can not be obtained through assigning all states equal weight. Moreover, agencies now engaged in promoting cooperation may have little expectation of being empowered to make binding decisions in matters of significance so long as equality in representation and voting power is maintained, and the future of world order appears to depend upon the development of such powers. With few exceptions, existing international agencies have resulted from a desire to advance the legitimate interests of all participating states rather than from a design of encroachment. A surrender of formal rights of equality in such organizations by the smaller states should tend to enhance their well-being rather than endanger it, inasmuch as it would contribute to the effective functioning of such bodies. Finally, in a very large number of organizations some form of majority decision already has been substituted for the unanimity rule either by frank constitutional provision to that effect or by the development of extra-legal practice in the agencies themselves. But in spite of the inappropriateness of political equality in all these cases, the demands of prestige, the slavish adherence by diplomats to the dogma of state equality, and an unreasoning fear of domination by other powers all contribute to its maintenance, and, consequently, to a retarding of the progressive development of international organization.

Although this survey has revealed more cases in which political equality is violated than strictly maintained, it will be appreciated, of course, that many of the departures noted are slight. The British Empire and Monaco have the same vote in the Hydrographic Conferences except when the Secretary-General and Directing Committee are being elected. Although the United States is assured of permanent representation in the Governing Body of the International Labor Organization and Cuba is not, the two states have the same number of votes in the Labor Conferences. Moreover, many of the schemes of plural voting have been adopted in a haphazard, irrational or even an opportunist fashion. Consequently, it is not surprising that the results are, in many cases, virtually indefensible. The combination of colonial representation with votes by categories of membership elected in the International Institute of Agriculture gives the British Empire possession of a total of twenty-two votes, the United States twenty-one, France nineteen, and Italy thirteen to only five for Germany. In the Postal Union, Portugal, Netherlands, Belgium, and Spain each control more votes than Germany or the Soviet Union.

In only a few cases has attempt been made to evolve for international bodies rational standards of representation to substitute for the unsatisfactory principle of equality. Yet if decisions are to be taken by less than unanimous vote by organizations having some power to impose obligations on member states, political expediency, as well as justice, demands that such standards be established. For even though experience within the League, as well as elsewhere, indicates that the small states make little attempt to take decisions over the opposition of the larger powers, the large states are unlikely to permit binding decisions in matters of significance unless they are equipped with a number of votes somewhat commensurate with their strength, interests, and responsibilities.

In view of the unsatisfactory condition in international practice in respect to representation, it is not surprising to find that almost every international body taking decisions by majority vote has, at one time or another, faced a struggle over the problem. In some cases the strife has been confined to the conference which established the organization. In others, it has continued long after. The more extended the powers the more bitter the struggle over votes, suggesting, of course, that more than prestige is involved. The experience of four organizations, the International Institute of Agriculture, the International Commission for Air Navigation, the Universal Postal

Union, and the International Telecommunications Union, illustrates the difficulty of reconciling the divergent views of governments in respect to multiple representation and voting privileges.

The Conference which assembled at Rome, May 28, 1905, for the purpose of drafting a constitution for the International Institute of Agriculture, was composed in large part of diplomatic officers, although a few of the delegates were agricultural technicians from government departments of agriculture.[39]   After the Conference had decided by vote of 27 to 4 that the Institute was to be an association of states rather than an association of delegates from agricultural societies,[40] three problems involving state equality soon emerged to face the members. First, was membership in the organization to be confined to fully sovereign states or might membership be extended to colonial areas? Second, upon what basis was representation to be accorded in the organs of the Institute? Third, what formula was to be used in determining voting power?

In regard to the first problem, the Conference had little alternative but to provide for representation of colonies inasmuch as Great Britain had repeatedly indicated the importance she attached to it.[41]   Consequently, the Conference wrote into Article 10 of the Convention the provision that colonies may, at the request of the state to which they belong, be admitted to form part of the Insti-

[39] Cf. Report of the British Delegates and the Minutes of the Proceedings at the International Conference of Agriculture at Rome, *B. P. P.,* 1906, XCVI.

[40] *Ibid.,* p. 116. The negative votes were cast by the representatives of Germany, Austria, Hungary, and Chile.

[41] See the Communication from T. H. Elliott, Board of Agriculture and Fisheries, to the Foreign Office; the British Foreign Secretary to the Italian Ambassador in London; the Instructions to the British Delegation to the Agricultural Conference of 1905, *B. P. P.,* 1906, XCVI. Also see Signor Cappelli's reference in the Conference to the views of the British delegation, *Minutes,* p. 121.

tute on the same conditions as independent states. This provision was accepted, but not with unreserved enthusiasm in all quarters. M. Kroupensky (Russia) observed " that by giving colonies the same rights as their mother countries, certain states with numerous colonies could, by paying for them, be assured of a majority, or in any case, a large number of votes, and influence unduly the decisions of the Institute." Cappelli (Italy) found two answers to this, neither very convincing. First, it would be too expensive for states to seek separate representation for their colonies merely to increase their voting power. Second, the colonies, considering their own particular interests, would in many cases vote independently of the mother country.[42]

In regard to the second problem, namely, the basis of representation in the organs of the Institute, it was immediately and generally conceded that equality of representation must be granted in the General Assembly which was intended to be the supreme organ of the Institute. Consequently, by terms of Article 3 each state was left free to send whatever number of delegates it cared to. Each member was authorized also to name one delegate to the Permanent Committee, although a Danish delegate pointed out that this would put a severe strain on the budgets of the small states, and a representative of Argentina suggested a committee of forty or more would be too large to perform executive functions well.[43] The Argentine delegate suggested that the Assembly elect a committee of twelve, but the Italians held this would result in the exclusion of the delegates of small states thus constituting a denial of equality and an injury to the susceptibilities of the smaller powers. They held the same end might be achieved without damage to the prestige of any by permitting adhering states to entrust their votes in the

[42] *Minutes,* p. 140.   [43] *Ibid.,* p. 146.

Committee to the representatives of another adhering power, provided that this Permanent Committee should never have less than fifteen members.[44] This suggestion was duly inserted in Article 7 of the Convention, and, in practice, has contributed directly to the domination of the Permanent Committee, and hence of the Institute, by one power.[45]

The question of weighted voting gave the Conference much more difficulty. It appears to have been understood by all that votes could not be distributed on a basis of strict equality. Most delegates appeared to favor linking voting power with financial contribution, as was ultimately done, the chief differences arising in respect to the exact formula to be applied. Only the delegate of Turkey criticized the principle applied. He observed that the function of the Institute was to develop agriculture. No relation existed between agricultural interest and financial resources. Adoption of the principle proposed would result in the policy of the Institute being formed by the states with greatest financial resources, not necessarily the states with greatest interest in agriculture. To this Cappelli (Italy) replied, declaring only administrative problems of the Institute to be involved in voting, each state remaining free on questions of policy.[46] This implied, of course, that unanimity would be requisite for decisions on policy in the General Assembly of the Institute.

In the actual preparation of the formula, the Conference experienced some difficulty in arriving at agreement. Cappelli first suggested six groups of states with votes ranging from one in the sixth class to eleven in the first with contributions from two units in the sixth up to sixty-

[44] *Ibid.*   [45] See below, p. 266.   [46] *Minutes,* p. 122.

18

four in the first.[47] Elliott (Great Britain) objected to this proposal, observing that Great Britain would be paying much more for each of her eleven votes than Ecuador would for her one vote.[48] After a plan more appealing to the large states had been introduced by the French delegation and rejected by the Conference as one likely to prevent the small powers from accepting membership, a compromise was reached. Five categories of membership were provided, each state being free to elect its own. Votes were to increase by arithmetical progression and contributions by geometrical progression.[49] The plan of plural voting applies in both Permanent Committee and General Assembly.

Although the prediction made by the Russian delegate in the Conference of 1905 to the effect that plural voting plus colonial representation would lead to the accumulation of large blocks of votes by a few great powers has been borne out, to some extent, in the practice of the Institute,[50] the records of neither the Permanent Committee

[47] *Ibid.* Cappelli's plan was as follows:

Groups of States	Votes	Units Subscription
I	11	64
II	9	32
III	7	16
IV	5	8
V	3	4
VI	1	2

[48] *Minutes,* p. 154.

[49] *Ibid.,* p. 156. The scale appears in Article 10 of the Convention as follows:

Groups	Votes	Units Subscription
I	5	16
II	4	8
III	3	4
IV	2	2
V	1	1

[50] At the present time there are 71 members of the Institute but some of these have neither paid dues nor participated in the control of the organization for years. Members, by groups, follow: Group I—Germany, Argentina, Brazil, China, Spain, United States, France, Great Britain,

nor the General Assembly reveal any concerted attack upon the system. This may be explained by three factors. First, the Institute possesses distinctly less power than several of the other well known public unions. By the terms of Article 9 of the Convention it is confined largely to the collection and publication of statistical information of agricultural interest. The final paragraph of the article provides that " all questions concerning the economic interests, the legislation, and the administration of a particular nation shall be excluded from consideration of the Institute." Moreover, Article 4 provides that the General Assembly must confine itself to consideration of " a programme proposed by the Permanent Committee and adopted by the adhering governments." [51] The *règlement* of the General Assembly further provides that the draft agenda proposed by the Permanent Committee must be submitted to the governments for approval at least three months before each session and that subjects not included and approved are beyond the competence of the body to discuss.[52] This provision, in effect, arms each state with a prior veto on any attempt by the Institute to extend the scope of its work. It likewise destroys much of the significance of the departures from equality.

Italy, Japan. Group II—Chile, Egypt, Hawaii, Philippine Islands, Virgin Islands, Porto Rico, Canada, India, Roumania. Group III—Algeria, Indo-China, French Morocco, Australia, Jugoslavia, Czechoslovakia, Mexico, Turkey, Netherlands. Group IV—Belgium, Bulgaria, Denmark, Finland, French West Africa, Greece, Eritrea, Irish Free State, New Zealand, Union of South Africa, Tunisia, Cyrenaica, Italian Somaliland, Tripoli, Norway, Poland, Portugal, Sweden, Switzerland, Venezuela, Dutch East Indies. Group V—Bolivia, Colombia, Belgian Congo, Costa Rica, Cuba, Ecuador, Esthonia, Madagascar, Guatemala, Haiti, Hungary, Latvia, Lithuania, Luxemburg, Nicaragua, Panama, Paraguay, Peru, Persia, San Marino, Siam, Uruguay. This gives the British Empire possession of a total of 22, the United States 21, France 19, and Italy 13.

[51] This provision, as well as the final paragraph of Article 9, was included on motion of T. H. Elliott (Great Britain) supported by delegates of France and Italy. Only the Cuban delegate opposed. *Minutes*, pp. 131-138.

[52] Arts. 4, 13 of Regulations of General Assembly.

Second, the General Assembly, unlike the conferences of many other public international unions, has never developed the practice of taking decisions by majority vote.[53] Majority decision in the Institute is confined to the Permanent Committee which is presumably engaged in administrative supervision. Consequently, in the General Assembly, though not in the Permanent Committee, the number of votes possessed by a power is of little significance.

Third, the question of formal equality has been somewhat overshadowed by a more pressing problem, namely, the tendency of administrative control of the organization to pass into the hands of the state in which the Institute is located. From the first, the Italian representative on the Permanent Committee has served as President, only Italian nationals have served as Secretary-General, and the remainder of the permanent staff, which the Regulations provide shall be international, has been almost exclusively Italian. On one occasion, when members of the Permanent Committee threatened selection of a Secretary-General not possessing Italian nationality, the President of the Permanent Committee is alleged to have called upon a large number of embassies and legations in Rome threatening denunciation of the treaty and withdrawal of housing facilities should the action be taken.[54] While the system of colonial representation and plural voting has assisted the Italian government to some extent in building up control, two other factors appear more important. The first of these is the provision of Article 7 of the Convention permitting adhering states to entrust their representation to another. The Italian delegate, or delegates of Italian nationality, have frequently represented as many as fifteen member states at one time. Latin American states, some far in arrears in dues payments, have been

---

[53] Majority decisions are taken in the committees of the General Assembly but in these bodies each state has one representative and one vote. Regulations of the General Assembly, Rule 6.

[54] A. Hobson, *The International Institute of Agriculture,* p. 302.

particularly prone to turn over representation to Italy. The second contributing factor is the practice followed by many states of sending to the Permanent Committee their diplomatic officers accredited to Rome. To many of these, a continuance of cordial relations with Italian officialdom appears more worthwhile than an attempt to break Italian domination over the Institute of Agriculture, an organization which appears of quite secondary importance.[55] So long as this condition exists little interest may be expected either in restoring abstract equality or in working out a rational plan of deviation therefrom.

The history of the International Commission for Air Navigation, unlike that of the Institute of Agriculture, is one of almost constant struggle over the principles of representation and voting power. This will be understandable when it is recalled that the Commission is authorized to amend the Annexes A to G of the Convention of 1919 by a vote of less than unanimity and that the amendments so adopted enter into force without ratification by the powers. Starting with wide departures from political equality, the Commission has been obliged to move steadily toward complete acceptance of the principle of political equality, a goal which was achieved when amendments to Article 34 proposed in protocols of June 15 and December 11, 1929, entered into force May 17, 1933.

In accordance with the practice generally followed in the Paris Peace Conference, the Aviation Commission which drew up the Convention of 1919, contained more representatives of the great powers than of the small states. The United States, the British Empire, Italy, Japan, and France named two members each, and Belgium, Brazil, Cuba, Greece, Portugal, Roumania, and Serbia were permitted one each.[56] A draft convention proposed

[55] Cf. Hobson, pp. 302 ff.
[56] *La Documentation Internationale; La paix de Versailles,* VIII, 7.

by the British Government was used as a basis for the
deliberations of the Commission. Article 23 of this draft
provided for marked departure from state equality in the
establishment of the International Commission, it being
proposed that the body should consist of two representatives each from the United States, the British Empire,
France, Italy, and Japan, with five being elected jointly
by all the other contracting powers.[57]   However, this undoubtedly was felt to be too flagrant a violation of state
equality; for the Legal Sub-Committee, consisting almost
exclusively of lawyers and diplomats named by the larger
powers, proposed a poorly devised substitute of its own.[58]
Each of the five first named states in the British plan was
to retain its two representatives and two votes, but the
remaining states, instead of electing five, were each to
have one representative, each representative possessing a
half vote up to a total of nine.   Thus the five great powers
would always be able to out-vote the smaller states.

When the Legal Sub-Committee's draft came before the
plenary session of the Commission it was challenged
immediately by the representatives of the small powers
both as an unwarranted violation of state equality and as
a clumsy device.[59]   A representative of the United States,
Admiral Knapp, then suggested a compromise which was
accepted unanimously except for Cuba,[60] and became, with
only slight change, part of the final Convention. Article
34 of the final text provided the International Commission
for Air Navigation should be composed of:

Two representatives of each of the following states: the United
States of America, France, Italy and Japan;

[57] The British Draft appears in *La Documentation Internationale,* VIII,
219 ff.
[58] Art. 34 of the draft submitted by the Legal Sub-Committee, *ibid.,*
p. 508.
[59] See particularly the remarks of Burlamaqui (Brazil), Marinkovitch
(Serbia) and de Mattos (Portugal), *ibid.,* pp. 56 ff.
[60] *Ibid.,* p. 59.

One representative of Great Britain and one of each of the British Dominions and of India.

Each of the five states first named (Great Britain, the British Dominions and India counting for this purpose as one state) shall have the least whole number of votes which, when multiplied by five, will give a product exceeding by at least one vote the total number of votes of all the other contracting States.

All the states other than the five first named shall each have one vote.

The resentment felt by some of the secondary and minor powers at this disregard of state political equality is evidenced by the formal reservations entered by the representatives of Cuba and Brazil at the time of adoption of the final draft by the Commission. Bustamante (Cuba) declared it inadmissible that an international organ should be created in which fifteen united powers could take no decision against a contrary opinion held by five powers.[61] The Brazilian delegate stated that his government could not allow to pass without protest this violation of the doctrine of state equality which Brazil had defended at the Hague and which she would continue to defend even after she had taken her proper position as a great power.[62]

Long before the Air Convention of 1919 had been sufficiently ratified to enter into force, it became apparent that the deviations from political equality were too great if general acceptance by the smaller powers was expected. In December, 1919, the representatives of seven states neutral during the World War [63] met at Copenhagen to formulate their objections to the terms of the Convention and to state the conditions under which they would adhere. They unanimously agreed to postpone adhesion until such time as the Convention had been amended to grant equality of voting privileges to all states.[64]

[61] *Ibid.*, p. 102.   [62] *Ibid.*, p. 108.
[63] Denmark, Finland, Netherlands, Norway, Spain, Sweden, and Switzerland.
[64] A. Roper, *La Convention Internationale du 13 octobre 1919*, p. 88.

As the Convention can be amended only on proposal of the International Commission, it was necessary for the powers to delay action until after July 11, 1922, when the Convention would be sufficiently ratified to bring this body into existence. At the first session of the Commission no action was taken because the large powers were unwilling to concede an equality of voting power and at the same time permit modifications of the Annexes by a three-fourths vote. Before the meeting of the second session, the group of World War neutrals, with the exception of Spain, arrived at a compromise plan which was submitted to the International Commission by the delegate of Belgium.[65] It was not until the fourth session (June 30, 1923), however, that the Commission decided to accept it. At this time amendment to Article 34 was proposed as follows:

> Each state represented in the Commission (Great Britain, the British Dominions and India counting for this purpose as one state) shall have one vote.
>
> Any modification of the provisions of any one of the annexes may be made by the International Commission for Air Navigation when such modifications of the provisions have been approved by three-quarters of the total possible votes which could be cast if all the states were represented; this majority must, moreover, include at least three of the five following states: the United States of America, the British Empire, France, Italy, Japan.[66]

This amendment entered into force December 14, 1926.[67] The concessions made by the great powers to the small in consenting to this were, of course, not extensive. The great powers retained their privilege of larger representation and, owing to the failure of the United States to ratify, no modification of the Annexes could be made if opposed by more than one of the larger powers. Substan-

---

[65] International Commission for Air Navigation, *Official Bulletin,* II, 38.
[66] *Ibid.,* IV, 15.   [67] *Ibid.,* XII, 17.

tially, the major states were as well equipped to defend their interests as before.

However, as ratification of the Convention continued to lag, an extraordinary session of the Commission was held in June, 1929, to which contracting and non-contracting powers alike were invited.   Its purpose was general revision of the Convention to encourage ratification by signatory states and accession by non-signatory states, particularly Germany.   At this conference, which was attended by twenty-two contracting and sixteen non-contracting states, it became apparent that German accession could not be expected unless she received full equality with the great powers.   Moreover, it appeared also that many of the secondary powers, notably Spain and Brazil, would not accept membership unless complete equality of all were established.[68]   Consequently, on June 15, 1929, the Commission proposed that Article 34 be amended to provide that each contracting state should have not more than two representatives on the Commission, and that modifications of the Annexes be effected by a three-fourths vote of the states represented at the session, the vote including at least two-thirds of the vote possible if all contracting states were represented at the meeting.[69]   This amendment entered into force May 17, 1933.[70]   Since the great powers had been stripped of their privileges there was no longer justification for providing that for voting purposes Great Britain, the Dominions and India should count as one. Hence, an amendment was proposed December 11, 1929, providing each state represented on the Commission should have one vote.[71]   This, too, became effective May 17, 1933.[72]

Thus complete equality in voting power and representation on the International Commission for Air Navigation

[68] Cf. Roper, p. 175.
[69] Official Bulletin, XVI, 33.
[70] Ibid., XXII, 56.
[71] Ibid., XVII, 27.
[72] Ibid., XXII, 56.

has been established through the process of amending the Convention. The concessions were made by the great powers in order to achieve a wider acceptance of the Convention, an end in which they have not been wholly successful.[73] The provisions for the amendment of the annexes by majority vote of the Commission constituted the chief obstacle to the granting of political equality, but the equality finally was achieved without sacrificing majority vote. However, it seems unlikely that the states would have consented to the majority provisions, written into the convention in 1919 by the military, naval, and air technicians on the Aviation Commission of the Peace Conference, if equality in representation and voting power had been provided at that time. The result of the establishment of political equality by amendment may well be that the larger states will combat any further extension in the application of the majority principle or in the competence of the Commission.

In 1874 the principle of "one state, one vote" was adopted to govern the functioning of the Postal Union. However, this principle of political equality is no longer adhered to by the Union. This will occasion no surprise considering the fact that membership in this union includes states of such varying population, industrialization, and general importance and that its Congress has authority to modify the Convention and attached Regulations by majority vote with ratification being reduced to theoretical importance only. Two devices are used to defeat strict equality. In the first place, some of the powers have been able to increase their own voices in the Congress by securing separate representation and voting privileges for their colonies. Second, the important work of shaping propositions for consideration by the plenary sessions of the Con-

---

[73] Only seven states have become parties since the proposal of amendments in 1929: Iraq (1931), Norway (1931), Finland (1932), Switzerland (1934), Spain (1935), Argentina (1935), Peru (1937).

gress takes place in committees. The Convention does not assure all members of the Union representation in the committees and the larger powers have, in one way or another, managed to secure representation on these bodies well above that of many of their smaller associates in the Postal Union. But neither of these practices has gone unchallenged.

As pointed out above, membership in the Universal Postal Union does not invariably carry representation and voting privileges. Sovereign states obtain membership by notifying the Swiss Government of their adherence to the convention.[74] Non-sovereign areas possessing postal administrations to some extent distinct from those of protecting states secure membership through notification of adherence given by the protecting states. Representation and voting privileges, however, are accorded by the Congress of the Union. They may be granted to or withheld from non-sovereign areas which have been accorded membership.[75]

At the present time France has three colonial votes, the United States, Japan, Netherlands, and Portugal two each, with Belgium, Spain, and Italy possessing one each.[76] The British Empire is now without any colonial vote as such, but Canada, the Union of South Africa, Australia, New Zealand, the Irish Free State, and India are all members with full voting privileges. The process of breaking down the rule of " one state, one vote," established by the Berne Congress of 1874, started just four years later at the Congress of Paris. At that time India was admitted to the Union, but to secure consent to a vote for India, seven other colonial votes had to be awarded. Once strict

---

[74] Art. 2 of the Convention.

[75] Cf. Arts. 8, 9, 10.

[76] Cf. Art. 8. Colonial voting is actually somewhat greater than this would suggest for a number of areas whose sovereignty certainly may be questioned are accorded full privileges. Among these are Iceland, Morocco, San Marino, Tunis, Vatican City.

equality for sovereign states was broken, subsequent Congresses found it difficult to check the expansion of voting power. States not immediately successful in obtaining colonial votes bolstered their claims by signing the Final Acts of the Congresses in their own names and in those of their colonies. More colonial votes were awarded at the Congresses of Lisbon (1885) and Vienna (1891), and a marked expansion took place at Washington (1897). By the time of the Rome Congress of 1906 colonial representation had grown to a total of eighteen. At Madrid in 1920 it was increased to nineteen in spite of the fact that Denmark had lost her colonial vote through sale of the Virgin Islands to the United States, and Germany, stripped of her colonies, had lost her colonial votes. The increase resulted from the awarding of two additional votes to Japan, one to Belgium for the Congo, and an additional vote to the United States for the Philippines. At the Congress of Stockholm in 1924, the delegations of several states without colonial possessions (Mexico, Switzerland, and the Soviet Union), opposed the awarding of a separate vote to the Irish Free State, thus indicating that further extension of the colonial vote would be difficult to obtain. The Irish Free State was granted a vote, but the Swiss delegate's assertion that " colonial votes are sought in order to obtain numerical superiority in the Congress " and that " many of the countries without colonies, among which are some very important ones " were beginning to feel unrest, was indicative of determination by some states to check the massing of votes around a few powers, if not to eliminate it altogether.[77] In fact, a considerable surface reduction of colonial representation and a slight real reduction was obtained by transferring the representation of India, Canada, Australia, and South Africa from the colonial

[77] *Documents du Congrès de Stockholm,* II, 208.

category to that of sovereign states and depriving the British Empire entirely of its vote for " other dominions and colonies," thus reducing the acknowledged colonial vote from 19 to 14.[78]

In view of the position taken in the Stockholm Congress, it is not surprising that a more determined assault was launched on colonial votes in the London Congress of 1929. Separate propositions for amendments of Article 8 of the Convention were introduced by the delegations of Argentina, the Soviet Union, and Uruguay. The Argentine proposition called for a strict limitation of voting rights to two classes of members: states fully sovereign, and dominions and colonies possessing a genuine parliamentary autonomy.[79] The plan of the Soviet Union called for the annulment of all supplementary votes awarded to groups of colonies not enjoying autonomy and not forming distinct territories, the granting of supplementary votes only to dominions and colonies enjoying real autonomy, and the replacing of the single vote given the Soviet Union by separate votes for each of the autonomous republics constituting it.[80] Uruguay's proposal was the most radical of all. It provided simply that each country should dispose of a single vote to the exclusion, by consequence, of votes for colonies, dominions, or possessions dependent upon those same countries.[81]

On the suggestion of the Preparatory Committee, the First Committee of the Congress took as a basis for discussion the proposition of Uruguay as it was the most far-reaching in its provisions. This decision was, perhaps, unfortunate for it made the issue not merely the elimination of the votes awarded to non-autonomous colonies but the elimination of those of the self-governing dominions as well. As the debate brought out, few delegates shared

---

[78] See the convention of 1924 in *B. & F. State Papers*, CXIV, 430.
[79] *Documents du Congrès de Londres*, I, 20.
[80] *Ibid.*, p. 24.   [81] *Ibid.*, p. 30.

Uruguay's desire to do this. The Argentine proposition would appear to have commanded much greater support and would not have served, as did the proposition of Uruguay, to confuse the issue.

When discussion was opened, the Swiss delegate promptly moved that for the present the Congress agree to maintain the *status quo* in supplementary votes.[82] He was supported by many delegates, most of them representing colonial areas or countries possessing colonial votes.[83] The arguments advanced by them for maintenance of the existing system of representation and voting power may be summarized as follows: The Universal Postal Union is not a union of independent states but rather a union of postal administrations. Many of the colonies and other possessions have postal administrations which are entirely independent of those of their mother countries. Many have demonstrated their independence by adhering to Arrangements to which the mother countries are not parties. The colonial delegation frequently votes in opposition to the mother country. Separate votes are required for colonial areas in order that they may defend their interests. Many of the areas have enjoyed such representation for a half century. The colonial delegates have made contributions of distinct value to the progressive development of the Union. Many of the areas are independent members of other international organizations, some even of the League of Nations.[84]

In the defense of the existing system the true reason for maintaining the colonial vote as distinct from the autonomous dominion vote, namely, its usefulness as a device for increasing the weight of some of the major

---

[82] *Ibid.*, II, 136.

[83] *Ibid.*, pp. 136-140.

[84] See particularly the remarks of the delegate of British India, *ibid.*, p. 138. Substantially the same arguments were used in defense of the system at the Congress of Stockholm. *Documents du Congrès de Stockholm,* II, 204-218.

powers in the Congress, was never mentioned. If any doubt existed in the Congress on this point it was dispelled by the defense of their plan submitted by the Soviet delegation and by the remarks of their delegation in the First Committee.[85] They asserted that, in common with most other delegations, they welcomed independent representation and voting privileges for all self-governing dominions and colonies but that they found very objectionable a system governed by no established principle which permitted certain favored countries to build up their own influence in the Congresses through the disposition of colonial votes in addition to their own. The chief arguments raised in defense of colonial representation were met by the declaration that in fact many of the colonies are represented by the delegation of the mother state and that where this is not the case the colonial delegation is generally composed of persons closely associated with the mother country's delegation. While colonies sometimes vote independently, the Soviet delegate asserted this was but rarely the case when important questions of principle were before the Congress. Finally, it was declared, the interests of colonial areas could be safe-guarded adequately by the delegation of the mother country itself. The Argentine delegation challenged the assertion that the Postal Union was merely a gathering of postal administrations. Those who hold this view forget, they asserted, that the decisions of the Congress, being ratified, are converted into law by the adopting states. The postal administrations are the elements which give the Union its physical make-up, but the high contracting parties are not the postal administrations, but the states themselves.[86]

[85] *Documents du Congrès de Londres,* I, 24, and *ibid.,* II, 150-151.

[86] *Ibid.,* I, 20. The terms of the Convention appear to substantiate the Argentine contention. Article 1 provides " the countries between which the present Convention is concluded." Article 13, " Each country is represented at the Congress by one or several plenipotentiary delegates." The Final Provisions declare " In faith whereof the Plenipotentiaries of

When the Swiss proposal for maintenance of the *status quo* was put to the vote in the committee, it was adopted by a vote of 42 to 9 with 7 abstaining.[87] This action prevented a vote in committee on any of the propositions suggesting change in Article 8. However, the matter did not end here, for the Soviet delegation then sought to induce the plenary session to adopt a *voeu* recommending that the next Congress take under consideration complete revision of the system of awarding colonial votes.[88] This was defeated, 15 voting for it, 35 against, with 24 abstaining. However, it affords a much better picture of the sentiment in the Congress than did the vote in the committee. Examination of the vote reveals the deeply entrenched position of the colonial powers.[89]

In the 1934 Congress at Cairo the question of colonial votes was again raised, the assault being led by the delegation of Argentina. Substantially the same arguments for and against colonial representation which had been advanced at Stockholm and London were again reiterated.[90] The result was again maintenance of the *status quo*.[91]

---

the governments of the above-named countries have signed the present Convention."

[87] *Ibid.*, II, 154.   [88] *Ibid.*, p. 565.

[89] *Ibid.*, p. 566. For the *voeu*: Brazil, Chile, China, Colombia, Cuba, Ecuador, Honduras, Mexico, Norway, Peru, Salvador, Turkey, U. S. S. R., Uruguay, Venezuela. Against: The Union of South Africa, Albania, Philippine Islands, Australia, Belgium, Belgian Congo, Bolivia, Spain, Spanish Colonies, France, Algeria, Indo-China, Other French Colonies, Great Britain, Greece, Hedjaz, British India, Iraq, Irish Free State, the Whole of the Italian Colonies, Japan, Korea, the Whole of the Other Japanese Dependencies, Morocco (exclusive of Spanish Zone), Morocco (Spanish Zone), New Zealand, Dutch Indies, Dutch Colonies in America, Portugal, Portuguese Colonies in Africa, Portuguese Colonies in Asia and Oceania, Roumania, Siam, Switzerland, Tunis. Abstentions: Germany, the United States, Insular Possessions of the United States other than the Philippines, Austria, Bulgaria, Canada, Denmark, Danzig, Egypt, Esthonia, Ethiopia, Finland, Hungary, Iceland, Italy, Latvia, Lithuania, Luxemburg, Netherlands, Persia, Poland, Saar Territory, Sweden, Czechoslovakia.

[90] Cf. *Documents du Congrès du Caire,* II, 192-213.

[91] The vote this time was 37 for, 13 against, with 8 abstentions. *Ibid.,*

In view of the marked discrepancy between the number of votes controlled by Portugal, the Netherlands, Belgium, and Spain on the one hand and Germany and the Soviet Union on the other, it seems safe to predict that the question of representation and voting power must continue to claim the attention of Postal Congresses. It seems unlikely that the solution will be a return to the complete equality of all contracting states. In a Congress taking decisions of a binding character by majority vote there is much to be said for awarding the United States and Great Britain more voting power than Iceland and Cuba.

The other deviation of importance from strict equality in the Congresses of the Postal Union is found in the constitution of the committees. Four of these bodies are used for preliminary consideration of the propositions submitted to the Congress.[92] The Postal Union has never accorded all members representation on all committees, a practice which is followed in many other public unions. Instead, an effort has been made to hold membership down to a point suitable for efficient deliberation. The number of seats on each committee is fixed by the Congress at the time it adopts its *règlement* and the seats are distributed by the President of the Congress, subject to final approval by the Congress itself. The major powers

p. 211. Those voting for maintenance of the *status quo*: Union of South Africa, Albania, United States, Possessions of the United States, Philippine Islands, Australia, Austria, Belgium, Belgian Congo, Bulgaria, Canada, Denmark, Egypt, Ecuador, Spain, Spanish Colonies, Finland, France, Algeria, French Colonies, Ireland, Italy, Italian Colonies, Japan, Korea, Lithuania, Netherlands, Dutch Indies, Persia, Poland, Portugal, Portuguese Colonies of Africa, Roumania, Sweden, Czechoslovakia, Tunis, Jugoslavia. Against: Brazil, Chile, Dominican Republic, Great Britain, Guatemala, British India, Latvia, Mexico, Nicaragua, Switzerland, U. S. S. R., Uruguay, Venezuela. Abstaining: Germany, China, Greece, Hungary, Norway, New Zealand, Peru, Turkey.

The British delegation explained they voted against because they favored equality for colonial powers. *Ibid.*, p. 211.

[92] The Congress of Cairo established a fourth committee although earlier Congresses had used only three.

are, as a rule, offered representation on all the committees. If they are not offered representation, their additional voting power enables them to force inclusion. Places on the first committee are most sought, as that body considers all propositions for amendment of the Convention and Detailed Regulations. Membership on the second, third, and fourth committees, which deal with the Arrangements, is generally less attractive and in some cases is deliberately passed over by delegations.[93]

The smaller powers have not always accepted exclusion of their delegations from the desirable committee assignments without protest. One of the first attacks upon the system was launched in the Congress of Rome in 1906 when the Greek delegation, supported by eight others, protested against a system which awarded all the committee assignments to the delegates of thirty states and entirely excluded those of twenty-seven from the preparatory work of the Congress.[94] The result of this and other protests has been a tendency for committee membership, particularly that of the first committee, to expand much more rapidly than the membership of the Union. At the Congress of Rome in 1906, the first committee had twenty-five members, at Madrid in 1920 it was increased to forty, at Stockholm in 1924 fifteen more were added, at London in 1929 it was increased to sixty-seven and at Cairo in 1934 to seventy-four. At the Congress of London, Ecuador, supported by Bolivia, Spain, the U. S. S. R., and Venezuela protested against non-representation of all members and submitted a plan for group representation. This was rejected by 21 to 9.[95]

[93] For example, in the Congress of London, the delegation of the U. S. S. R. asked to be relieved from service on the third committee as it had no interest in the subjects to be dealt with there. *Documents du Congrès de Londres*, II, 24.

[94] *Documents du Congrès de Rome*, II, 564.

[95] *Documents du Congrès de Londres*, II, 23.

An examination of the committee assignments through several Congresses reveals that the complaints of the small states have not been made without reason. At the Congress of London, for example, while a dozen or more very small powers such as Ecuador, Costa Rica, Esthonia, Ethiopia, and Nicaragua were entirely without representation on the important first committee, the United States and France each had three places, and Portugal, Belgium, Spain, Italy, Japan, and the Netherlands all had two places each. Great Britain was, of course, represented on the committee as were each of five Dominions and India.[96]

Mention should also be made of the advantage afforded some powers through membership on the important Preparatory Commission established by the Congress of Stockholm in 1924 and continued by subsequent Congresses. It is the practice for each Congress to designate by majority election countries to name members. The superior voting strength, as well as the prestige of the more important powers, assures them of membership on this important body.[97]

The Congresses of the Telecommunications Union, like those of the Universal Postal Union, have been troubled by the problem of colonial votes. The Union was founded at Madrid in 1932. This action was taken after both the International Telegraph Conference, which met at Paris in 1925, and the International Radiotelegraph Conference, which met at Washington in 1927, had decided in favor of combining the conventions relating to the two subjects. The Radiotelegraph Convention of 1906 permitted colonial representation subject to the qualification that

---

[96] *Ibid.,* p. 25.

[97] At the Congress of Stockholm the following states were selected: Germany, Belgium, France, Great Britain, Hungary, Italy, Netherlands, Portugal, U. S. S. R., Spain, Sweden, Switzerland and the United States. (Clark, *International Communications,* p. 54.) At the Congress of London: Germany, France, Great Britain, Japan, Belgium, Switzerland, the United States, the U. S. S. R., Spain, Sweden, Uruguay, Italy, Netherlands, and Canada. (*Documents du Congrès de Londres,* II, 264.)

" the number of votes at the disposal of one Government, including its colonies, possessions or protectorates, shall in no case exceed six." [98] The revision of 1912 carried the same article with the addition of a list of thirty-four dependencies or groups of dependencies, each of which was to be considered as possessing representation and voting privileges. This gave the United States, Great Britain, Germany, France, and Russia each five votes for their dependencies; Italy, Netherlands, and Portugal had two each; and Belgium, Spain, and Japan were permitted one each.[99] At the Washington Radio Conference of 1927 no agreement could be reached on a plan for voting in future Conferences, and so the Convention carried no provision on that subject.[100] In the Administrative Conferences of the International Telegraphic Union, which had been held from time to time to revise the Regulations attached to the Convention of 1875, a limited colonial voting had been permitted under the following provisions:

> In the deliberations, each administration has a right to one vote, subject to the condition, in the case of different administrations of the same government, that a claim for it has been made through the diplomatic channel to the government of the country where the conference is to be held, before the date fixed for its opening, and that each one has a special and distinct representation.[101]

In the absence of provisions covering voting in the Radio Convention and inasmuch as serious doubt existed as to whether the provisions of the Telegraph Convention of 1875 could cover Plenipotentiary Conferences, the joint Radio and Telegraph Conference of Madrid in 1932 referred the question of voting to a committee for examina-

---

[98] Art. 12, *B. & F. State Papers,* XCIX, 321.

[99] *B. & F. State Papers,* CV, 219.

[100] Cf. I. Stewart, " The International Radiotelegraphic Conference of Washington," *A. J. I. L.,* XXII, 28.

[101] Art. 16, *B. & F. State Papers,* LXVI, 19.

tion.[102]   An American proposal, which had been circulated in advance of the Conference, in pursuance of an obligation to attempt to find agreement undertaken by request of the Washington Conference of 1927, suggested the right to vote " be limited to independent countries and to territorial units possessing a large measure of autonomy as evidenced by their eligibility for membership in the League of Nations, and which send to international conferences delegations not subject to the control of another delegation." This proposal had received the approval of 42 governments, 11 had not replied, and 4 had opposed.[103] No attempt was made to push this proposal to adoption by majority vote of the Conferences for fear of disrupting the Union.[104]

The deliberations in the committee and in the plenary sessions revealed wide variation in the views held in respect to colonial voting. The Swiss delegation suggested the signatories be divided into two groups. The first group should be composed of sovereign states and states not fully sovereign but eligible for membership in the League of Nations. The second group should be composed of units whose independence or near independence is not so apparent. On the production of documentary evidence establishing independence in the field of communications, any territory in this class might be assigned a vote by the Congress.[105] The Greek delegation favored one vote for each sovereign state or each state consisting of mother country and colonies.[106] The Soviet delegation charged that the insistence upon separate votes for colonies, protectorates,

---

[102] *Documents de la Conférence Radiotélégraphique Internationale de Madrid* (1932), II, 42.

[103] *Ibid.,* p. 40. The states opposed were the four chief beneficiaries of colonial representation: France, Belgium, Netherlands, and Portugal.

[104] Cf. I. Stewart, "The Madrid International Telecommunications Convention," *Air Law Review,* V, 236.

[105] *Documents de la Conférence de Madrid,* II, 435.

[106] *Ibid.,* p. 828.

and other dependent territories was designed to reenforce the influence of the mother countries.[107] They demanded a separate vote for each of the republics constituting the Soviet Union if plural voting were to be continued.[108]

The principle of colonial voting was defended by the delegation of the Portuguese colonies, the arguments advanced resembling closely those used in the Postal Union congresses. In the first place, the principle of colonial voting had been long recognized, and to deprive the colonies of their votes would appear " unconstitutional." Second, the interests of the colonies and mother country were sometimes opposed. Third, the colonial communications administrations were generally quite independent from those of the mother country and were sometimes more important. Fourth, the colonial delegates had never used their votes in obstructive fashion. On the contrary, their representatives had contributed much to the Radio and Telegraph Conferences of the past.[109] Finally, the delegation offered a rather novel compromise solution. Certain named colonies were to retain their votes but they should be counted only if opposed to the votes of the states to which they belonged. If the colonial vote coincided with that of the mother country, only a single vote would be recorded for the state and its colonies.[110] Needless to say, this proposal found little favor among the metropolitan states.[111]

No agreement could be reached in the committee in respect to the awarding of votes nor could a sub-committee, consisting of representatives of the United States, Italy, Great Britain, France, and the Dutch Indies, find a solution acceptable to all. Consequently, the American delegation, supported by France, suggested a provisional plan

---

[107] *Ibid.,* p. 831.
[108] *Ibid.,* p. 505.
[109] *Ibid.,* p. 832.
[110] *Ibid.,* p. 902.
[111] It was rejected in committee by 6 votes for to 9 against. *Ibid.,* p. 487.

for the Conference of Madrid, it being understood that permanent solution again would be sought through the diplomatic channel.[112] The following temporary voting plan was then adopted, the Soviet delegation opposing:

1. Exclusively, for the Plenary Assemblies of the Conferences of Madrid, and this provision not constituting a precedent, the countries, or the whole of the countries mentioned below and participating in these Conferences, have a right to vote. They are: The Union of South Africa, Germany, Argentina, Austria, Australia, Belgium, Bolivia, Brazil, Canada, Chile, China, the Vatican City, Colombia, Switzerland, the Belgian Congo and the Ruanda-Urandi Mandated Territories, Costa Rica, Cuba, Denmark, Danzig, Dominican Republic, Egypt, Ecuador, Spain, the Spanish Zone of Morocco and the Whole of the Spanish Possessions, the United States, the Whole of the Colonies of the United States, Ethiopia, Finland, France, the Whole of the French colonies and countries under French Mandate, Great Britain, the Whole of the British Colonies and Territories under the Sovereignty or Mandate of Great Britain, Greece, Guatemala, Honduras, Hungary, British India, Netherland Indies, Ireland, Italy, the Whole of the Italian Colonies, Japan, the Whole of the Japanese Colonies and Territories under Mandate, Latvia, Liberia, Lithuania, Luxemburg, Mexico, Nicaragua, Norway, New Zealand, Panama, Paraguay, Netherlands, Peru, Persia, Poland, Portugal, the Whole of the Portuguese Colonies, the French Protectorate of Morocco and Tunis, Roumania, Sweden, Czechoslovakia, Turkey, the U. S. S. R., Uruguay, Venezuela, Jugoslavia.

2. Exceptionally, based on the traditions of preceding conferences, Germany and the U. S. S. R. have the right to a supplementary vote. . . .

.   .   .   .

4. Each delegation may vote only for the country or the whole of the countries it represents. However, the delegations of Spain, the United States, and Great Britain may also vote for the whole of their colonies and possessions.

A delegation, which for some serious reason might be pre-

[112] *Ibid.*, p. 494.

vented from being present at meetings, has the right to entrust its vote or votes to another delegation. However, a single delegation may not, in these conditions, assemble and avail itself of the votes of more than two delegations, including its own vote, or votes.

In conformity with its opposition to unprincipled plural voting, the Soviet delegation formally renounced the second vote awarded to it by the plan adopted in the Conference.[113]

Inasmuch as the plan adopted at the Madrid Conference in 1932 was for that conference only and was not intended to constitute precedent of a binding character, the problem of voting arose again at the Cairo Telecommunications Conference of 1938. The Inter-American Radio Conference held at Havana in 1937 had provided one vote for each state meeting the following qualifications: (1) a permanent population, (2) a defined territory, (3) government, and (4) capacity to enter into relations with other states.[114] Some attempt was made to induce the Cairo Telecommunications Conferences to adopt this principle of restricting voting power to fully sovereign or independent states, but the principle again was opposed by the numerous colonial powers. Instead, the following resolution was adopted:

1. That for future plenipotentiary and administrative conferences the same rules apply with regard to voting as were applied at the Madrid and Cairo Telecommunications Conferences.

2. That consequently the countries listed in Article 21 of the Internal Regulations of the Cairo Conferences will, as a matter of right, be entitled to vote at future telecommunication conferences.

3. That at the first assembly of future plenipotentiary and administrative conferences countries that are not now listed in Arti-

[113] *Ibid.,* p. 112.
[114] H. B. Otterman, " Inter-American Radio Conferences, Habana, 1937," *A. J. I. L.,* XXXII, 569.

cle 21 may ask to be included in the list of countries entitled to vote.

4. That in case of countries whose independence and sovereignty are well recognized, such requests shall be acceded to as a matter of course by the first plenary assembly.

5. That the case of other countries making such requests shall be referred to a special committee on the right to vote for consideration and recommendation to the plenary session.[115]

The problem which troubled earlier Telecommunication and Radio Conferences was thus resolved for the time, but inasmuch as it carries on the irrational scheme adopted as a temporary expedient at Madrid in 1932, it appears safe to predict that the question will again arise to plague future Conferences of the Union.

The experiences of the organizations which have been considered suggest that although considerations of prestige are not unimportant in causing conflict over the award of votes, the practical issue of control is the more compelling cause. Whenever the majority is empowered to take decisions in matters of some consequence directly or indirectly binding upon the totality of participating states, difficulty in respect to voting weight appears. There is conflict between two forces. The small states are reluctant to yield their equality and the large states are reluctant to continue majority decisions unless their voting strength is somewhat commensurate with their interests and responsibilities. For the most part, the deviations from equality have appeared in somewhat disguised form in order that the susceptibilities of the small states intent upon maintaining their prestige might not be injured. Where inequality in representation and voting strength has been openly provided, it has resulted generally, as in the International Commission for Air Navigation, in non-participation by many of the small powers. Moreover, the indirect meth-

[115] F. C. de Wolf, "The Cairo Telecommunication Conferences," *A. J. I. L.,* XXXII, 562.

ods designed to accomplish the same end, in a form more palatable to the small powers, have themselves created additional problems, for they seldom result in a distribution of voting strength which can be defended upon rational grounds. Therefore, to the friction between large and small states is added that between states of substantially equal position which find themselves differently treated through application of the device selected.

It does not seem that the solution can be found in the return to the principle of one vote for every sovereign state, a principle which has been urged repeatedly in the congresses and conferences of many of the organizations considered. To return to this principle might, in many cases, provoke return to the rule of unanimity or at least serve to prevent any further development in the direction of majority decision, for such a solution seems to ignore completely the realities of the international state system. Enormous differences exist among sovereign states in respect to size, population, and strength and in respect to interest in the various activities undertaken by permanent international bodies. Such considerations can not be ignored if effective international government is to be developed. The small and weaker powers and those whose interests are minor must cede their political equality in return for substantial additions to their well-being in the form of more effective performance of the functions undertaken by the international bodies in question.

If it be granted that the principle of equality is an unsatisfactory basis on which to award voting strength in international bodies, one is confronted immediately by the difficulty of supplying an alternative principle. Clearly, it can not be the drawing of a line between great and small powers. Not only is such a line of demarcation distasteful to the smaller powers, causing them to refrain from participation, but, in addition, it fails to consider the extent and degree of interest by members of the international community in the activity of the international body in question. It may well be that a state generally accorded secondary rank as a world power has greater interest in the suppression of cattle diseases or in the regulation of an international waterway than have certain other states enjoying great power status. Nor does it appear that either financial contribution or possession of colonial areas offers a satisfactory basis for standards of representation and voting strength. As the representative of Turkey long ago pointed out in the conference founding the International Institute of Agriculture, no necessary connection exists between financial resources and interest in the activity of an international organ. Colonial voting appears likely to be yet more unsatisfactory inasmuch as certain powers of first rank and wide interests are without colonial possessions, while several states of only secondary importance have numerous areas whose claims may be advanced.

In view of the great variations in the functions of international bodies, it seems neither desirable nor possible to develop for all bodies one standard of representation and voting power. Rather, for each international organization there should be developed a formula for representation given in terms of the interest of the states, or of the groups within states, in the activities of the particular international body. Such formulas need not ignore the relative strength of states, their ability to make financial contributions, their colonial possessions, their population or any of the other factors which may now be used in assigning voting strength, but they should in addition include some tests designed to determine interest in the activities of the particular organization in question. In short, if the desired discrimination is to be made among states in the award of votes, the award should not be based upon a single factor which may or may not be strictly relevant to state interest in the function, but upon consideration of all factors which appear to have direct bearing upon that point. The use of such formulas would avoid injury to the prestige of the smaller states which generally, but not always, should have less representation and voting strength than the larger powers and, at the same time, permit a distribution in accord with international realities. Although such formulas will naturally be difficult to construct, the feasibility of the suggestion is evidenced by the successful construction by the first Conference of the International Labor Organization of a formula for determining the eight states of chief industrial importance for permanent representation in the Governing Body. The criteria included consideration of such things as total industrial population; proportion of industrial population to the total population; total horse power, steam and water; horse power per inhabitant; length of railways in proportion to area; and tonnage of merchant marine.

Use of a formula is not, of course, strictly essential to the awarding of voting strength on the basis of interest in the activity of the international body. The Sugar Conference held in London in May, 1937, laid down in the terms of the agreement the number of votes to be exercised by each state delegation, this determination being made in accordance with interest as a producer or consumer of sugar. However, use of a formula, even though it entails certain difficulty both in construction and in application, as the experience of the International Labor Organization indicates, seems preferable inasmuch as it affords a means for changing the allotment of votes as membership changes or as the interests or the capacities of the participating states change.

CHAPTER XI

SUMMARY AND CONCLUSIONS

The international society is composed of states each of which, in accordance with widely accepted legal theory, is sovereign. From this doctrine of sovereignty is derived the principle that new rules of law depend for their validity upon consent. However, it does not follow, as it is sometimes asserted to follow, that each rule to have validity must rest upon unanimous acceptance by the states on which it is intended to impose legal obligation. Sovereign states may unite in the establishment of permanent international organs possessing authority to regulate matters of common concern and they may consent, either expressly or tacitly, to accept as binding decisions reached in these organs by some form of majority vote, without in any sense compromising their own independence or sovereignty. The establishment of permanent organs with power to adopt new rules within a limited field and the surrender of the *liberum veto* in respect to the decisions of these organs involves essentially no greater limitation upon the freedom of conduct of states than does the acceptance of any other treaty obligation. It follows, therefore, that states in the international community, just as individuals within the domestic community, may, where they see fit, establish governmental organs and consent to a rule of law in respect to these organs whereby the view of the majority stands as the view of the whole, binding upon all, including the dissenting minority. Indeed, it may be said that the very achievement of order in the international community appears to require, first, the creation of organs competent to take decisions on matters of common concern which will be binding upon all, and second, the adoption of rules within these organs which make decision possible.

In respect to the first need, little progress has been made. Although the states forming the international community have by joint action established many permanent international agencies, the powers which these bodies may exercise have been restricted closely by convention provision. But few have authority to take decisions which impose direct legal obligations upon the participating states. Where such powers have been granted, as in the Convention establishing the International Commission for Air Navigation, they are confined always within narrow limits and they seldom extend to matters which could be considered of major significance. For the most part, the permanent international agencies which have been established have been confined to the supervision of international offices or bureaus which are themselves primarily agencies for the collection and distribution of information, to the enactment of administrative regulations, to the adoption of resolutions of an advisory character or to the adoption of draft conventions or other agreements *ad referendum.* However, resolutions of an advisory character are in some cases virtually as effective as decisions purporting to carry legal obligation, and in a few cases, notably that of the Congresses of the Universal Postal Union, decisions reached *ad referendum* are in fact treated as having legal validity from the date established by the enacting authority, without awaiting ratification by the member states.

Within this narrow sphere in which permanent international organization operates, procedural rules are generally of such a nature as to permit rapid decision. The rule that decisions may be taken by some form of majority action has been accepted much more widely than is generally appreciated. Strict adherence to the rule of unanimous consent has become unusual. The present survey has revealed but few permanent bodies composed of repre-

sentatives of states or administrations which take all decisions on matters of consequence by unanimous vote.[1] To
be sure, in a number of bodies, unanimity is required for
some decisions of importance but other decisions may be
taken by some form of majority vote.[2] It should be added
that certain bodies nominally reaching decision by majority may, on occasion, be thrown back on unanimity by
reason of certain convention stipulations. For example, in
a few cases decisions reached by majority require unanimous approval by the participating powers before they can
have any legal validity [3] and in some other cases decisions
are obligatory only for those states voting for them.[4] But
the fact remains, that in a very much larger number of
permanent international bodies in which states or administrations are represented, all decisions of consequence
which the organ is permitted to take are reached by some
form of majority vote.[5]

---

[1] The Conference of the Union for the Protection of Industrial Property, the Conference of the Union for the Protection of Literary and
Artistic Works, the General Assembly of the International Institute of
Agriculture, the Governing Board of the Pan American Union, and the
Permanent Advisory Commission for Military, Naval and Air Questions
fall in this class. Where special diplomatic conferences are called to
revise conventions of public unions decisions are frequently, if not generally, by unanimous consent.

[2] In this category should be included the Council and the Assembly of
the League of Nations, the European Commission of the Danube, the
International Commission of the Danube, the International Commission
of the Elbe, the General Conference of the Metric Union, the International
Sugar Council, the Cape Spartel Lighthouse Commission, the Committee
of Control of the Tangier Zone, and the Permanent Technical Hydraulic
System Commission of the Danube.

[3] As in the International Commission of the Office of Epizootics and
the International Commission of the International Bureau on Intelligence
on Locusts.

[4] As in the Central Commission for Navigation of the Rhine.

[5] Included are the International Commission for Air Navigation, the
Committee of Experts of the Railway Union, the General Conference of
the Relief Union, the Conference of the International Hydrographic
Bureau, the Conference of the International Labor Organization, the
Governing Body of the International Labor Organization, the General

In a few cases majority decision rests upon express convention provision to that effect. This is true, for example, of the Conference of the International Labor Organization, the Baltic Geodetic Commission, and the General Council of the International Relief Union. Much more frequently, the conventions specify that decisions in respect to certain matters may be reached by majority, the organs being left free to determine the vote essential for decision in other cases. This is the case in respect to the International Commission for Air Navigation and the Governing Body of the International Labor Organization. In yet other conventions, such as those creating the Council and Assembly of the League of Nations, the Permanent Technical Hydraulic System Commission of the Danube, the Committee of Control of the Tangier Zone, and the International Sugar Council, the drafters apparently attempted to provide for all decisions, in some cases specifying majority vote and in others unanimity. The many additional exceptions which have developed in the practice of the Council and Assembly of the League of Nations to the general rule of unanimity laid down in Article 5 of the Covenant illustrate how difficult it is to hold active organs to an apparently explicit, but narrow, rule.

In many other cases, the terms of the conventions forming the basic law of permanent international bodies are silent on the vote necessary for decision, providing either

Conference of Communications and Transit, the Baltic Geodetic Commission, the Permanent Committee of the International Office of Chemistry, the Technical Organizations of the League of Nations, the Congress of the Universal Postal Union, the Congress of the Postal Union of the Americas and Spain, the International Committee of the International Office of Public Health, the Conference of the Telecommunications Union, the International Conference of American States, the Executive Committee of the International Institute of Refrigeration, the Permanent Committee of the International Institute of Agriculture, the Advisory Committee on Traffic in Opium and other Drugs, the Advisory Committee on Protection of Children and Young People, and the Administrative Council of the International Exhibitions Union.

explicitly or by implication for determination of the matter by the organs themselves. This is true, for example, in respect to the Conference of the Union for the Protection of Industrial Property, which adheres strictly to the rule of unanimous consent, as well as to the Congress of the Universal Postal Union, the Congress of the Postal Union of the Americas and Spain, the Permanent Committee of the International Office of Public Health, the Conference of the Telecommunications Union, the Permanent Committee of the International Institute of Agriculture, and many other bodies which use majority decision. Where majority decision has been established in such cases it generally rests upon express provision in the internal regulations. Although such regulations are susceptible to change by majority action, majority decision has in many cases hardened into a constitutional practice from which it would be difficult to deviate. In at least one case, that of the Permanent Committee of the International Office of Public Health, majority decision rests entirely upon practice.

Not only does it appear that majority decision has been accepted somewhat more widely than generally has been appreciated, but the trend of the last twenty years may be said to be definitely toward a more complete acceptance of the rule. Specific authorization of majority rule appears much more frequently in post-war conventions than in those drafted earlier. With certain notable exceptions, majority decision in bodies established in the pre-war period has developed from internal usage. For the most part, those organs which adhere strictly to the rule of unanimous consent for all important decisions are following practices formed in the pre-war period, only one such organ, the Permanent Advisory Commission on Military, Naval and Air Questions, being a post-war creation.

In general, the increased acceptance of majority decision in the international sphere results from the same factors

20

which produced majority decision within the domestic sphere. Within states the emergence of a recognized community of interest accompanied by substantial agreement upon the general ends to be sought in the social order made possible the acceptance of majority rule as the most convenient way of arriving at decisions. In the absence of a recognized community of interest and of agreement upon objectives, majority decision is impossible for the reason that the minority sees no reason for acquiescing in the decisions which might be reached by the majority. This may be illustrated by observing that in the domestic sphere the emergence of strong parties committed to ends which are incompatible with those sought by other influential groups in the community, results in the termination or suspension of democratic government. Those in control generally are unwilling to risk substitution of policies diametrically opposed to their own. Agreement is lacking upon fundamental points and, consequently, majority decision becomes impossible.

The situation is not different in the international sphere. In respect to many matters such as boundaries, markets, raw materials, and treatment of minority groups, no general agreement has been reached. Consequently, international organs are not endowed with authority to take by majority vote decisions in respect to such matters which are binding upon the international community. If states recognize a common interest in the regulation of these matters they have yet to agree upon the fundamental principles to be observed in such regulation. But in respect to an increasing number of other matters a common interest has been recognized and fundamental principles have been agreed upon. Within that sphere of agreement, a sphere which in many cases is extremely narrow, majority decision is possible and is generally adopted as the most convenient method for reaching decision. Thus rules applying to postal communications, to technical regulations for aircraft in time of peace, to notification of epidemics, to the distribution of relief in case of disaster, and to many other matters may be laid down by majority vote. Or again, majority decision may be used for establishing the scale of river tolls, but unanimity may continue to be insisted upon for any change in the principles to be applied in determining that scale. The field in which states have perceived the existence of a common interest is yet pitifully small but the slow, yet perceptible, extension of majority rule bears witness to its growth.

Although the extension of majority decision has resulted primarily from the emergence of a recognized community interest, several other factors appear to have hastened the trend. First, where technical delegates rather than diplomatic officers have been granted chief responsibility either for the establishment or the operation of an international organ, the result generally has been a much more complete acceptance of the majority principle. Thus the Congress of the Universal Postal Union, composed primarily of persons drawn from the postal administrations of the participating states, developed majority rule while the Conferences of both the Union for the Protection of Industrial Property and the Union for the Protection of Literary and Artistic Works, composed primarily of diplomatic officers, have adhered strictly to the unanimity rule. The chief function of all three has been revision *ad referendum* of the basic conventions of the unions. The concern of a technical delegate is with the construction of a procedure which may function efficiently in achieving the objectives in view. He sees little reason for adhering to practices which may have been followed in earlier diplomatic gatherings. To him the advantages of the *liberum veto* appear distinctly illusory when balanced against a method of decision which promises rapidity of action. This view is further substantiated by the part which the technical delegates played in securing the adoption of majority vote for decision in the International Commission for Air Navigation, in the Conferences of the International Labor Organization, in the Permanent Committee of the International Office of Public Health, and in other bodies as well. It is appreciated, of course, that the placing of technical delegates, rather than diplomatic officers, in a position of influence is itself indicative of an agreement by participating states which makes majority decision possible.

The popular idealism which characterized the Peace Conference period also appears to have been a factor causing wider acceptance of majority decision in permanent international organs. In an atmosphere which permitted serious proposal by the representatives of one great power, supported by those of another, of a proposition whereby Labor Conferences would be authorized to enact legislation directly binding upon all states, it is not surprising that old procedures designed to safeguard state sovereignty should have been thrust aside rather generally. Statesmen proposed and governments accepted certain departures from unanimity which probably could have been neither proposed nor accepted at any other time.

Finally, the trend toward majority decision appears to have been hastened in some cases by political considerations. The attempt to extend majority action in the Central Commission for the Navigation of the Rhine, for example, may be attributed largely to a determination on the part of France, and to a lesser extent of the other victorious powers, to prevent Germany from using her representation on the Commission to block fulfillment of the provisions of the settlement in respect to the Rhine. Many of the departures from unanimity provided for the Council of the League of Nations likewise may be attributed to a determination to prevent any former enemy or neutral state from using its place on the Council to sabotage the fulfillment of the terms of the peace. Adoption of majority rule in such circumstances is not indicative of any general willingness to accept as binding decisions reached by majority vote of international representative bodies.

Recognizing that majority decision in permanent international bodies received artificial stimulus both from the popular idealism of the Conference period and as a result of political considerations growing out of the World War, the wide acceptance of the practice is, nevertheless, indicative of a growing acceptance in the international community of the idea that the group will may properly be ascertained through some form of majority action. This is true in spite of the fact that in a few cases majorities were never able to perform all of the acts the drafters of the conventions intended, and in spite of the inactivity forced upon some international organs as a result of the rise to power of governments in certain states committed to programs quite incompatible with international government. Undoubtedly, majority government now is suffering a recession. However, it is possible that the present situation is but of transient character. All the gains that have been made may not be lost.

Aside from the increased number of international organs now taking decisions by some form of majority vote, other evidences exist to suggest some tendency toward substitution of the majority principle for that of unanimity for determining the will of the whole.

In the first place, in many of the permanent organizations which yet cling to unanimity for all or part of their decisions of consequence, considerable dissatisfaction has developed with the rule. As previously noted, the Conferences of the Union for the Protection of Literary and Artistic Works have been driven to the adoption of various devices to escape the consequences of unanimity, devices now recognized as producing other evils. In the most recent Conference of the Union for the Protection of Industrial Property serious consideration has been given to modification of the unanimity rule. In response to the resolution of the Assembly of the League of Nations adopted July 4, 1936, in which it was recommended that the Council invite the members of the League to send to the Secretary-General " any proposals they may wish to make in order to improve . . . the application of the principles of the Covenant," seventeen out of forty-three governments replying suggested some modification of the unanimity rule.[6] Eleven governments suggested the votes of the parties should be ignored in reckoning unanimity under Article 11.[7] One (Norway) suggested majority vote should suffice under Article 11, and another (Latvia) suggested majority decision under the article should be considered. Four governments recommended that decisions to request advisory opinions from the Permanent Court should be taken by majority vote.[8] One (Peru) suggested majority decision under Article 15, paragraph 4. Two (Colombia and Lithuania) favored majority decision under Article 10 to make that article workable. Five suggested some form of majority decision under Article 16.[9] Two (Bulgaria and Peru) favored a qualified majority under Article 19 and one (Norway) believed that a majority should suffice under the article since the Assembly is authorized to advise rather than to decide. In short, within those bodies yet adhering to the rule of unanimous consent, the conviction appears to be widely held that successful functioning necessitates substantial modification of the rule.

In the second place, even the Permanent Court of Inter-

---

[6] *O. J.,* 1936, Special Supplement No. 154 (League Doc. A. 31. 1936. VII). Some of the replies were made directly to the Secretary-General and others were in the nature of statements in the Assembly.

[7] Belgium, United Kingdom, China, Colombia, Esthonia, Finland, France, Sweden, Canada, Denmark, the U. S. S. R.

[8] Denmark, Finland, Norway, Sweden.

[9] Esthonia, Liberia, Lithuania, U. S. S. R., Latvia.

national Justice, which could scarcely be expected to play a leading part in the enactment of new procedures for international bodies, has encouraged rejection of the rigid unanimity rule. In connection with the dispute between Great Britain and Turkey the Council asked the opinion of the Court on whether a resolution of the Council laying down the frontier of Iraq should be by unanimous or majority vote and whether the representatives of the parties to the dispute should take part in the vote. The terms of the Treaty of Lausanne, under which the Council was acting, are silent on the matter, but Article 5 of the Covenant carries the express stipulation: " Except where otherwise expressly provided in this Covenant . . . decisions at any meeting of the Assembly or of the Council shall require the agreement of all the Members of the League represented at the meeting." It would appear that if the letter of the Covenant were to be observed, absolute unanimity was requisite. The Court, however, took no such view. Nor did it boldly declare in favor of majority decision as it might have done in order that there be no frustration of the purpose of the treaty. It did, however, express the opinion that in cases of actual dispute laid before the Council, the principle of exclusion of the interested parties provided for in Article 15, paragraphs 6 and 7, and in Article 16, paragraph 4, might properly be applied by analogy. The Court declared:

It should be observed that the very general rule laid down in Article 5 of the Covenant does not specifically contemplate the case of an actual dispute which has been laid before the Council. On the other hand, this contingency is dealt with in Article 15, paragraphs 6 and 7, which, whilst making the limited binding effect of recommendations dependent on unanimity, explicitly states that the Council's unanimous report need only be agreed to by the Members thereof other than the representatives of the parties. The same principle is applied in the cases contemplated in paragraph 4 of Article 16 of the Covenant and in the first three paragraphs which, in accordance with a resolution of the Second Assembly, are to be inserted between the first and second paragraphs of that article.

It follows from the foregoing that, according to the Covenant itself, in certain cases and more particularly in the case of a settlement of a dispute unanimity is applicable, subject to the limitation that the votes cast by representatives of the interested parties do not affect the required unanimity.

The Court is of the opinion that it is this conception of the rule of unanimity which must be applied in the dispute before the Council. . . . [10]

In no sense is the opinion of the Court indicative of a view that majority vote or even qualified unanimity should be substituted for strict unanimity in all cases. No suggestion is made that the Council is entitled to decide the substance of disputes without the concurrence of the members. It suggests, rather, that in cases comparable to those arising under Article 15, paragraphs 6 and 7, qualified unanimity might suitably be used. The opinion is, nevertheless, indicative of an appreciation on the part of the Court that strict adherence to the rule of unanimous consent in all cases may lead to the stultification of the Covenant. Therefore, the letter of the Covenant was disregarded by the Court to arrive at an interpretation which would make treaty and Covenant effective.[11] The way was opened for the Council to hold that the votes of the parties to a dispute were not required for valid resolutions under Article 11, and encouragement was given to those who seek more complete approximation of majority rule in the relations of states.

A third indication of the breakdown of rigid adherence to the rule of unanimity in all dealings among states is found in the terms of many post-war multilateral conven-

[10] *Publications of the P. C. I. J.*, Series B., No. 12, p. 31.
[11] Cf. H. Lauterpacht, *The Development of International Law by the Permanent Court of International Justice*, pp. 47-50.

tions which provide for no permanent administrative organs of their own. An increasing number of these provide for consideration of revision upon the suggestion of some fraction of the contracting parties. Although as a general rule, unanimity continues to be requisite for the actual adoption of revision, the acceptance by states of an obligation to *consider* revision when suggested by some part of the parties to a convention, marks a distinct advance over pre-war practice which generally recognized no obligation to consider revision save with the express consent of all parties. A large number of conventions provide for revision upon request of one contracting party supported by not less than one-third of all the contracting parties.[12] According to the provisions of other conventions, revision may be demanded by one-fourth of the contracting governments [13] or upon demand of a fixed number of parties.[14] In yet other cases, the Council of the League of

[12] Art. 34, Convention for Limiting the Manufacture and Regulating the Distribution of Narcotic Drugs, July 3, 1931, *L. N. T. S.,* CXXXIX, 303; Art. 22, Convention relating to the Transmission in Transit of Electric Power, Dec. 9, 1923, *L. N. T. S.,* LVIII, 315; Art. 22, Convention relating to the Development of Hydraulic Power, Dec. 9, 1923, *L. N. T. S.,* XXXVI, 75; Art. 13, Agreement concerning the Preparation of Transit Cards for Emigrants, June 14, 1929, *L. N. T. S.,* XCIV, 227; Art. 9, Convention and Statute of the Regime of Navigable Waterways of International Concern, April 20, 1921, *L. N. T. S.,* VII, 35; Art. 15, Convention regarding the Measurement of Vessels Employed in Inland Navigation, Nov. 27, 1925, *L. N. T. S.,* LXVII, 63; Art. 10, Convention and Statute on the International Regime of Ports, Dec. 9, 1923, *L. N. T. S.,* LVIII, 285; Art. 21, Convention Establishing an International Relief Union, July 12, 1927, *L. N. T. S.,* XIII, 247.

[13] Art. 7, Agreement concerning Manned Lightships not on their Stations, Oct. 23, 1930, *L. N. T. S.,* CXII, 21; Art. 8, Agreement concerning Maritime Signals, Oct. 23, 1930, *L. N. T. S.,* CXXV, 97.

[14] Revision upon the request of not less than three contracting parties is provided by Art. 16, Convention on Taxation of Foreign Motor Vehicles, March 30, 1931, *L. N. T. S.,* CXXXVIII, 151; by Art. 41, Convention for the Unification of Certain Rules relating to International Carriage by Air, Oct. 12, 1929, any party may after two years call for a conference of revision, *L. N. T. S.,* CXXXVII, 13; by Art. 29, Convention regarding the Regime of the Straits, July 20, 1936, the parties agree to consider

Nations is authorized to decide whether a conference for revision shall be assembled when a request is made by a participating state through the Secretary-General and is supported by at least six other contracting states.[15] By the terms of another convention, the Council is authorized to consider the desirability of summoning a conference of revision when request is made by at least one-third of the contracting states.[16] In yet another case, the Council of the League is charged with the duty of summoning a conference of revision when requested by any two contracting parties, all the contracting parties agreeing to be represented at any such conference convened.[17]

Finally, provision has been made in at least one postwar convention of recent date, the Convention regarding the Regime of the Straits, signed at Montreux, July 20, 1936, and ratified November 9, 1936, by Bulgaria, France, Great Britain, Greece, Roumania, Turkey, the Union of Soviet Socialist Republics, and Jugoslavia,[18] for revision of certain articles by majority vote. By terms of Article 29 of the Convention any contracting party may request

revision at five year intervals when requested by one party supported by one other, or, in case of certain articles, one supported by two others, Cmd. 5249 and *A. J. I. L.,* Supplement, XXXI, 1.

[15] Art. 8, Convention on Stamp laws in Connection with Cheques, March 19, 1931, *L. N. T. S.,* CXLIII, 9; Art. 18, Convention for the Settlement of Certain Conflicts of Laws in Connection with Bills of Exchange and Promissory Notes, June 7, 1930, *L. N. T. S.,* CXLIII, 319; Art. 9, Convention providing for a Uniform Law for Bills of Exchange and Promissory Notes, June 7, 1930, *L. N. T. S.,* CXLIII, 259; Art. 19, Convention providing for a Uniform Law for Cheques, March 19, 1931, *L. N. T. S.,* CXLIII, 357; Art. 8, Convention on Stamp Laws in connection with Bills of Exchange and Promissory Notes, June 7, 1930, *L. N. T. S.,* CXLIII, 339; Art. 17, Convention for the Settlement of Certain Conflicts of Laws in connection with Cheques, *L. N. T. S.,* CXLIII, 409.

[16] Art. 30, International Convention relating to the Simplification of Customs Formalities, Nov. 3, 1923, *L. N. T. S.,* XXX, 371.

[17] Art. 18, Convention for the Regulation of Whaling, Sept. 24, 1931, *L. N. T. S.,* CLV, 363.

[18] Cmd. 5249; *A. J. I. L.,* Supplement, XXXI, 1.

revision at the expiration of each five year period from the
date of entry into force of the Convention. If modification of Articles 14 or 18 is desired, the request must
be supported by one other contracting state. If modification of any other article is sought, the support of two
other states is necessary. Should it be found impossible,
following any valid request for revision, for the parties to
agree through diplomatic channels upon amendments, the
powers agree to assemble in conference. " Such a conference may only take decisions by a unanimous vote, except
as regards cases of revision involving Articles 14 and 18,
for which a majority of three-quarters of the high contracting parties shall be sufficient." [19] The three-quarters
majority must include three-quarters of the Black Sea
powers which are parties, including Turkey.

Opinions may vary concerning the significance of the
many departures in international organization from political equality and from the obstructive rule of unanimity.
It is apparent, however, that the discarding of the rule of
unanimity has contributed markedly to the success of many
permanent international bodies. In general, those which
have been most successful over a period of years are the
ones which have substituted majority decision for the rule
of unanimous consent, at the same time permitting some
modification of political equality. The factual experience
of the organizations reviewed in this study indicates that
concessions, such as modification of the unanimity rule
and political equality, are prerequisite to the construction
of effective international government and hence indis-

---

[19] Article 14 fixes the maximum aggregate tonnage of all foreign naval
forces which may be in course of transit through the Straits and Article 18
fixes the tonnage which non-Black Sea powers may have in that sea in
time of peace and the duration of their stay.

pensable to the solution of the problem of peaceful change. But however desirable such concessions may be, it by no means follows that states are now prepared to make them to a sufficient extent or with sufficient rapidity to meet the need. Although the sphere of international control by majority decision has been extended, it yet falls far short of covering the greatest sources of international conflict and tension, particularly those leading to war.

BIBLIOGRAPHY

BOOKS

Bailey, S. H., *The Anti-Drug Campaign*, London, 1935.

Brierly, J. L., *The Law of Nations*, Oxford, 1936.

Burke, E., *Appeal from the New to the Old Whigs*, "The Works of the Right Honorable Edmund Burke," 9th ed., Boston, 1889.

Calhoun, J. C., *A Disquisition on Government*, "The Works of John C. Calhoun," New York, 1853-1856.

Chacko, C. J., *The International Joint Commission*, New York, 1932.

Chamberlain, J. P., *Regime of International Rivers*, New York, 1923.

Clapp, E. J., *The Navigable Rhine*, London, 1911.

Clark, Keith, *International Communications*, New York, 1931.

Colegrove, K. W., *International Control of Aviation*, Boston, 1930.

Conwell-Evans, T. P., *The League Council in Action*, Oxford, 1929.

Davies, Lord, *Nearing the Abyss*, London, 1936.

Dickinson, E. D., *The Equality of States in International Law*, Cambridge, Massachusetts, 1920.

Dunn, F. S., *Peaceful Change*, New York, 1937.

———, *The Practice and Procedure of International Conferences*, Baltimore, 1929.

Eagleton, C., *International Government*, New York, 1932.

Eisenlohr, L. E. S., *International Narcotics Control*, London, 1934.

Éles, G. T., *Le principe de l'unanimité dans la Société des Nations*, Paris, 1935.

Fauchille, P., *Traité de droit international public*, 2 vols., Paris, 1921-1926.

Federalist, The, 6th ed., eds. J. and G. S. Gideon, Washington, 1845.

Florinsky, M. T., *The Saar Struggle*, New York, 1934.

Follett, M. P., *The New State*, New York, 1918.

Frangulis, A. F., *Théorie et pratique des traités internationaux*, Paris, 1936.

Genet, R., *Traité de diplomatie et de droit diplomatique*, 3 vols., Paris, 1932.

Greaves, H. R. G., *The League Committees and World Order*, London, 1931.

Grotius, Hugo, *De Jure Belli ac Pacis*, "The Classics of International Law," ed. J. B. Scott, Oxford, 1925.

Haelling, G., *Le Rhin*, Paris, 1930.

Hall, A. B., *Popular Government*, New York, 1921.

Harley, J. E., *International Understanding*, Stanford University, 1931.

Hill, N. L., *International Administration*, New York, 1931.

———, *The Public International Conference*, Stanford University, 1929.

Hobson, A., *The International Institute of Agriculture*, Berkeley, 1931.

Howard-Ellis, C., *The Origin, Structure and Working of the League of Nations*, Boston, 1928.

Keen, F. N., *A Better League of Nations*, London, 1934.

Ladas, S. P., *The International Protection of Industrial Property,* Cambridge, Massachusetts, 1930.

Lauterpacht, H., *The Development of International Law by the Permanent Court of International Justice,* London, 1934.

——, *The Function of Law in the International Community,* Oxford, 1933.

Locke, J., *Two Treatises on Civil Government,* "The Works of John Locke," 12th ed., 9 vols., London, 1824.

Lorwin, L. L., *Labor and Internationalism,* New York, 1929.

Manning, C. A. W., ed., *Peaceful Change,* London, 1937.

Mill, J. S., *Representative Government,* ed. A. D. Lindsay, London, 1910.

Miller, D. H., *The Drafting of the Covenant,* 2 vols., New York, 1928.

——, *My Diary at the Conference of Paris,* 21 vols., New York, 1924-1927.

Moore, J. B., *Digest of International Law,* 8 vols., Washington, 1906.

Morley, F., *The Society of Nations,* Washington, 1932.

Myers, D. P., *Handbook of the League of Nations Since 1920,* Boston, 1930.

Newfang, O., *The Road to World Peace,* New York, 1924.

Normandin, A., *Du statut juridique des associations international,* Paris, 1926.

Nys, E., *Le droit international,* 3 vols., Bruxelles, 1912.

Ogilvie, P. M., *International Waterways,* New York, 1920.

Oppenheim, L. F. L., *International Law,* 5th ed., 2 vols., ed. H. Lauterpacht London, 1935-1937.

Pignochet, A., *La Commission Internationale de Navigation Aerienne,* Paris, 1936.

Pillet, A., *Le Régime International de la Proprieté Industrielle,* Paris, 1911.

Pradier-Fodéré, P., *Cours de droit diplomatique à l'usage des agents politiques de ministere des affaires étrangeres des états européens et américains,* 2 vols., Paris, 1881.

Radovanovitch, V. M., *Le Danube et l'application du principe de la liberté de la naviagtion fluviale.* Genève, 1925.

Ray, J., *Commentaire du pacte de la Société des Nations,* Paris, 1930.

Reinsch, P. S., *Public International Unions,* Boston, 1911.

Riches, C. A., *The Unanimity Rule and the League of Nations,* Baltimore, 1933.

Rogers, L., *Crisis Government,* London, 1934.

Roper, A., *La Convention Internationale du 13 octobre 1919,* Paris, 1930.

Rousseau, J. J., *The Social Contract.* Translation by H. J. Tozer, London, 1895.

Satow, E., *A Guide to Diplomatic Practice,* 2d ed., 2 vols., London, 1922.

Sayre, F. B., *Experiments in International Administration,* New York, 1919.

Schmeckebier, L. F., *International Organizations in which the United States Participates,* Washington, 1935.

Schücking, W., *Der Staatenverband der Haager Konferenzen,* München, 1912.

Schücking, W. and Wehberg, H., *Die Satzung des Völkerbundes*, 2d ed., Berlin, 1931.
Scott, J. B., *The Hague Peace Conferences of 1899 and 1907*, 2 vols., Baltimore, 1909.
Shotwell, J. T., ed., *Origins of the International Labor Organization*, 2 vols., New York, 1934.
Smith, Herbert A., *The Economic Uses of International Rivers*, London, 1931.
Streit, C. K., *Union Now*, New York, 1939.
Strupp, K., *Eléments du droit international public universel, européen et américain*, Paris, 1927.
Stuart, G. H., *The International City of Tangier*, Stanford University, 1931.
Temperley, H. W. V., *A History of the Peace Conference of Paris*, 6 vols., London, 1920-24.
Tobin H. J., *The Termination of Multipartite Treaties*, New York, 1933.
Tombs, L. C., *International Organization in European Air Transport*, New York, 1936.
Van Eysinga, W. J. M., *La Commission Centrale pour la Navigation du Rhin*, Leiden, 1935.
Wilcox, F. O., *The Ratification of International Conventions*, London, 1935.
Williams, J. F., *Chapters on Current International Law and the League of Nations*, London, 1929.
———, *Some Aspects of the Covenant of the League of Nations*, London, 1934.
Wilson, F. G., *Labor in the League System*, Stanford University, 1934.
Woolf, L. S., *International Government*, 2d ed., London, 1916.
Wright, Quincy, *Mandates Under the League of Nations*, Chicago, 1930.
Zimmern, A., *The League of Nations and the Rule of Law*, London, 1936.

ARTICLES

Akzin, B., "Membership in the Universal Postal Union," *American Journal of International Law*, XXVII (1933), 651-674.
Baty, T., "The History of Majority Rule," *Quarterly Review*, CCXVI (1912), 1-28.
Eagleton, C., "Reform of the Covenant of the League of Nations," *American Political Science Review*, XXXI (1937), 455-472.
Garbini, M., "Summary of the Work of the Universal Postal Union Since 1874," *International Conciliation*, 1927, 437-443.
Garner, J. W., "Le developpement et les tendances recentes du droit international," Académie de Droit International, *Recueil des Cours*, 1931, 599-714.
———, "Limitations on National Sovereignty in International Relations," *American Political Science Review*, XIX (1925), 1-24.
Heinberg, J. G., "History of the Majority Principle," *American Political Science Review*, XX (1926), 52-68.

Heinberg, J. G., "Theories of Majority Rule," *American Political Science Review,* XXVI (1932), 452-469.

Hewes, A., "Functional Representation in the International Labor Organization," *American Political Science Review,* XXII (1928), 324-338.

Hill, N. L., "Unanimous Consent in International Organization," *American Journal of International Law,* XXII (1928), 319-329.

Hostie, J., "Examen de quelques règles du droit international dans le domaine du communications et du transit," Académie de Droit International, *Recueil des Cours,* 1932, II, 403-518.

Hudson, M. O., "The Development of International Law since the War," *American Journal of International Law,* XXII (1928), 330-350.

Jenks, C. W., "The Revision of International Labor Conventions," *British Yearbook of International Law,* XIV (1933), 43-64.

———, "The International Labour Organization," *British Yearbook of International Law,* XVII (1936), 178-183.

Kaufmann, W., "L'Institut International d'Agriculture," Académie de Droit International, *Recueil des Cours,* 1924, II, 189-191.

———, "L'Union Internationale pour la Protection de la Propriété Industrielle," *Recueil des Cours,* 1924, II, 198-204.

Krehbiel, E., "The European Commission of the Danube," *International Conciliation,* 1918, No. 131, 543-565.

Morrellet, J., "Legal Competence of the International Labor Organization," *Annals,* CLXVI (March, 1933), 46-52.

Ostertag, F., "International Unions for the Protection of Industrial, Literary and Artistic Property," *Michigan Law Review,* XXV (1926-27), 107-123.

Otterman, H. B., "Inter-American Radio Conferences, Habana, 1937," *American Journal of International Law,* XXXII (1938), 569-574.

Politis, N., "L'Organisation de l'Union Internationale des Sucres," *Revue de science et de législation financières,* 1904.

Sherman, G., "The International Organization of the Danube under the Peace Treaties," *American Journal of International Law,* XVII (1923), 438-459.

Shotwell, J. T., "The International Labor Organization as an Alternative to Violent Revolution," *Annals,* CLXVI (March, 1933), 18-25.

Sly, J. F., "The Genesis of the Universal Postal Union," *International Conciliation,* 1927, 393-436.

Spicer-Simson, G., "The International Hydrographic Bureau," *Geographical Journal,* LIX (1922), 293-303.

Stewart, I., "The International Radiotelegraphic Conference of Washington," *American Journal of International Law,* XXII (1928), 28-49.

———, "The Madrid International Telecommunications Convention," *Air Law Review,* V (1934), 236-266.

Stone, J., "The Rule of Unanimity: The Practice of the Council and Assembly of the League of Nations," *British Yearbook of International Law,* XIV (1933), 18-42.

Stuart, G. H., "The International Lighthouse at Cape Spartel," *American Journal of International Law,* XXIV (1930), 770-776.

Turkel, H. R., "International Postal Congresses," *British Yearbook of International Law*, X (1929), 171-180.

Vitta, C., "Le droit sanitaire international," Académie de Droit International, *Recueil des Cours*, 1930, III, 547-667.

Wilk, Kurt, "The International Sugar Régime," *American Political Science Review*, XXXIII (1939), 860-878.

Williams, J. F., "The League of Nations and Unanimity," *American Journal of International Law*, XIX (1925), 475-488.

——, "Sanctions Under the Covenant," *British Yearbook of International Law*, XVII (1936), 130-149.

Williamson, F. H., "The International Postal Service and the Universal Postal Union," *Journal of the Royal Institute of International Affairs*, IX (1930), 68-80.

Wolf, F. C. de, "The Cairo Telecommunication Conferences" *American Journal of International Law*, XXXII (1938), 562-568.

Wright, Q., "Article 19 of the League Covenant and the Doctrine ' Rebus Sic Stantibus '," *Proceedings of American Society of International Law*, 1936, p. 55-73.

TREATY COLLECTIONS

British and Foreign State Papers, London.

Carnegie Endowment for International Peace, *The Treaties of Peace, 1919-1923*, 2 vols., New York, 1924.

Great Britain, Foreign Office, *Treaty Series*, London, 1892—

Hertslet, Sir Edward, *Commercial Treaties*, 31 vols., London, 1827-1925.

——, *The Map of Europe by Treaty*, 4 vols., London, 1875-1891.

Hudson, Manley O., *International Legislation*, 6 vols., Washington, 1931-1937.

League of Nations, *Treaty Series*, London, 1920—

Malloy, William M., comp., *Treaties, Conventions International Acts, Protocols and Agreements between the United States of America and Other Powers, 1776-1909*, 2 vols., Washington, 1910-23.

Martens, G. F. von, *Recueil des principaux traités*, Gottingue, 1817-35.

——, *Nouveau recueil général de traités*, Deuxiéme Série, Göttingen-Leipzig, 1876-1908.

Oakes, A., and Mowat, R. B., *The Great European Treaties of the Nineteenth Century*, Oxford, 1918.

DOCUMENTS

La Commission Européenne du Danube et son œuvre de 1856 à 1931, Paris, 1931.

Commission Permanente sur la Régime des Sucres, Procès-verbaux, Bruxelles, 1903-1913.

Conference on Central American Affairs, 1922-23, Washington, 1923.

Conférence Internationale pour l'Etablissement du Statut Définitif du Danube, 2 vols., Paris, 1920.

21

Convention of the Universal Postal Union, His Majesty's Stationery Office, London, 1935.

Correspondence Respecting the Formation of an International Copyright Union, *British Parliamentary Papers,* 1906, XCVI.

La Documentation Internationale; La paix de Versailles, VI, VIII, Paris, 1931—.

Documents de la Conférence Radiotélégraphique Internationale de Madrid, 1932.

Documents de la Conférence Télégraphique Internationale de Paris, 1925.

Institut International d'Agriculture, *Actes de la . . . Assemblée Générale,* Rome, 1909—

———, *Conférence Internationale d'Agriculture,* Rome, 1905, Procèsverbaux.

———, *Regulations of the General Assembly,* Rome, 1934.

———, *Statuts,* Rome, 1934.

International Agreement regarding the Regulation of Production and Marketing of Sugar, His Majesty's Stationery Office, 1937. Cmd. 5461.

International Commission for Air Navigation, *Extraordinary Session, June, 1929, Draft Minutes,* Paris, 1929.

———, *Official Bulletin,* Paris, 1922—

International Hydrographic Conference, *Statutes of the International Hydrographic Bureau,* Monaco, 1932.

International Labor Office, *International Labor Conference,* Geneva, 1920—

———, *Minutes of the Governing Body,* Geneva, 1920—

———, *Official Bulletin,* Geneva, 1919—

———, *Report of the Director,* Geneva, 1938.

League of Nations, *Official Journal,* 1920—

———, *Records of the Assembly,* Plenary, 1920—

———, *Records of the Assembly,* Committees, 1920—

———, *Monthly Summary,* 1920—

———, *Committee on Amendments to the Covenant; First Report to the Council.* (League Doc. A. 24. 1921. V.)

———, *Rules of Procedure, Health Committee.* (League Doc. C. 10. M. 7, 1924. III)

———, *Report on Danube Navigation submitted to the Advisory and Technical Committee for Communications and Transit.* (League Doc. C. 444 (a). M. 164 (a). 1925. VIII)

———, *Committee on the Composition of the Council.* (League Doc. C. 299. M. 139. 1926. V)

———, *Documents of the Preparatory Commission for the Disarmament Conference,* Series 3. (League Doc. C. 740. M. 279. 1926. IX)

———, *Minutes of the Conference of States Signatories of the Protocol of the Statute of the Permanent Court of International Justice, 1926.*

———, *Rules of Procedure adopted at the Economic Conference of 1927.* (League Doc. C. 356. M. 129. 1927. II)

———, *Slavery Convention, 1926.* (League Doc. C. 210. M. 83. 1927. VI)

———, *Statute of the Organization for Communications and Transit, 1927.* (League Doc. C. 558 (c). M. 200 (c). 1927. VIII)

League of Nations, *Minutes of the Committee for the Amendment of the Covenant of the League of Nations in order to Bring It into Harmony with the Pact of Paris.* (League Doc. C. 160. M. 69. 1930. V)

——, *Acts of the Conference for the Codification of International Law,* I. (League Doc. C. 351. M. 145. 1930. V)

——, *Rules of Procedure, Committee on Traffic in Women and Children.* (League Doc. C. 247. M. 129. 1933. IV)

——, *Application of the Principles of the Covenant of the League of Nations, Communications from Governments.* (League Doc. A. 31. 1936. VII)

——, *Study of the Proposals Submitted by Members of the League.* (League Doc. C. 376. M. 247. 1936. VII)

——, *Ratification of Agreements and Conventions Concluded under the Auspices of the League of Nations.* (League Doc. A. 6 (a). 1937. Annex I. V)

——, *Statute of the Organization for Communications and Transit,* 1938. (League Doc. C. 95. M. 48. 1938. VIII)

Office International d'Hygiène Publique, *Comité Permanent, Procès-verbaux.* Paris, 1919-1920.

——, *Statuts.*

——, *Vingt-cinq ans d'activité de L'Office International d'Hygiène Publique,* Paris, 1933.

Office International du Vin, *Actes de la Conférence Internationale du Vin,* Paris, 1932.

——, *Textes de l'Arrangement International et des Règlements,* Paris, 1928.

Pan American Union, *Bulletin,* 1893—.

——, *The International Conferences of American States, 1889-1928.*

——, *Fifth International Conference of American States, Santiago, Chile, 1923.*

——, *Sixth International Conference of American States, Havana, 1928.*

——, *Seventh International Conference of American States, Montevideo, 1933.*

——, *Regulations of the Inter-American Conference for the Maintenance of Peace, Buenos Aires, 1936.*

——, *Status of the Treaties and Conventions Signed at International Conferences of American States and Other Pan American Conferences,* 1938.

Permanent Court of International Justice, *Publications,* Series A/B.

——, Series D, No. 1, 2d ed.

——, Annual Reports, Series E.

Report of the British Delegates and Minutes of the Proceedings at the International Conference on Agriculture at Rome, 1905, *British Parliamentary Papers,* 1906, XCVI.

Rijndocumenten, 's-Gravenhage, 1918.

L'Union Internationale des Poids et Mesures, *Comptes rendus des séances de la Conférence Générale,* Paris, 1890-1913.

L'Union Internationale des Poids et Mesures, Comité International, Procès-verbaux des séances, Paris, 1890.

L'Union Internationale pour la Protection des Œuvres Littéraires et Artistique, *Actes de la Conférence Internationale*, Berne, 1884.

————, *Actes de la 2me Conférence Internationale*, Berne, 1885.

————, *Actes de la 3me Conférence Internationale*, Berne, 1886.

————, *Actes de la Conférence de Berlin, 1908*.

————, *Actes de la Conférence de Rome, 1928*.

L'Union Internationale pour la Protection de la Propriété Industrielle, *Actes de la Conférence de Paris*, 1883.

————, *Actes de la Conférence de Rome*, 1886.

————, *Actes de la Conférence de Madrid*, 1890.

————, *Actes de la Conférence de Bruxelles*, 1900.

————, *Actes de la Conférence de Washington*, 1911.

————, *Actes de la Conférence de La Haye*, 1925.

————, *Actes de la Conférence de Londres*, 1934.

Union Postal de los Américas y España, *Congreso de Panamá*, 1937.

Union Postale Universelle, *Documents du Congrès Postal International*, Berne, 1874.

————, *Documents du Congrès Postal de Rome, 1906*.

————, *Documents du Congrès Postal de Madrid, 1920*.

————, *Documents du Congrès Postal de Stockholm, 1924*.

————, *Documents du Congrès Postal de Londres, 1929*.

————, *Documents du Congrès Postal du Caire, 1934*.

INDEX